A GLORIOUS
HARVEST

A GLORIOUS HARVEST

Robust Recipes from the Dairy, Pasture, Orchard, and Sea

Henrietta Green

Americanized text by Miriam Rubin

Special photography by Jess Koppel

Sedgewood® Press

New York, New York

To Coco, my god-daughter — in the
hope that she will grow up to be a keen
and informed cook.

First published in 1992 by
Conran Octopus Limited
37 Shelton Street
London WC2H 9HN

Art Director: Mary Evans
Design: Paul Welti
Project Editor: Denise Bates
Recipe Editor: Lewis Esson
Americanizer: Norma MacMillan
Editorial Assistant: Lynne Drew
Picture Research: Jessica Walton
Production: Julia Golding
Illustrations: Lynne Robinson

U.S. edition published by
Sedgewood ® Press
150 East 52nd Street
New York, NY 10022

Vice-President, Editorial Director: Elizabeth P. Rice
Editorial Project Manager: Maryanne Bannon
Project Editor: Miriam Rubin
Recipe Editor: David Ricketts

Typeset by Servis Filmsetting Limited
Printed and bound in Hong Kong

All correspondence should be addressed to Sedgewood ® Press.

ISBN: 0-696-02366-0

Distributed by Meredith Corporation
Des Moines, Iowa

This book may not be sold outside the United States of America.

Contents

Introduction

Whenever I tell people that I am a food writer, they invariably reply "Then you must be a good cook." Without wishing to blow my own trumpet, I suppose I am; but what I really aspire to is to be an excellent shopper.

Not everyone can shop well, some people are just not interested. They find it boring and a waste of time; their ideal is to rush into the nearest supermarket, grabbing from the nearest shelves, and loading their cart sky-high, while praying that the contents will see them through the week. And, knowing the busy pressurized lives most of us lead, who can blame them?

But shopping really is the key to successful cooking, as without good ingredients you do not stand a chance. Not so long ago, cooking was a complicated process; hours were spent in the kitchen creating elaborate dishes, transforming ingredients with intricate preparations, and tucking them up in blankets of rich sauces. So, what did the initial quality matter if the taste was so heavily disguised?

Nowadays, the trend has moved away from this complicated approach and back to the more robustly flavored food that we generally think of as cooking from the country. Our appetites crave fresher, purer flavors, simpler dishes, such as those which you will find in *A Glorious Harvest*, where the true nature of the ingredients shines through. The actual preparation and cooking may be simpler but, and it is a very large but, to achieve the right balance and effect and to wheedle and coax out the flavors, the ingredients have to be of the best possible quality – which neatly brings us back to shopping.

In order to shop well, you need to know how and what to buy. I have spent years championing quality products and have acquired a reputation for an understanding and discernment of the cornucopia of ingredients found in Britain and elsewhere. I have visited endless farms, nurseries, factories, and smaller specialty producers; wherever I go, I talk about the products in an attempt to get to grips with how and to what standards they are grown or produced. So many different factors can affect eating quality, and I believe that only when armed with a knowledge of the roots of a product can you reach a better understanding of its nature. To this end, I explain in this book the different grades, cuts, varieties, and standards of the ingredients generally available, so anyone can make an informed choice when buying.

Most of us are well served by supermarkets; they are remarkably convenient, and although they have done sterling work in raising their standards and expanding their range of varieties, too often their produce, aimed at a mass market, is bland and lacks strength of flavor. So, I generally prefer to shop in smaller local stores; it is not that small is necessarily better, but you can usually get more helpful, personal, and flexible service. If you give advance notice, a good butcher will cut and trim meat to your specifications, a fishmonger will order the fish you need and fillet it, giving you the bones for a stock; a delicatessen will discover the right cheese and a keen greengrocer will buy in those special herbs. Search out the stores where service is paramount and remember, if you are not happy with the quality, do not be afraid to say so and stand your ground. After all, it is you the customer who must be satisfied.

Other sources of good food are farm stands, which often stock unusual varieties of vegetables straight from the farm, pick-your-own farms, where you can be sure of the freshness and, of course, farmers' markets. But do not be put off by the inevitable grumpy dragons manning the stalls who tell you "not to touch". Examine the produce and if it is blemished, complain. Another useful tip is to scour the back pages of magazines for mail order sources (see page 250) where you can find such interesting delicacies, such as smoked trout, farmhouse cheeses, free-range geese for Christmas, and even oysters delivered in prime condition by overnight carrier. In spite of what the supermarkets would have you believe, buying from small specialty suppliers is not necessarily more expensive.

If you think that this all sounds like hard work, believe me, it is worth it in the end. I have already said that I think the right shopping is as important as the cooking; sometimes I even spend more time on shopping than on the actual food preparation.

All my recipes reflect this new approach to food, where the raw ingredients are of paramount importance. Just as you would always expect food straight from the farm to be fresh and in peak condition, so I urge you to seek out this quality when you are cooking from *A Glorious Harvest*. My style is for strong vibrant flavors and — as the saying goes — you can't make a silk purse out of a sow's ear. Neither can you make fine meals from poor quality ingredients.

The Recipes

Soups

Appetizers

One-Course Meals

Vegetables and Salads

Fish and Shellfish

Beef, Lamb, and Pork

Poultry and Game

Breads and Cakes

Desserts

Pickles, Preserves, and Sauces

Basic Recipes

The Vegetable and Herb Garden

Country food would be unimaginable without fresh,
seasonal vegetables, each one marking in its way the
passing of the year, from the first asparagus of spring
or the tender peas and beans of summer to the golden-
fleshed pumpkins of fall.

Vegetables

In spite of the temptation presented by the glorious array of out-of-season vegetables on sale throughout the year, as a general principle I try to buy fresh homegrown vegetables in season. Not only does it make sense financially, as they are bound to be cheaper, but it is when they are at their best.

Homegrown produce hangs for sale on a garden fence.

The only frozen vegetable I buy is sweetcorn. I cannot see the point of any other frozen vegetables; and the only canned vegetables I keep are dried peas and beans, for emergencies, and tomatoes.

Vegetables are categorized by the part of the plant we eat: There are roots and tubers, leaf vegetables, stalks and stems, and vegetable fruits and seeds.

Vegetable Stock

Many recipes call for a vegetable stock, and this may be made with almost any vegetable — even the water used in the cooking of vegetables may be added. The stock can be refrigerated for up to 3 days or frozen.

MAKES ABOUT 5 CUPS

2 carrots, trimmed
2 stalks of celery, with their leafy tops
1 whole leek, including the green leaves
2 tomatoes
1 onion
small bunch of flat-leaf parsley
1 tbsp butter
1 tbsp olive oil
1 bay leaf
2–3 whole black peppercorns
strip of lemon zest

Coarsely chop all the vegetables and the parsley.

Melt the butter with the oil in a large pot over medium heat. Add the vegetables and sauté them for 3–5 minutes, until soft.

Add the bay leaf, peppercorns, and lemon zest with water to cover (about 5 cups). Bring to a boil. Cover, lower the heat, and simmer gently about 1 hour.

Let cool, then strain before use.

What price perfection?

Fresh vegetables are essential for a balanced diet, and over the last few years we have come to expect them to be perfectly formed, regularly shaped, and free from any blemishes. In order to achieve these high standards, farmers and growers are forced to wage chemical warfare with herbicides, insecticides, and fungicides. The trouble is that the chemicals are absorbed into the vegetables, and, as a result, we are absorbing them into our bodies; it is no longer even enough just to wash or peel them. Although the experts find it difficult actually to pinpoint the harmful effect they may have on our health, I cannot think of anyone who claims that these chemicals are beneficial.

Now, I do not want to be an alarmist, but it is a situation that is escalating as the quantities used are increasing. Unless things change, in my opinion, they may soon get out of control. The first thing to realize is that the pesticide residue is part of the price we pay for perfect vegetables. So we should think about changing our views on exactly what it is we want. We should also realize that not even all the chemicals permitted by law are necessarily safe; scientific testing is improving, and our governments are having to knock several chemicals off their approved list.

We, the consumers, should demand to know what is being used. Equally, we should demand that more money is spent on developing biological pesticides, whereby insects rather than chemicals are introduced to control other insects.

Pesticide residues are everywhere in the ecosystem, so much so that minimal amounts are even found in organically grown vegetables – vegetables grown to a sustaining system, without the use of chemicals and where the land is revitalized.

Growing your own vegetables is one way of knowing what they have been treated with.

Several of Britain's major supermarket chains are doing sterling work monitoring pesticide residues, but they should be encouraged to publish their findings.

One thing I do want to make clear is that when I mention lowering the standards of vegetables, I am only talking about their eye appeal – this does not mean that I would ever recommend buying old wrinkled vegetables which have been bruised by bad handling. Vegetables should be fresh and pert, plump and full. As they get old and tired they start to lose their moisture, and so they sag and wrinkle.

Roots and Tubers

Most of the root vegetables are in season during the winter, and are well suited to winter dishes, such as soups, stews, gratins, and braises.

RUTABAGAS are known in my country as SWEDES. They can be added to stews, or peeled and roasted with meat, or boiled and then mashed with lashings of cream, butter, and freshly ground black pepper. They are deep purple from the stem end, to about two-thirds of the way down, then they are yellow to the root. Rutabagas must be peeled as they are usually coated with paraffin to increase their shelf life; and once peeled, they are golden yellow in color. The larger the rutabaga, the more likely it is to be coarse and woody in texture. So choose medium-size rutabagas that are firm to the touch and feel heavy for their size.

In cooking, rutabagas and TURNIPS are almost interchangeable, although the former tend to have a coarser flavor. They are bright white in color, with a purple stripe at the stem end, and large turnips always need peeling before cooking. Baby turnips may sometimes be found in specialty stores and farm markets. They are crisp, sweet, and nutty flavored, and often need only to be lightly scrubbed before being boiled or steamed in a matter of minutes. If their young green leaves are still attached, don't throw them away: You can steam them and toss with a good olive oil and a little lemon juice to serve as a salad. Don't use this method with larger turnip greens, however, as these need longer cooking, and usually prior blanching in order to be tender.

The young leaves of SALSIFY and SCORZONERA (black salsify), also known as the "oyster plant," as its roots are said to taste like oysters, and are, in Europe, eaten in salads. In the States, salsify is quite rare, and the leaves rarer still, but the long white roots may be boiled, baked, or made into soups.

PARSNIPS make the most amazing velvety soup (see page 16), as do JERUSALEM ARTICHOKES. Buy these crisp-fleshed roots with as few knobby bits as possible – they will not affect the taste but they make peeling much more difficult – and, as soon as you have peeled them, drop them into water acidulated with lemon juice or vinegar, otherwise they will discolor. Then boil them in a mixture of milk and vegetable stock, flavored with parsley, peppercorns, and a bay leaf. Once they are tender, purée them in a food processor until smooth.

KNOB or CELERY ROOT or CELERIAC should also be soaked in acidulated water after peeling. This is especially important if you are making *céleri rémoulade,*

Turnips promise robust winter stews and creamy purées.

that favorite dish of French *traiteurs*, in which blanched shredded celeriac is tossed in a pungent mustard-flavored mayonnaise. Do not be put off by the scabby appearance of the root, as underneath its pock-marked skin lies a treasure trove of nutty juiciness, which I sometimes use instead of celery when cooking. Avoid the large knobs as they can be tough, woody, and sometimes even wooly in texture.

HORSERADISH is a very mis-shapen root and is not always easy to come by: When you see it fresh, snap it up. It will keep for ages in the refrigerator, if you peel and grate it and put it in a jar with a little white wine vinegar.

CARROTS and POTATOES, the most popular root vegetables, which are dealt with in more detail later, should be stored in a cool, dark place — but remember that the refrigerator is too cold for potatoes!

Gratin of Mixed Root Vegetables

Make sure that your vegetables are all fresh and firm: If they are flabby, they will break down while baking. Slice them into uniform-sized pieces so they will all take about the same time to cook.

SERVES 8

4 garlic cloves
1 tbsp butter
1 lb new, thin-skinned potatoes, thinly sliced
¼ lb carrots, trimmed and thinly sliced
½ lb celeriac (celery root), peeled and thinly sliced
½ lb parsnips, peeled and thinly sliced
¼ lb rutabaga, peeled and thinly sliced
1 tsp grated nutmeg
salt and freshly ground black pepper
1½ cups heavy cream

Preheat the oven to 400°F.

Cut one of the garlic cloves in half and rub the cut sides all over the inside of a 10- to 12-inch ovenproof gratin dish, then grease it with the butter. Finely chop the remaining garlic.

In a large bowl, toss the potatoes, carrots, celeriac, parsnips, rutabaga, and chopped garlic to mix them together. Season with the nutmeg and plenty of salt and pepper.

Arrange half of the vegetables in an overlaping layer in the gratin dish; pour on a little of the cream, then arrange another layer of vegetables on top. Pour on the remaining cream so that the vegetables are well covered.

Bake about 40 minutes, or until the vegetables are tender but not too soft and the top has turned golden brown. Let stand about 10 minutes before serving.

Parsnips

Although some supermarkets sell parsnips washed and bagged, I never trust them in this state. Somehow wrapping them in plastic makes them go flabby and the moisture trapped in the bag can cause them to sprout. It is far better to go to a farmer's market to buy them still covered with earth: It may make more work, but they will probably be fresher. Choose the plump shapes, as you will get more slices of a similar size, and avoid those which are too enormous and fat, as they will almost certainly have a woody central core which you will have to throw away.

Parsnips should always be peeled and they may be sliced and baked, roasted with meat, or boiled and then puréed in a food processor with copious quantities of heavy cream (or crème fraîche for a sharper flavor), butter, and pepper for a meltingly delightful purée. They may also be very thinly sliced, using a mandoline grater or the slicing disk of a food processor, and deep-fried in oil to make the most unusual "chips."

Curried Parsnip Soup

SERVES 6

1 tbsp coriander seeds
1 tsp cumin seeds
1 small dried red chili pepper
1 tsp ground turmeric
pinch of fenugreek
4 tbsp butter
2 parsnips, peeled and chopped
1 onion, finely chopped
1 large garlic clove, chopped
1 tbsp all-purpose flour
1 quart Chicken Stock (see pages 106–7), plus extra
$\frac{2}{3}$ cup heavy cream
salt and freshly ground black pepper
small bunch of fresh chives, chopped

Grind the coriander, cumin, chili pepper, turmeric, and fenugreek together in a food processor or pound them in a mortar with a pestle. As you will not need all this mixture for the recipe, store all but 1 tablespoon in a small, airtight jar in a cool, dark place for future use.

In a large saucepan, melt the butter over low heat, and add the parsnips, onion, and garlic. Cover the pan and cook gently 10 minutes.

Stir in the flour and the tablespoon of spice mixture. Cook 2 minutes longer, stirring from time to time. Pour in the stock and let simmer about 15 minutes, or until the parsnips are tender.

Process the liquid and solids in a food processor until smooth, then add a little extra stock or some water to dilute to a good soup consistency. Return the soup to the pan and reheat it gently. Then stir in the cream and adjust the seasoning.

Serve scattered with chives.

Carrots

Carrots are rich in vitamin A and have a high sugar content. Grown in many states in the U.S., the largest producer is California, followed by Texas. If you can find out where the carrots are from, do so, because the farther west the carrots are grown, the sweeter the flavor. Avoid carrots grown in Canada, as they have a tendency to be woody. Carrots are available year-round, although there may be some decline in availability in the summer months. While many varieties of carrots exist, they are sold by their shape, not by the variety. Although they are most usually retailed in plastic bags, they are also available in unwrapped bunches, with the leafy green tops still attached. Remember that the tops, while attractive, are not edible, and should be removed either in the store or at home, because they will draw moisture from the roots, so the carrots won't stay fresh as long.

Baby carrots are sold topped and in plastic bags, or in good little bunches with the tops still on. Both are good on crudité platters, or steamed and tossed with a little olive oil or butter, chopped fresh mint, and a good grinding of black pepper.

Larger carrots should always be peeled and, when choosing them, avoid any with pitted surfaces, or which seem to weigh heavy for their size — a sure sign of a woody center. With small young carrots you need not bother with peeling as their skin is so soft; a light scrub or scrape under running water should be enough to clean them. They may then be eaten raw or steamed or cooked in stock or butter in a matter of minutes.

Glazed Carrots with Sauternes

Use firm, brightly colored carrots for this dish, so they hold together well and have a sharp color that glistens under the rich glaze.

If it seems an extravagance to use such a special wine as a Sauternes for cooking, try any of the lesser-expensive sweet dessert wines, such as vin santo, Beaumes-de-Venise, or Loupiac. The remainder of the bottle can be chilled and served with dessert.

SERVES 4

2 tbsp butter

1 lb carrots, trimmed, peeled and cut into 1-inch long sticks

$\frac{2}{3}$ cup Chicken Stock (see pages 106–7)

$\frac{2}{3}$ cup Sauternes, or other dessert wine (see above)

salt and freshly ground white pepper

Melt the butter in a large saucepan which has a tight-fitting lid over medium heat. Stir in the carrots to coat them with the butter.

Add the stock and wine. Season to taste, cover the pan, and cook about 20 minutes, or until tender.

After 15 minutes or so, remove the lid to check the liquid. As you want it to be thick and syrupy, you may need to simmer it uncovered for the final 5 minutes to reduce the sauce. However, do make sure the carrots do not stick and burn by stirring occasionally and lowering the heat if necessary. Otherwise, replace the lid for the last 5 minutes of cooking.

Beets

Beets are classified as a salad root, and in my country, they can be bought already boiled for salads. This strikes me as a shame for several reasons. First of all, I dislike beets in a salad: their velvety texture is quite wrong for mixing with salad greens. Far more importantly, if you buy them already cooked, or if you buy them raw without the leafy greens attached, you miss out on the delicious (and nutritious) stems and leaves which can be lightly poached in water, then cooled and dressed in vinaigrette for a salad.

When buying beets, choose even-sized ones — neither too big, nor too small — which have an unbroken skin and which feel firm to the touch, and show no sign of wrinkling. Any greens should be unblemished.

Beets au Gratin

SERVES 4

6 beets, each weighing about 4 oz
butter, for greasing
¾ cup finely grated Parmesan cheese
salt and freshly ground black pepper
¾ cup heavy cream
3 tbsp soft bread crumbs

Carefully scrub the beets, making sure the skins are not punctured. Cut off their roots and leaves, leaving only about 2 inches of stem and root to make sure they bleed as little as possible while cooking.

Put them in a saucepan, cover with water, and bring to a simmer over medium heat. Continue to simmer about 40 minutes, or until tender.

Preheat the oven to 375°F and lightly butter a 6- to 8-inch gratin or baking dish.

Drain the beets in a colander and let cool. Peel them by rubbing off their skins or, if particularly thick, using a sharp knife. Cut them into slices about ¼-inch thick.

Sprinkle ¼ cup of the Parmesan over the bottom of the prepared gratin dish. Arrange half of the beet slices on the bottom of the dish, season to taste, and sprinkle with another ¼ cup of the Parmesan. Repeat the layers once more. Pour the cream over, so it covers the beets. Scatter the bread crumbs on top.

Bake about 15 minutes, or until the juices start to bubble at the side of the dish and the top is golden brown. Serve immediately.

With such a wide range of potatoes available, it is important to choose the correct variety for each method of cooking opposite.

Potatoes

The potato comes from the same botanical family as Deadly Nightshade and what we eat are the tubers which form on the plant's underground stems. These tubers are vital for the plant's survival and reproduction, as it is in them that the plant stores carbohydrates and water.

Potatoes consist mostly of carbohydrate and fiber and also contain vitamin C and iron. It is their cell structure and the proportion of starch to dry matter that affects the texture when cooked: "waxy" potatoes, with a lower starch content, boil and deep-fry beautifully, but are generally hopeless for mashing and not always successfully baked; "floury" potatoes, on the other hand, are ideal for purées and for mashing, as they collapse on boiling. So, whether you are boiling, steaming, baking, or roasting, it is important to choose the right variety of potato.

British potatoes fall into three categories: "earlies" with a waxy texture; "second earlies," more of an all-purpose type of potato; and "maincrop," generally a more floury potato. By regulation, all potatoes sold in stores in Britain must be identified by name, which makes shopping much easier. There is no similar regulation in the States.

Potatoes in the U.S. separate into two basic categories: OLD POTATOES and NEW POTATOES. Contrary to popular misconceptions, "new" potatoes are not a variety but simply potatoes which come to market directly from the field without first being placed in storage. They are generally harvested when smaller in size, have thin skins, are usually round in shape, and range in color from deep red to a creamy white. Their texture is waxy, and they are the best bet for boiling, then serving with butter and chives, or for potato salads, because they hold their shape well. If you can buy them freshly dug, they are superb. There's no need

to peel new potatoes; a good scrub is all they need, and this has the advantage of retaining the nutrients which are close to the skin. Varieties to look for are: the Long White, from California, available from May to September, which also bakes well; Round White, grown in the Midwest and the East; and Round Red, grown in Florida, Texas, Arizona, and California, which is generally available from February through the summer. Sometimes small-sized, old, round, white potatoes are dyed red and sold as new red-skinned potatoes to bring a higher price, but these are not the real thing. Tiny white and red baby, or fingerling, potatoes may sometimes be found in the markets, and these are really a wonderful treat.

Old potatoes, with their floury texture, are the choice for baking, mashing, and French fries (what we in Britain call chips). Most widely known is the Russet potato. It is often called an Idaho potato, due in part to the fact that most, but certainly not all, are grown in the state of Idaho. Round, white all-purpose potatoes are generally grown east of the Mississippi, with the greatest producer being the state of Maine, which explains why they are often called Maine potatoes. Sold most of the year, especially from autumn to spring, these potatoes are good used for mashing.

Other interesting varieties to look for are Finnish Yellow or Yukon Gold, which are golden fleshed with a buttery texture and flavor, good boiled, fried, and baked; and purple potatoes, rather surprisingly violet-purple in color, these are small-sized potatoes, good baked and fried.

Whether each variety has its own inherent taste is a matter of some controversy, as so many factors affect flavor – such as soil, climate, weather pattern, farming practices, and the degree of maturity – that it is impossible to isolate any predominant factor.

PAPER BAG POTATOES

When buying potatoes, choose the variety and size appropriate for the cooking method. Make sure they are fresh and firm, with unbroken skin (except for some new potatoes), with no green areas and sprouting roots.

Paper Bag Potatoes

As the potatoes for this recipe should be quite small, I use tiny new red- or white-skinned potatoes or fingerling potatoes. I always leave the skin on, as it firms up while the flesh softens to a creamy whip. You can use any mixture of fresh herbs and even add a little grated lemon zest; just make sure your mixture is not too overpowering or it will drown the taste of the potatoes.

SERVES 4–6

24 small potatoes, scrubbed
1 tbsp finely chopped fresh flat-leaf parsley
1 tbsp finely chopped fresh rosemary
1 tbsp finely chopped fresh thyme
⅛ tsp coarse sea salt or kosher salt
4 tbsp butter, diced

Preheat the oven to 350°F.

Put the potatoes on a large sheet of parchment paper or foil large enough to enclose them and scatter with the herbs. Sprinkle with the sea salt and dot with the butter. Fold the paper over loosely, so the potatoes are not wrapped too tightly, but the package is sealed.

Bake for 45 minutes.

Lift the package out of the oven, taking care not to tear it, and put it on a serving plate. Cut the package open with a knife or scissors just before serving, so the heady aroma can be fully appreciated.

Henrietta's Roast Potatoes

At the risk of sounding conceited, I really do think I make the best roast potatoes ever. To be fair, they are not really roast potatoes in the classic sense, with a crisp outside and a silky soft center. Mine are crisp right through, more like huge, crunchy French fries.

For the right effect, it is very important what fat and potatoes you use. I go for goose or duck fat; otherwise it should be an olive oil. As for the potato, a firm, floury variety is best.

SERVES 4–6

1½ *lb potatoes (see above), peeled and quartered*
2 *tbsp all-purpose flour*
coarse sea salt or kosher salt and freshly ground black pepper
3 *tbsp duck or goose fat (see page 117) or olive oil*

Preheat the oven to 400°F.

In a saucepan over medium heat, cook the potatoes in lightly salted boiling water about 5 minutes, or until just slightly soft. Drain them and let cool slightly.

Put the flour in a paper bag and add a generous pinch of salt and black pepper. Shake a few potatoes at a time so they are well coated.

Put them in a roasting pan large enough to hold them in a single layer. Dot or pour over 2 tablespoons of the fat or oil, and then give the pan a good shake.

Roast on the top shelf of the oven at least 2 hours, or until very crisp throughout, turning occasionally so they cook evenly. Baste with the remaining fat if they look in danger of drying up.

If you are roasting meat or poultry at the same time, use the fat from that to baste the potatoes. If you want to cook the meat or poultry at a lower temperature, it will not affect the potatoes. Just start them off at 400°F for about 30 minutes, then turn the oven down to the required temperature.

The Onion Family

No kitchen can ever afford to be without the onion and its relations, such as garlic, shallots, and leeks. Essential to most savory dishes, they lend a sweet sharpness, an extra bite, and a considerable depth of flavor.

The best ONIONS for cooking are the Spanish or Bermuda onions, with their caramel-colored, papery skin, or the smaller, sharper-flavored Globe or Yellow onions. Red onions are imported into Britain from France or Italy, but in the States are grown in Texas, California, Michigan, and New York state, as well as being imported from Italy. They seem to lose their sweet taste, their texture, and, sadly, even their color if cooked for any length of time. It is wiser to restrict their use to salads or *gremoladas* (see page 136), so their full flavor can shine through. White onions also have a milder flavor and I rarely use them. However, what I do find immensely useful are the white pearl onions; their shape and size make them delightful in stews, braises, and sauces, and they are never too overpowering.

When buying onions, they should be firm to the touch, unblemished, and quite dry. If you leave them in the light too long, they will go soft and sprout vibrant green shoots; if this happens, throw away the onion, but save the shoots and use them as you would chives.

SCALLIONS, also known as GREEN ONIONS or SPRING ONIONS, are not just sold in the spring, but are available all year round. Scallions are the most gentle of all onions, and are particularly handy if you want to cook something very quickly, as they will soften and lose the raw edge of their flavor in minutes. They are often used raw in salads, and are an essential ingredient in Oriental cooking.

SHALLOTS can be used instead of onions, but they

should always be stewed rather than being fried in butter, as frying makes them bitter. Shallots resemble miniature onions, but their flavor is a cross between garlic and onions. They have a papery outside skin, which ranges in color from a reddish to a yellow-brown.

GARLIC is grown in Britain, but it really needs the relentless sun of a place like California or Mexico to give it any real intensity of flavor. The variety of garlic grown most widely in California is called Creole; its papery skin is white to off-white in color, and the flavor is on the mild side. Mexico grows the Italian variety of garlic, which has a purple-tinged skin, a stronger flavor, and is available from April to June. Garlic should never be kept too long as it tends to dry out or sprout green shoots in the middle of the cloves, which can cause them to become quite bitter.

LEEKS may either be boiled, poached, sautéed, or stir-fried, to be eaten as a vegetable, or added to stocks, soups, and stews for extra flavor. For some inexplicable reason, I have developed an irrational prejudice against fat leeks and prefer to buy them thinner, even though it means more work cleaning them. It is a good idea to buy untrimmed leeks, then you can tell exactly how fresh they are; if their tops have faded from their natural bright green to an unsightly yellow and are dry and papery, it means they are on the way out. Equally, check their centers, as sometimes they may have a thick, woody core which makes them useless for anything but stocks. And see if they bend – a flexible leek is one without a thick core. Baby leeks are mild and really need nothing more than a quick steaming to bring out their succulent flavor.

Onion Marmalade

Some recipes for onion marmalade result in quite a thin mixture which can be served in quite large quantities to be eaten as a vegetable.

The version given here is very dense, bold, and sweet. It should probably be thought of more as a chutney, and served quite sparingly. It can be eaten hot, straight from the pan, or cooled, packed into a sterilized jar, and kept for up to four weeks in the refrigerator. Spanish onions are best for this recipe as they soften down easily and absorb the alcohol while still holding their shape.

SERVES 8

3 tbsp olive oil
$1\frac{1}{2}$ lb Spanish or Bermuda onions, thinly sliced
$\frac{3}{4}$ cup superfine or granulated sugar
coarse sea salt or kosher salt and freshly ground pepper
1 cup dry red wine
$3\frac{1}{2}$ tbsp sherry wine vinegar
2 tbsp crème de cassis (black currant liqueur)

Heat the oil in a large, heavy-bottomed skillet over medium heat. Add the onions and cook them about 15 minutes, until they are golden brown.

Stir in the sugar and season to taste. Turn down the heat to low, cover the skillet, and cook, stirring occasionally, 10 minutes longer, or until the onions have softened and turned a slightly deeper brown. Check the onions, and if at any time they look in danger of burning, add 1–2 teaspoons of water.

Stir in the wine, vinegar, and crème de cassis, and cook uncovered, stirring frequently, 30 minutes longer, or until the onions have absorbed most of the liquid and reduced to the consistency of jam.

The distinctively French way of transporting onions.

Roast Garlic

For some, the idea of eating a whole head of garlic seems a rather curious idea. However, once you have plucked up the courage to try it, you will realize just how good it is. The curious thing is that roast garlic does not really taste like garlic at all; it is far creamier, milder, and softer than you could possibly imagine. It goes wonderfully well with roast lamb, chicken, and other roast meats.

The best garlic to use comes from plump heads because the fuller the clove, the juicier the result. Forget about the smaller heads with tiny cloves because extracting the purée can be so difficult that you will probably lose patience. Spread the purée on bread, mix with potatoes, or dab a forkful of meat or poultry with a little.

SERVES 6

6 heads of garlic
olive oil, for brushing

Preheat the oven to 350°F.

Using a pastry brush, paint each head of garlic all over with olive oil. Cut out 6 small squares of aluminum foil and wrap up each garlic head.

Put them on a baking sheet and bake them about 35 minutes, or until soft.

To extract the purée, remove the papery outer skin of the bulb, then slit the skin of a clove with a knife and ease out the pulp or press down on it to squeeze it out.

If you are roasting lamb, simply scatter I unwrapped head per person at the base of the roast and cook them in the pan juices for the last 35 minutes of the meat's cooking time.

ROAST GARLIC

Brassicas

Members of the brassica, or cruciferous, family include a wide range of vegetables. Some of the cultivated varieties, such as cauliflower and broccoli, are known to have been eaten by the ancient Greeks and Romans, and cabbage was certainly grown by the Saxons and Celts, so they must number among the green vegetables with the longest culinary traditions.

Always choose CABBAGE with a firm, compact heart and fresh outer leaves which are a light to medium green, without yellowing or discoloration, and which show no sign of frost or insect damage. The varieties of green cabbage you will find most often are the Domestic, which is an early to mid-season crop, and the Danish, which is available from July through March. Savoy, that most elegant of cabbages with its fine-veined crinkly leaves, has a short season. With a flavor milder than its smooth-leaved cousins, it can be shredded raw for salads and makes a welcome change to the ubiquitous cole slaw, usually made with the crunchy, but dull, Domestic or Danish cabbage.

RED CABBAGE, essentially a winter vegetable, is now grown all the year round, and can be braised for hours for a rich, earthy flavor, as well as being pickled or turned into a robust warm salad.

Red cabbage apart, no cabbage should ever be cooked for very long – the actual time will depend on the variety and how thickly it has been shredded. As a general rule, however, it only needs just enough time to soften the texture while still retaining the crunchiness. It can be poached in stock or water, sautéed in butter, steamed, or stir-fried.

The BRUSSELS SPROUT is the one member of the brassica family I try to avoid, as I find its flavor bland and I don't really care for its texture. However, the thousands of kitchen gardens in Britain sporting fine examples of the species are living proof that not everyone agrees with me and, of course, no Thanksgiving table is complete without them. Choose brussels sprouts when tightly formed and pale to deep green; if

A firm, creamy white head is a sure sign of freshness in a cauliflower.

the leaves are yellowing, it means they are not fresh. Be sure to cook them briefly to preserve their texture.

I much prefer the nuttier flavor of KALE, a loose-leaf plant which may be cooked exactly as cabbage. Again, the leaves should be firm, free of blemishes, and a good, clear, even color. The best CAULIFLOWERS to buy are those with firm creamy white, unmarked tight heads; as they age, they droop, turn a grayish yellow, and the florets separate and fall apart.

Unlike cauliflower, BROCCOLI, the Italian member of the brassica family, produces spears of deep green which are actually made up of clusters of flower buds. The stems should be tender, so watch out for any signs of woodiness as this means they are tough. The color should be velvety green, sometimes with a slight purple cast. If the flower buds have started to run to yellow, they are way past their best. Nearly all of the fresh broccoli produced in the U.S. is grown in California, and available all year round. Broccoli needs only a gentle heat when cooking. And, if possible, it should be steamed, instead of coming in direct contact with the cooking liquid. The florets and stems require different cooking times, but can be successfully cooked together if you first peel the stems with a knife.

KOHLRABI, if left to grow too long, also turns woody, so choose the smaller, sweeter ones. It should be peeled and sliced, and can be eaten raw or lightly boiled like cabbage. It also makes a good substitute for turnip with its sweet, if less-fiery, flavor.

Warm Red Cabbage Salad

Choose a firm head of red cabbage. One way of testing is to press on it gently; if it retains an imprint of your fingers, it is old and flabby and not worth buying.

To prepare any head of cabbage, pull away the loose outer leaves and any of the top leaves that may have been scarred. Cut it in half and then cut away the base of the stem in a deep "V" shape to get rid of the core. To shred, cut with the grain to whatever thickness you want. Then rinse it in a colander, and drain it thoroughly.

SERVES 4

½ cup walnuts
2 tsp walnut oil
salt and freshly ground black pepper
2½ tbsp olive oil
1 red onion, thinly sliced
1 garlic clove, finely chopped
2½ tbsp balsamic vinegar
1 small head red cabbage, weighing about 1 lb, finely shredded (see above)
¼ lb semisoft goat cheese, cubed
1 firm red apple, cored and thinly sliced
1 tbsp finely chopped fresh flat-leaf parsley
½ tsp finely chopped fresh marjoram

Preheat the oven to 350°F.

In a bowl, toss the walnut halves in the walnut oil and season to taste. Spread them on a baking sheet and toast, stirring occasionally, in the oven 5–7 minutes, or until they begin to smell nutty. Remove them from the oven and let cool.

Heat the olive oil in a large skillet over moderate heat. Add the onion and garlic and sauté gently about 2 minutes. Then stir in the vinegar and cook 30 seconds more. Add the cabbage and continue cooking, stirring constantly, about 3 minutes or until the cabbage is just wilted. Season well with salt and pepper plus a little more vinegar, if necessary, to sharpen the flavor.

Carefully stir in the goat cheese, apple, parsley, marjoram, and walnuts, so as not to crush the goat cheese or break it up. Toss together briefly and remove from the heat.

Serve immediately.

Fruiting Vegetables

These vegetables form a rather loose collection; what they do have in common, however, is that what we eat is the fruit containing the seeds. If the fruit is underripe, it will be too firm and lacking any inherent flavor; but if it is overripe, the seeds will be too large and tough, and the flesh pulpy.

SUMMER SQUASH are an edible gourd of the melon and cucumber family. Summer squash are available in markets year round, with the peak production in spring and early summer. Most are grown in Florida, but they are also a favorite of gardeners. ZUCCHINI, an elongated green, thin-skinned squash, is popular and extremely prolific. If you have a friend with a garden, you may have been the happy (or not so happy, depending on the size of the squash) recipient of a basket of this vegetable. Zucchini can grow to gargantuan proportions in a matter of days (or sometimes overnight). A new strain of canary-yellow-skinned zucchini may be found in farmer's markets; its flavor is nearly identical to green zucchini. Yellow straight-necked and yellow crooked-neck summer squash are also available all year.

When buying summer squash, choose those with taut, glossy skins, that are small to medium in size. They should be left unpeeled, but their skins may be sandy, so scrub them lightly with a vegetable brush. To cook: Cut them in half lengthwise, brush with oil and broil; or slice and then steam, fry, or sauté them. I also particularly like the nutty, scalloped pattypan squash.

PUMPKINS and other WINTER SQUASHES generally do need to be peeled before cooking; they may be baked with the skin on, but the skin is not eaten. They have a firmer, more floury texture and are a good source of iron, riboflavin, and vitamins A and C. Like all squash, they make terrific chutneys and soups.

SWEET BELL PEPPERS may also be yellow, orange, or deep dark purple, although the most common colors are red or green. I have never understood the attraction of eating these raw as, although crunchy and succulent, they have no length or depth of flavor. I prefer them grilled, broiled, or roasted, when their sweetness starts to caramelize. Buy them when firm and fleshy with thick walls, and avoid any with wrinkled skins. Always remove the seeds and any white pith before use.

The closely related CHILI PEPPERS, of which there are hundreds of varieties, add bite to a wide assortment of dishes. Remember that most of the chili's heat is in the seeds and ribs due to a substance called capsaicin.

EGGPLANT are available throughout most of the year, with Florida and New Jersey growing the largest crops. Usually one sees the large, purple variety, but also found on a smaller scale are the smaller Italian eggplant, and the long, thin, pale violet-colored Japanese eggplant, along with Large White and Baby White eggplants. Even if they are very large, I never bother to peel or salt them, although some people say it is essential for removing their bitterness. Eggplants should be glossy and look blown up like a balloon; once they begin to sink and their skin starts to wrinkle, they are no longer worth buying.

CORN comes from the corn stalk. Mature plants are sold on the cob and should be wrapped in the pale green husks. For the freshest corn, it should have been picked no more than a few hours before you purchase it, so buy it from a reputable farm stand or farmer's market, and check that the leaves are supple, the silk moist, but not slimy at the top of the ear, and the ears plump, with tightly packed kernels. To husk, pull off the leaves and silk, then break off the base of the cob. To cook, plunge into boiling water and simmer 4–5 minutes, until just tender.

Golden-orange pumpkin adds a welcome touch of color to fall dishes.

Zucchini-Corn Chowder

If I can, I like to mix zucchini and yellow summer squash for this soup for an extra dash of color. When they are in season I sometimes also use other summer squashes, such as pattypan and chayote, for their varied skin colors.

Corn is one of the very few vegetables I recommend buying frozen. The idea of going to all the trouble of husking fresh ears and cutting the kernels, only to add them to a soup, seems a little unnecessary. Unlike most frozen vegetables, moreover, frozen corn has a very good taste and texture.

Serve the flavorful, country-style soup as an appetizer before a main course of roast meat, or on its own with chunks of Whole-wheat bread (see page 191).

SERVES 4

5 cups milk
$1\frac{1}{2}$ cups frozen corn kernels, thawed
3 tbsp all-purpose flour
1 small onion, finely chopped
$1\frac{1}{2}$ tbsp finely chopped fresh coriander (cilantro)
$1\frac{1}{2}$ tbsp finely chopped fresh mint
3 large fresh basil leaves, finely chopped
6 coriander seeds, crushed
piece of cinnamon stick, about 2 inches long
$\frac{1}{2}$ lb zucchini (see above), diced
2 tomatoes, peeled, seeded, and chopped
juice of 1 lime
salt and freshly ground black pepper

Put about $\frac{2}{3}$ cup of the milk along with 1 cup of the corn into a food processor and add the flour. Process until smooth, then strain the mixture into a large saucepan.

Add the remaining milk, the onion, $\frac{1}{2}$ tablespoon each of the fresh coriander and mint, the ·basil, coriander seeds, and cinnamon. Slowly bring to a boil over low heat, stirring constantly.

Add the zucchini, half of the prepared tomatoes, and the remaining corn to the pan. Simmer for about 10 minutes, or until the zucchini is tender.

Stir in the remaining chopped tomato and the lime juice (if this curdles the milk, do not worry as it gives the soup a "chowder" look). Remove the cinnamon stick, season to taste, and garnish with the remaining finely chopped herbs.

Stewed Cucumbers

The long, smooth hothouse or European cucumber is, as you would expect, grown indoors or under a frame. Juicy and crisp, it is the best kind to use for cooking as its skin may be eaten. This allows a contrast of taste and texture between the sweet, melting flesh and the slightly bitter, harder skin. If you find this too overpowering, peel the skin off lengthwise in alternating strips, rather than removing it all.

The shorter, fatter cucumber more commonly found in stores may be used but you will need three of them and they should be peeled, whether you are cooking them or serving them raw. Kirby or pickling cucumbers won't need peeling, but as they are small, use six of them.

SERVES 4

2 hothouse or European cucumbers
3 tbsp butter
2 onions, chopped
$\frac{1}{2}$ cup Chicken Stock (see pages 106–7)
$3\frac{1}{2}$ tbsp dry white wine
salt and freshly ground white pepper
$\frac{1}{2}$ tsp ground mace
$1\frac{1}{2}$ tbsp all-purpose flour

To prepare the cucumbers, trim off the ends and cut them lengthwise in half. If you don't like the seeds, scoop them out with a teaspoon.

Cut the cucumber halves into 1-inch pieces and divide these again into quarters or sixths, depending on how fat the cucumbers are.

ZUCCHINI-CORN CHOWDER left, *GRISSINI (SEE PAGE 192)* center, *LETTUCE AND CHERVIL SOUP (SEE PAGE 41)* right.

Melt 2 tablespoons of the butter in a heavy-bottomed saucepan over medium heat. Add the onions and cook them gently about 5 minutes, or until they are soft but have not changed color.

Add the cucumbers and cook a few more minutes, then pour in the stock and wine and season with salt and pepper to taste and the mace. Bring to a boil, cover, reduce the heat, and cook gently about 10 minutes, or until the cucumbers are tender.

Meanwhile, mash the remaining tablespoon butter with the flour in a small bowl to make a thick paste. Remove the pan from the heat and stir in the paste, a little at a time. Return the pan to the heat and, stirring constantly, simmer 2–3 minutes longer, until the sauce thickens. Adjust the seasoning and serve.

Tomatoes

Tomatoes are usually a disappointment unless ripened naturally in the sun; those grown commercially in greenhouses, picked when green and force-ripened are all too often wooly, watery, and lacking in flavor and sweetness; absolutely no match for a vine-ripened tomato. There are many varieties available in season; your best bet is to seek out a local farm stand or farmer's market and choose what looks best. A good tomato will have a high red color, it will feel just a bit firm, but with no soft spots, and it will have a fresh fragrance. If you cannot buy really ripe tomatoes, you can let them ripen further at home at room temperature. Unless they are ripe and ready to eat, never, never refrigerate a tomato.

Out of season, the best advice is to not use fresh tomatoes; if you must, you can sometimes find flavorful tomatoes which are imported from Israel, or choose cherry tomatoes or Italian plum or Roma tomatoes. Even out of season, these will generally have flavor, especially when cooked.

Recently yellow-skinned tomatoes, in varying shapes and sizes, have been appearing in stores, but since they are low-acid, you may discover that their exciting color has no match in their taste. For some sauces, canned tomatoes work just fine.

To peel tomatoes for cooking: First cut a small cross on the bottom, put them in a bowl, and pour some boiling water over them. Leave them in the water for a couple of minutes, then drain and refresh in cold water, and slip off their skins.

Green Tomato, Raisin, and Mint Chutney

Among all the thousands of chutneys, this is one of my favorites because it has a sharp, clean flavor that, unlike many others, is neither too cloying nor too sweet.

This recipe is also a good way of using up unripe, or green, tomatoes which are too hard and bitter to be eaten raw, and fail to ripen even if left on a sunny windowsill or wrapped in paper bags. As with all chutneys, the ingredients must be a good quality.

MAKES FOUR 1-PINT JARS

$3\frac{1}{2}$ lb green tomatoes, cut into medium dice

1 lb onions, finely chopped

1 lb (3 cups) dark, seedless raisins

3 cups sugar

1 cup cider vinegar

$3\frac{1}{2}$ oz fresh ginger, peeled and finely sliced

1 tsp cayenne

$\frac{1}{2}$ tsp salt

1 cup coarsely chopped fresh mint leaves

Put all the ingredients except the mint in a large heavy-bottomed saucepan or kettle and bring to a simmer. Simmer, uncovered, about 1 hour, stirring occasionally with a wooden spoon, taking care not to break up the vegetables or to let the mixture bubble too fiercely.

Stir in the mint and simmer 15 minutes longer, or until the vegetables are just tender but not too soft.

Have ready 4 warm, dry, sterilized 1-pint glass canning jars. Pack the hot chutney loosely into the jars, leaving $\frac{1}{2}$-inch headspace. Cover with tops. Cool and refrigerate for up to 4 weeks. For storage up to 6 months, process the jars, when still hot, in a boiling-water bath, following manufacturer's instructions, to prevent spoilage and mold. Cool. Check seals, and store in a cool, dark place.

Fresh garden peas are one of the true pleasures of summer.

Peas and Beans

These vegetables are all members of the legume family – plants which bear their seeds in pods that split open when ripe.

There are numerous varieties of fresh peas. The type I most often find in British markets is known as the ENGLISH PEA or GREEN PEA. These peas are grown for the seeds inside their pods, and the pods are not eaten. Choose pods which are a clear bright green, full and swollen, but still quite soft, as hard pods are an indication of over-mature peas. As a general guideline, to obtain a given weight of shelled peas, you need to buy two and a half times the weight of peas in the pod. Once shelled, the peas should be eaten as soon as possible, for their sugar quickly turns to starch.

As the name suggests, every bit of the EDIBLE-PODDED PEA or MANGE-TOUT PEA may be eaten. Again there are different varieties, the most common being the sugar snap pea and the snow pea. The best ones to buy are the small- to medium-sized pods which are crisp and bright green. Snow peas are flat-podded, with just a hint of teeny weeny peas showing through the paper-thin pods, while sugar snaps are rounder and plumper. If they are still very young, you should not even need to trim off the strings. When fresh, the pods are crisp and a vibrant green; as they age, they start to flop and lose their intensity of color.

Both the English and edible podded pea can be simmered in water, stewed in butter (with a little chopped lettuce for added sweetness), or stir-fried in olive oil or stock.

Especially if you live in the American South, you are probably familiar with table peas, which include such varieties as Crowder peas and black-eyed peas (both are sometimes called cow peas). The pods are not for eating, and the peas must be cooked to be tender, but they are truly delicious when simmered with a smoked ham hock.

In the States, the most popular GREEN BEANS are the snap bean, and the yellow wax bean. Snap and green beans are available year round, wax beans have a shorter season, and are found fresh in markets from October to April. Less often seen are purple beans, which when cooked, turn as green as ordinary green beans.

FRENCH BEANS are the preferred green bean on the Continent; small and thin, they can vary in color. In the States, they are considered a gourmet item and carry a very hefty price tag, as they are usually imported from France.

All beans should be firm and supple, and sound crisp when snapped in half. To prepare green beans: Trim off the ends and cut to the required size, or leave them whole. Then cook them until tender in boiling water or sauté them in butter. Very young, or baby, FAVA BEANS are so tender you may eat them shells and all. However, larger fava beans, and other members of the shell-bean family, such as cranberry and lima beans, must be shelled, and sometimes skinned (see Pasta with Spring Vegetable Sauce, overleaf).

LEGUMES are dried peas and beans and are a very important feature in cooking. Many types are available in the States, and these include: Yellow and green

SPLIT PEAS; CHICK-PEAS; several different hues of LENTILS; white beans, such as NAVY, CANNELLINI, and GREAT NORTHERN BEANS; BLACK-EYED PEAS; LIMA BEANS; and SOYBEANS. Except for split peas and lentils, legumes need overnight soaking prior to cooking. One thing it is important to remember is not to salt the beans until after they are cooked, as salt can keep them from becoming tender.

Pasta with Spring Vegetable Sauce

One of the nicest pasta sauces is made with sweet and tender baby vegetables, which hardly need any cooking at all. If you can find them, use baby fava or lima beans and just toss them whole, uncooked, into the sauce; otherwise, if buying the larger pods, buy $2\frac{1}{2}$ times the weight of the beans needed, avoiding any which have badly marked pods or which are very swollen because this means the beans inside will probably be too large and consequently too tough. Their skins can also be quite tough which ruins the effect of the soft buttery bean inside, so you should remove them as explained below.

You could also use all snow peas instead of shelled green peas. In fact, when I make this sauce I use whatever sweet-flavored and tender baby vegetables I can find. So I suggest you make up your own mixture and merely think of this recipe as a guide.

It is, however, essential to use the right shape of pasta. Noodles made in flat, wide ribbons, like tagliatelle, are the best because they are the right shape to trap the small vegetables on their surface; if you use spaghetti, the vegetables will just slide to the bottom.

SERVES 4

10–12 oz dried, wide-noodle pasta (see above)
2 oz ($\frac{1}{3}$ cup) shelled fava or lima beans
6 tbsp extra-virgin olive oil
3 scallions, trimmed and cut into 1-inch pieces
2 baby leeks, trimmed and cut into 1-inch chunks

$\frac{1}{4}$ cup coarsely chopped fresh flat-leaf parsley
3 whole green peppercorns
2 tbsp Chicken Stock (see pages 106–7) or water
3 tbsp dry white wine
6 baby carrots, trimmed
2 oz snow peas
$\frac{1}{3}$ cup shelled fresh green peas
1 oz baby spinach leaves (about $\frac{1}{2}$ cup)
1 tsp balsamic vinegar
coarse sea salt or kosher salt and freshly ground black pepper

Cook the pasta in a large saucepan of lightly salted boiling water until just tender but still firm to the bite.

While the pasta is cooking, put the fava or lima beans in a saucepan, cover with lightly salted water, and bring to a boil over medium heat. Simmer 30 seconds to 1 minute to loosen the skins. Drain and refresh them immediately under cold running water. When they are cool enough to handle, skin the beans by gently slitting them open and pressing them out with your fingers.

Heat 3 tablespoons of the oil in a large heavy-bottomed skillet over medium to low heat. Add the scallions, leeks, 2 tablespoons of the parsley, and the peppercorns, and cook gently 2–3 minutes. Pour in the stock and white wine and simmer 1 minute. Then stir in the carrots, snow peas, and green peas, and cook 2–3 minutes longer. Add the beans, then the spinach leaves and cook just long enough to wilt the leaves.

Using a slotted spoon, transfer the vegetables to a warm bowl. Turn up the heat to medium, add the remaining 3 tablespoons oil and the balsamic vinegar, and simmer about 3–4 minutes to allow the sauce to reduce slightly. Season with the salt and pepper to taste.

Drain the pasta well, transfer it into a large serving bowl, and add the vegetables. Pour the sauce over the pasta, sprinkle with the remaining parsley, give the pasta a good toss, and serve.

PASTA WITH SPRING VEGETABLE SAUCE

Stalks, Stems, and Leaves

CARDOONS, rarely seen in the shops, are one of the most underrated of vegetables. A member of the thistle family and closely related to the artichoke, it is the stalk rather than the flowerheads or choke which is eaten. The stalks are cut when still young and tender, lightly blanched and eaten like celery in soups, salads, and hearty stews.

ASPARAGUS, a member of the lily family, is grown in over 20 states in the U.S., with California supplying the greatest amount, and is found from February to June. There is always a great debate as to which asparagus (called "grass" in the trade), is better, the thick spears, or the thin ones. Whichever you buy, they should be firm, taut, fleshy, and with not a hint of woodiness, and with the tips still tightly closed. In my country, and in the U.S., green stems are preferred, whereas milky white asparagus, with tips tinged with purple is eaten on the Continent. This is not a question of variety, but rather of the way the asparagus is grown. The former are left to sprout in beds, whereas the latter are covered up in soil to blanch them and to prevent the stalks from turning green by being exposed to sunlight. Some people find the pale ones too astringent and prefer the slightly grassier flavor of the green; whereas others think that only white ones are worth eating.

The ideal way to cook asparagus is in a tall asparagus pot, so that it stands upright, allowing the stalks to boil in water while the tips are gently steamed. Failing that, lay the spears flat and either simmer in a large skillet, or steam them in a steamer. Serve them hot with melted butter or cold with vinaigrette.

CELERY is available all year round in the States, with California providing three-quarters of the crop,

White asparagus is blanched to keep the stems white.

and the remainder from Florida, New York, Michigan, and other states. The celery head should be neat and hold tightly together. The stalks should be resilient and firm; if they droop and bend they are no longer fresh. Watch out for stalks which are too thick, as they may be tough and stringy.

If possible, buy celery with its leaves still attached, as not only are these a good indication of the freshness of the plant (they start to go blotchy and lose their color within days), they are also very useful chopped as an additional flavoring in stocks, soups, and stews. Raw celery can be eaten in salads, or served to accompany cheese, or it may be braised or baked *au gratin* and served as a vegetable.

FENNEL, at times incorrectly called anise, and not to be confused with the herb fennel, which comes from a slightly different plant, is a short, stocky plant with an edible swollen leaf base. It is sold from autumn through spring, and it has a slight anise taste and a crisp texture when fresh, but rapidly goes rubbery with age. Fennel is usually sold trimmed of most of its feathery tops. It should be snowy white, with green-tinged stalks, plump and firm, with the layers tightly wrapped around each other; avoid any which are soft to the touch. Chop fennel to eat raw in salads, or braise whole or halved bulbs, brush with olive oil and broil or roast.

SORREL, also called SOUR GRASS, is available in some parts of the States year round, but more likely, you will find it in the spring and summer. Sorrel is used as a flavoring ingredient for sauces, and marries especially well with salmon or eel (see page 75), and for soups. Shav, a soup common to Jewish cooking, gets its sharp flavor from sorrel. To prepare sorrel, tear the leaves from their stems, cut them into julienne strips, and sauté in butter, or simmer in stock; the leaves will lose their green color, and will be reduced to a purée.

SPINACH is an invaluable leaf vegetable, sold year round, which is rich in vitamins A and C, and in iron. The tiny baby leaves are lovely added raw to salads; cook larger, older leaves with only the water clinging to them, until they are wilted. As spinach cooks down almost to nothing, allow about 6 oz per person. Make sure the leaves are bright to dark green, firm rather than wilting, and free of slime and insect damage. Spinach should always be very thoroughly washed. Some people like to tear off the stems, but I never bother, particularly as they add texture. However, if the stems are very large, or rather dry-looking, they should be removed. New

Zealand spinach has recently been making appearances in U.S. grocery stores. Despite its name, it is grown in California, not in New Zealand, but it is notable for its large, flat, easier-to-clean leaves, as opposed to the curly leaves of the spinach more commonly found.

SWISS CHARD is a member of the beet family, and available from spring through autumn, with the best supply from June to October. It is a very good source of vitamins A and C, and of potassium and iron. Chard is easily distinguished by its glossy leaves and thick white ribbed stems. Tasting something like asparagus, these stems are sometimes stripped of their leaves and steamed on their own. Red Swiss Chard has deep-red stems and leafy ribs. Buy chard when the leaves are bright and evenly colored, with soft tender stems; if left too long in the ground, they will toughen and become far too stringy. Prepare and cook like spinach.

Roast Vegetables with Thyme

Once you have cut the fennel bulb, it will start to discolor and turn brown, so, unless you are using it immediately, soak it in a bowl of acidulated water.

Beefsteak or plum tomatoes are much better for roasting than other varieties. Not only do they taste better but, because of their texture, they will hold together better.

SERVES 6–8

6 fennel bulbs
6 beefsteak or 10 plum tomatoes
pinch of granulated sugar (optional)
7 garlic cloves
$\frac{1}{4}$ cup olive oil
$\frac{1}{3}$ cup dry white wine
2 small dried chili peppers
4–6 small sweet red onions, peeled
3 celery stalks, trimmed and cut into 6-inch pieces
3–4 sprigs of fresh thyme
2 sprigs of fresh rosemary
coarse sea salt or kosher salt and freshly ground black pepper

Preheat the oven to 350°F.

Trim the tops of the fennel and, if necessary, peel off a layer of the tougher outer leaves. Using a sharp knife, cut the bulbs lengthwise in half and, making a deep "V," cut away the central core. Wipe the tomatoes, cut small crosses in their tops, and, if they are not very sweet, sprinkle a pinch of sugar into the cross.

Cut the garlic cloves in half and rub one of the cut sides all over the inside of a deep ovenproof gratin dish or a large roasting pan. Using a pastry brush, lightly paint the inside of the dish with a little olive oil. Then pour in the wine and add the chili peppers. Arrange the fennel, tomatoes, onions, and celery in the dish in a single layer, tucking in the remaining garlic. Brush the tops of the vegetables with the remaining oil, tuck in the sprigs of herbs, and season.

Bake in the preheated oven about 45 minutes or until the vegetables are tender, occasionally basting them with their juices and brushing them with extra olive oil if necessary, to stop them from going too brown and drying out.

Remove the chili peppers for serving.

Artichokes

The Green Globe artichoke, grown on the Central coast of California, specifically from Castroville, is the main variety of artichoke sold in the States. They are available year round, with peak supplies found from March to May, and from October to November.

Globe artichokes probably originated in the Mediterranean region, and are thought to have been eaten as long ago as Roman times. The artichoke grown in California is a thistle, and a member of the sunflower family. You may also find baby artichokes in your markets at certain times of the year; if they are very young and tender, the entirety may be consumed.

With the larger artichokes only certain parts may be eaten, namely the base of the leaves and the heart — once the spiky choke on top of it has been removed. Always choose artichokes when fresh and firm, with their leaves closely layered together. If their tips are going brown, they are past their best and the leaves will be rather tough. Although restaurants go to an inordinate amount of trouble trimming the leaf tops and removing the choke, I never bother.

Recently, in a restaurant in Brittany, I came across "artichoke crisps" which were quite superb and well worth copying. The chef had simply sliced the raw heart very finely on a mandoline grater and then deep-fried the slices in groundnut oil.

Globe Artichokes with Fava Beans

SERVES 4

4 globe artichokes
1 large lemon, halved
1 tbsp olive oil
3 sprigs of fresh flat-leaf parsley
3 whole black peppercorns
coarse sea salt or kosher salt and freshly ground black pepper
5 oz baby fava beans in their pods
2 hard-boiled eggs, shelled
$\frac{2}{3}$ cup extra-virgin olive oil
2 tsp finely chopped fresh summer savory or marjoram
1 tsp drained and finely chopped capers

Rub the artichokes all over with the cut halves of the lemon. Pack the artichokes right side up, into a non-aluminum saucepan, and fill it with just enough water to come up to the tips of their leaves — you do not want to drown them. Add the ordinary olive oil, parsley sprigs, peppercorns, and a generous pinch of salt.

Bring the water to a boil over medium heat, then lower the heat, and simmer, covered, for 35–45 minutes, depending on the size of the artichokes. To test if they are cooked, break off a leaf and check the texture of the fleshy base; it should be soft and yielding while the rest of the leaf is still firm. When they are ready, drain the artichokes in a colander and turn them upside down to allow any water inside to drain away.

Shell the fava beans, put them in a saucepan, and cover with lightly salted water. Bring to a boil and simmer over medium heat 30 seconds to 1 minute to loosen skins. Drain and refresh them immediately under cold running water. When they are cool enough to handle, skin by gently slitting them open and pressing them out with your fingers.

Cut one of the eggs in half, remove and reserve the yolk, then coarsely chop the other whole egg with the remaining white.

Press the reserved yolk through a strainer into a bowl and slowly beat in the extra-virgin olive oil, a few drops at a time, to make a thickish mixture.

Stir in the juice from the lemon halves, along with the chopped egg, summer savory, and capers. Fold in the skinned fava beans carefully, so you do not break them up, and season the mixture to taste.

Arrange the drained artichokes on a serving plate and gently separate the top leaves to make a small opening. Remove the fuzzy chokes with a teaspoon. Spoon some of the bean mixture into the artichokes, and refrigerate to chill. Serve the artichokes with the rest of the bean mixture in a bowl.

GLOBE ARTICHOKES WITH FAVA BEANS

Salad Vegetables

When thinking of a salad, most people start with lettuce. Thankfully, however, the range of salad greens available has increased over the last few years, beyond the dreams of gastronomy. Where once we had to make do with lank, vapid lettuces, like Boston lettuce, we now have a whole range of differently colored and textured plants to chose from.

LETTUCES are generally classified into several different types, categorized by shape and structure. CRISPHEAD LETTUCES usually refers to the crisp, but sadly flavorless, Iceberg lettuce. BUTTERHEAD LETTUCES, of which the most common types include Boston and Bibb lettuces, have soft, pliable leaves. LOOSE-LEAF LETTUCES, which grow in loose bunches on a common stem, include the red and green leaf lettuces. ROMAINE or COS LETTUCE has long leaves which form into elongated heads, and a crisp texture. The small inside leaves are quite sweet and

tender, but you may wish to remove the thick stems of the outer leaves.

Other interesting salad greens include members of the ENDIVE family. The three types most commonly found are: Belgian endive, which has bud-like shoots that are forced and blanched to give them their succulent texture and pale white leaves, sometimes tipped with the palest of yellow green; curly endive, sometimes mistakenly called chicory, which grows into loose heads and has lacy, spiky, leaves with green tips; and escarole, which also grows in loose heads, but has wide, flatter leaves, that are dark to pale green in color. Besides being used in a salad, escarole is often braised with garlic and olive oil and served as a vegetable.

Radicchio, a red-leafed member of the endive family, grows either in round, tight heads, which look like miniature red cabbages, or in narrow, tapered heads, which resemble Belgian endive but are streaked with purple. Radicchio may also be brushed with a fruity olive oil and roasted, broiled, or grilled.

More unusual additions to a salad, found in gourmet greengrocers and at farmer's markets, are baby lettuces, or smaller loose-leaf lettuces. Some types to look for

Lollo rosso lettuce

are: lollo rosso, with its ruffled red-tipped leaves; red and green salad bowl, both good, mild lettuces; red oak-leaf lettuce; and frisée, a blanched lettuce, which is pale yellow in color and has slightly bitter, spiky leaves. You may also find a salad mixture, called mesclun, which is a beautiful mixture of baby lettuces, tender bitter greens, herbs, and edible flowers.

Then there are the SINGLE-LEAF SALAD PLANTS, such as MÂCHE or LAMB'S LETTUCE, a low-growing plant with roundish, silky textured leaves, which are slightly nutty in taste; pungent ARUGULA or ROCKET, with a spicy flavor, which can turn quite overpowering in larger, older leaves but is especially good with citrus fruits; peppery WATERCRESS, which should never be touched when the leaves have wilted or turned yellow; and PURSLANE, which grows wild in many a garden, and has juicy, mild-flavored leaves and stems.

RADISHES are classified as salad roots and they can be round or cylindrical, red or white, purple and black. Although they are usually eaten raw, I was recently served them lightly blanched as a vegetable and they made interesting, if slightly curious, eating. I prefer to eat them on their own, spread lavishly with a sweet unsalted butter. You can also buy radish sprouts, very sweet-looking sprigs, which can add an interesting flavor to a salad, without the interruption of its texture. Like the other salad root, BEETS (see page 17), I would never dream of adding radishes to a salad.

Lettuce and Chervil Soup

You can usually tell just how fresh lettuce is by the pertness of the leaves. Another means, which is more reliable when buying Boston or bibb lettuce, is to turn the head upside down and examine the base of its stem: if it is still chalky white and exuding a milky substance, it has been cut within a few hours. It soon dries up, however, and the base starts turning brown, getting darker as it ages.

Romaine lettuce seems to retain its firmness and shape longer

than most other lettuce, but once its leaves start to separate and pull apart or turn brown at the edges, it will have lost the sweet flavor that makes it so good for this soup. Several cookbooks suggest that you can use tired lettuce for cooking, but do not be tempted.

SERVES 4–6

2 tbsp butter
1 large onion, finely chopped
1 garlic clove, finely chopped
$\frac{1}{2}$ lb romaine lettuce, leaves broken into pieces
small bunch of fresh chervil or flat-leaf parsley
$1\frac{1}{2}$ tbsp all-purpose flour
1 quart Chicken Stock (see pages 106–7), plus a little extra, or water
$\frac{2}{3}$ cup heavy cream
1 egg yolk
salt and freshly ground black pepper

In a large saucepan, melt the butter over medium heat. Add the onion and garlic and cook 5 minutes to soften. Stir in the lettuce leaves and the chervil or parsley, reserving a few sprigs for garnish, and cook 1–2 minutes. Sprinkle with the flour and, using a wooden spoon, stir it into the mixture. Cook 1 minute longer, then gradually stir in the stock, and simmer 5 minutes, or until lettuce is tender.

Process in a food processor until smooth. If you prefer your soup ultrasmooth, pass it through a strainer. Return to the pan and slowly reheat the soup. Depending upon how thick it is, you may need to add a little extra stock or water.

Beat the cream and egg yolk together in a bowl. Remove the soup from the heat. Stir a little of the hot soup into the cream mixture. Slowly add the cream mixture to the soup, stirring constantly. Season and gently heat the soup to just below a simmer. Do not let it boil.

Serve sprinkled with the reserved sprigs of chervil or flat-leaf parsley.

Wilted Green Salad with Prosciutto

For a green salad like this with a warm dressing, use a mixture of greens that wilt easily, such as mâche, arugula, chard or Swiss chard, baby spinach or ordinary spinach torn into small pieces, dandelion leaves, escarole, oak-leaf lettuce, or flat-leaf parsley.

SERVES 6

2 tbsp red wine vinegar
coarse sea salt or kosher salt and freshly ground black pepper
1 large shallot, finely chopped
1 garlic clove, finely chopped
6 tbsp extra-virgin olive oil
9–12 oz of mixed salad leaves (see above)
12 thin slices of prosciutto, cut into slivers

Pour the vinegar into a wok or large skillet, add a generous pinch of salt, and stir until dissolved. Add the shallot and garlic. Simmer over medium heat 2–3 minutes, but do not let it brown.

Then stir in the olive oil, add plenty of black pepper, and heat the dressing for a few minutes, or until it is warmed through.

Add the mixed greens and toss and stir them until they are just wilted but have not gone entirely limp. Using a slotted spoon, transfer the greens to a large salad bowl and scatter with the prosciutto. Then pour the dressing left in the wok over the top. Serve at once while the dressing is still warm.

Putting together a salad

Salads are a very personal matter because what they are made from must depend on your taste and sense of color. I like my salads leafy, with a good contrast of sweet and bitter, and crisp and soft. I always keep a plastic bag in the refrigerator full of different salad greens, wrapped in damp paper towels to keep the greens fresh. This way I can pick and choose from them to make an assortment to suit my mood. Nowadays, some gourmet stores sell the salad mixture called mesclun, which is trimmed and washed; while this is convenient, I find it is not nearly as much fun.

I usually start with a full-flavored lettuce, such as red leaf or romaine, tearing the leaves by hand into bite-size pieces as I do not believe in cutting them with a knife.

Then I may add some frisée or curly endive for texture, Belgian endive for bitterness, and radicchio for color. There are plenty of other leaves and herbs that I also like to include, although not all together at the same time: Chives or, for a more delicate flavor, their purple flowers; opal basil; chervil for its nuttiness; flat-leaf parsley for a hint of chlorophyl; hyssop flowers for their color; sorrel for its lemony bite; nasturtium leaves or arugula for a dash of peppery flavor; purslane for its texture; and baby spinach leaves — the list is endless, and none of my salads are ever alike.

Allow a total of about $1\frac{1}{2}$–2 oz per person, and tear the leaves by hand into similar bite-size pieces. Once I have made up my mix, I wash it in cold water and then use an invaluable salad spinner to remove the water.

Basic Vinaigrette

1 tsp Dijon-style mustard
$\frac{1}{3}$ cup extra-virgin olive oil
1 tbsp white wine vinegar
coarse sea salt or kosher salt and freshly ground black pepper

In a bowl, beat the mustard with a few drops of the olive oil until smooth.

Then slowly beat in the rest of the oil and the vinegar until the dressing is thick and creamy.

Season to taste with salt and pepper.

Variations

1 Replace the vinegar with the juice of 1 lemon.

2 Add 1 finely chopped shallot.

3 Add 1 tablespoon of finely chopped fresh herbs, such as flat-leaf parsley, chives, or tarragon.

Tomato, Honey, and Garlic Dressing

$\frac{1}{3}$ *cup tomato juice*

1 tsp honey

1 small garlic clove, finely chopped

1 tsp balsamic vinegar

$\frac{1}{3}$ *cup extra-virgin olive oil*

coarse sea salt or kosher salt and freshly ground black pepper

2 fresh basil leaves, finely chopped

In a large bowl, beat together the tomato juice, honey, garlic, and vinegar. Gradually beat in the oil until the dressing is thick and well blended.

Season with salt and pepper and stir in the basil.

Yogurt Dressing

$\frac{1}{3}$ *cup thick plain yogurt (see page 53)*

1 tsp Dijon-style mustard

$\frac{1}{3}$ *cup extra-virgin olive oil*

juice of $\frac{1}{2}$ lemon

coarse sea salt or kosher salt and freshly ground black pepper

1 tbsp finely chopped fresh coriander (cilantro)

In a large bowl, beat the yogurt with the mustard until smooth. Gradually beat in the oil and lemon juice until the dressing is thick and smooth.

Season with salt and pepper and stir in the coriander.

From left to right: *TOMATO, HONEY, AND GARLIC DRESSING; HERB VINAIGRETTE; YOGURT DRESSING; GREEN SAUCE (SEE OVERLEAF).*

Herbs

Fresh herbs are essential in cooking, for their tastes, smells, and colors. Every keen cook should have a herb garden or, at the very least, a sunny windowsill packed with pots. When cutting or plucking sprigs or leaves from a herb plant, try to use either the tips, side shoots or lateral leaves, to encourage new growth.

Many supermarkets stock a good range of fresh herbs. Because of the evaporation of their volatile oils, however, they start to lose their intensity of flavor after a few hours, even if they are kept chilled. Nevertheless, they are still better than dried herbs in most preparations, even, if admittedly, more expensive.

Always buy cut herbs when they look perky, and avoid any which show signs of wilting or if the leaves are changing color.

When you get fresh herbs home, wrap the herbs in damp paper towels and keep them in the refrigerator.

The flowers of herbs such as chives can be used in salads or salad dressings for extra color.

Bunches of parsley or basil can be stored in a jar of fresh water loosely covered with a plastic bag in the refrigerator. (Change the water every couple of days, as this keeps the herbs fresher and prevents the water from smelling stale.)

Some herbs, particularly the woody stemmed perennials like thyme, rosemary, bay leaves, hyssop, fennel, and sage, do dry quite successfully. The soft-stemmed herbs which mostly die back during the winter or need re-seeding, such as parsley, mint, basil, tarragon, chervil, and cilantro (or coriander), should really only be used fresh, although they can sometimes be frozen successfully for adding to hot dishes.

To chop herbs, I find the quickest way is to snip them with a pair of scissors, either directly into the food or into a small cup (for the herbs with larger leaves, just fold the leaves up and then snip them into tiny pieces) – it is a lot less work.

There are several superb combinations of herbs and other foods, which work because they are complementary and balance each other's flavors. Examples include eggs with sorrel, chicken with tarragon, lamb with rosemary, peas with mint, tomatoes with basil, fava beans with summer savory, rhubarb with sweet cicely (to eliminate some of its tartness), dill with salmon, and mackerel with fennel. Nevertheless, I am all in favor of cooks experimenting for themselves, as this is the only way that their repertoire of herbs can be broadened.

I also think that cooks should use varying amounts of herbs, according to their feel for them and the taste they prefer. This is why I do not always specify the amount exactly – a "large bunch" means a handful to one and a few sprigs to another. I have deliberately left it vague and urge you to achieve the balance you like rather than blindly follow my directions. The pungency of herbs also varies according to the time of year, so amounts can never be exactly prescribed.

With few exceptions, however, I do insist (although it goes without saying that you are free to ignore my prejudice) on using Italian flat-leaf rather than curly leaf parsley. I know that curly parsley is more available, both in Britain and in the States, but I just do not like its grainy coarse texture and its overwhelming flavor. It should only really be used with very bold-flavored and coarse or chewy textured ingredients, as in Jambon Persillé (see page 155). Flat-leaf parsley is far softer and subtler and enhances the flavor of food rather than overwhelming it.

I personally never use dried herbs, bay leaves apart, and if I cannot get the fresh herb I need for a particular recipe, I will substitute another fresh herb of a similar flavor. If you choose to use dried herbs, however, keep them in a cool dry place away from the light. Also remember, that they fairly rapidly lose any flavoring power they had, so buy them in small quantities from shops with a rapid turnover, and replace them on a regular basis.

Green Sauce

This is a very powerful sauce of Italian origin and it is usually served with plainly boiled meats, such as beef or tongue, or sausages. You could also use it to dress hard-boiled eggs or the meat of a chicken that has been boiled for stock (see page 106), or even to give a boost to a mild, soft cheese.

SERVES 4

6 canned anchovy fillets, drained
¼ cup finely chopped fresh flat-leaf parsley
8 cocnichons or sour gherkins, finely chopped
2½ tbsp capers, drained and finely chopped
1 small garlic clove, finely chopped
grated zest and juice of ½ lemon
6 tbsp extra-virgin olive oil
coarse sea salt or kosher salt and freshly ground black pepper

Coarsely chop the anchovies into small pieces, then pound them to a smooth paste in a mortar with a pestle, or blend them in a small food processor.

Put the paste into a large bowl along with the parsley, cocnichons, capers, garlic, and lemon zest and juice. Stir the ingredients together.

Beat in the olive oil a little at a time, until the sauce is thick and smooth. Check the seasoning (because of the anchovies you may not need any salt but add plenty of pepper). Let stand at least 30 minutes before serving.

The Dairy

Whether from the cow, sheep or goat, milk is the
essential component of all dairy products, producing
rich cream and yogurt and golden yellow butter. And,
countless local cheese-making skills transform it into
literally hundreds of different cheeses.

Milk

Milk is not only one of our most complete foods in itself, but it is also used as the basis of all dairy products. While we in the West generally drink and process milk from the cow, ewe, and goat, it is the milk of the buffalo and yak which finds favor in India and Tibet respectively. And in northern Africa, the milk from the camel is used.

The composition of milk varies according to the type and breed of animal, as well as its condition and diet. Among the nutrients it contains are calcium (two 8-oz glasses of milk will provide 60 percent of the recommended daily allowance), phosphorus, magnesium, and zinc, along with fat, protein (principally casein which makes up 82 percent of the protein milk), and vitamins A, D, and riboflavin, and carbohydrates in the form of the sugar lactose.

Once collected, fresh cow milk is subjected to various treatments: Most milk sold in Britain and in the U.S. is pasteurized to kill off any harmful bacteria. The exact process varies, but involves either heating the milk to a temperature of 145°F for at least 30 minutes, or to at least 161°F for 15 seconds, and then rapidly cooling it down to 40°F or lower. The milk is then usually homogenized by forcing it through a fine aperture, which breaks down the fat globules, and disperses and distributes them evenly throughout the milk.

Milk may also be skimmed to reduce its fat content. This was once done by hand: After the milk had been left to stand overnight, the dairymaid would skim off the cream which had risen to the surface, using a wooden skimmer. Now the process is highly mechanized and the milk is spun in a centrifuge to separate off the heavier fat globules.

In the States, milk used to be delivered in glass bottles by the milkman, and either left on the front step or in the milk chute, but those times are long gone. Nowadays, most people buy their milk in cartons or plastic jugs from the supermarket. There are, however, small dairies popping up, producing additive-free milk sold in glass bottles. The milk is pasteurized, but not homogenized, so the cream rises to the top. If there is such a dairy in your area, I urge you to support their efforts and to pay the higher price for this superior product.

In Britain, fresh cow milk is graded according to its fat content and processing: CHANNEL ISLAND or GOLD TOP has a legal minimum of 4.9 percent fat and is the only milk to come from specified breeds, in this case Jersey and Guernsey cows.

LOWFAT MILK sold in the United States has a milk fat level of between $\frac{1}{2}$ to 2 percent, and this is marked clearly on the carton. SKIM MILK or NONFAT MILK undergoes the same processing, but it has a milk fat content of less than $\frac{1}{2}$ percent. Lowfat and skim milk can be used for cooking, but they have a tendency to burn unless warmed over a low heat. Also, children under two years of age should consume whole milk, rather than lowfat or skim, because their growing bodies need the fat the whole milk provides.

Interestingly, skim and lowfat milk contain slightly higher levels of calcium than does whole milk. However, anyone who wishes to increase their calcium intake can choose a calcium-added milk, which boosts the amount of calcium in an 8-oz glass from 300 to 500 milligrams, which is half of the recommended daily allowance. Equally, if anyone has difficulty digesting milk, they could try ACIDOPHILUS MILK (also called sweet acidophilus milk), which is made by re-introducing the natural bacteria lactobacillus acidophilus that has been killed off during pasteurization,

Guernsey cows, whose milk goes to produce an extra creamy milk.

which makes milk easier to digest.

BUTTERMILK was traditionally a by-product of butter-making, but it is now commercially made by adding a buttermilk culture to skim or lowfat milk and sometimes a bit of salt for flavor. The result is a slightly thickened product with a light acidic taste, useful for baking biscuits and bread, and in salad dressings. Buttermilk is also available in powdered form, which is convenient for baking.

RAW (unpasteurized) fresh milk is not widely available in either Britain or the United States. You may be able to buy it from health-food stores or from small dairies. It is subjected to scrupulous testing, and the farms which sell it, along with the herds it comes from, must be inspected regularly in order to be certified to sell the milk. Raw milk is favored by the cognoscenti as it is thought to be fuller flavored and more nutritionally beneficial. Also sold on a small scale is GOAT MILK, found in some health-food stores.

Fresh milk is perishable and it should be refrigerated as soon as you bring it home from the market, ideally at a temperature of 40°F or less. Be sure to reseal the container after opening to prevent the milk from absorbing the flavors of other foods in the refrigerator.

The life of fresh milk can also be prolonged by certain industrial processes: ULTRA-PASTEURIZED MILK has been heated to a higher temperature than that ordinarily used for pasteurization in order to extend its shelf life, but this milk must be refrigerated; while UHT (Ultra High Temperature) milk, available whole, lowfat, and skim, is processed in a similar manner. It is then packaged in sterile containers, and may be stored without refrigeration for up to three months. Once opened, however, it should be treated as fresh milk.

Both SWEETENED CONDENSED MILK and EVAPORATED MILK are concentrated by high heat. POWDERED DRY MILK is milk which has had the moisture removed, and is available in two forms, whole, and nonfat. It is reconstituted by adding water.

Cream

Originally cream was skimmed by hand from the milk. Now it is generally produced by industrialized centrifugal separation. Like milk, most cream is pasteurized and homogenized, or it may be ultra-pasteurized. Cream may also contain stabilizers and emulsifiers. The different varieties of cream are named according to the percentage of milk they contain. The higher the milk fat content, the less likely it is to curdle when cooked, and easier it is to beat.

HEAVY CREAM, also called HEAVY WHIPPING CREAM, contains at least 36 percent milk fat. When beaten to stiff peaks, it doubles its original volume. Once whipped, it holds its texture for some time.

LIGHT WHIPPING CREAM, sometimes also called WHIPPING CREAM, contains at least 30, but not more than 36 percent milk fat.

ULTRA-PASTEURIZED CREAM can be heavy or light whipping cream, or half-and-half, that has been briefly heated to a temperature up to 300°F to give it a longer shelf life. However, once the container is opened, the cream lasts as long as pasteurized cream, but takes longer to whip than pasteurized cream.

The best way to whip cream is to first make sure it is well chilled, then put it in a chilled bowl and use a balloon whisk to aerate it rather than a rotary beater, which actually wears away the fat membrane and causes the cells to stick together.

LIGHT CREAM, also called COFFEE or TABLE CREAM, contains at least 18, but no more than 30 percent milk fat. It does not whip successfully, but it is good used as a pouring cream over puddings and desserts. As its fat content is low, it is much more likely to curdle when added to a hot liquid. To prevent this

Creams vary greatly in consistency and fat content, with golden-yellow British clotted cream the richest of all.

from happening, first stir a little of the hot mixture into the cream, then slowly stir the cream mixture into the hot liquid; and never let it boil or reheat it.

HALF-AND-HALF is very light, a mixture of milk and cream, that contains at least 10.5, but no more than 18 percent milk fat. Use it in coffee or on breakfast cereal but do not use it for whipping.

CRÈME FRAÎCHE is made by adding a culture to cream to thicken it and give it a distinctive light acidic flavor without souring it. Its fat content can vary and depends on the cream used.

To make crème fraîche
Heat 1 cup heavy whipping cream (not ultra-pasteurized) in a small saucepan over low heat until warm, from 90–100°F. Pour the cream into a small bowl or a jar and stir in 2 tablespoons buttermilk. Cover and let stand at room temperature 24–30 hours, without stirring, until it has thickened. Stir well, then cover and refrigerate. It will keep in the refrigerator for a week or two.

SOUR CREAM, the popular topping for baked potatoes, is made by adding a bacterial culture to cream with a milk fat level of at least 18 percent. It is incubated at 72°F, until a portion of the lactose is converted to the desired level of lactic acid, which gives it a tangy flavor and thickens it. Then, it is packaged, chilled, and aged 12–48 hours before being shipped to stores. It may also contain gums and emulsifiers to improve the texture and extend the shelf life.

Yogurt

Yogurt is a soured milk which is thought to have originated among the nomadic tribes of Eastern Europe. Their yogurt was very rich and acidic, and an entirely natural product in the sense that it was not manufactured. Whole milk was left to ferment and, as there was no temperature control, it would occasionally separate, and turn very sour indeed.

The yogurt made now is far milder. It is made with whole, lowfat, or skim milk, and sometimes cream. Cow milk is what is mainly used, but it may also be made with goat milk. First the milk is pasteurized and homogenized, and then it is inoculated with a lactobacillus bulgaricus and streptoccus thermophilus bacteria until the right amount of milk sugar turns to acid and the yogurt thickens. It is then cooled to prohibit further bacterial growth.

The fat content of yogurt depends on the milk from which it was made. Yogurt which is made from whole milk contains at least $3\frac{1}{2}$ percent milk fat; LOWFAT yogurt contains between $\frac{1}{2}$ and 2 percent milk fat; and NONFAT yogurt, less than $\frac{1}{2}$ percent. Yogurt is an excellent source of calcium, riboflavin, and protein, and depending on the type, can be low in calories and fat.

When buying yogurt, read the label to see if it contains active cultures. Yogurt is sometimes pasteurized after being cultured which destroys these friendly bacteria, helpful to those who are lactose intolerant.

You may be able to find Greek-style yogurt in Middle Eastern specialty stores. It is generally thicker than the more commercially available yogurt. You can also thicken yogurt yourself. Line a strainer with dampened cheesecloth or several sheets of white paper towels, or fit a cone-shaped coffee filter with a piece of filter paper, then spoon in the yogurt. Let it drain for 15 to 30 minutes, or longer, if you wish. The drained yogurt will be thicker and will taste richer.

Goat milk is used to make yogurt, as well as various cheeses.

Cooking with yogurt

As with cream in cooking, the higher the fat content of yogurt, the easier it is to add it to a hot liquid without fear of curdling. To be on the safe side you should stir a little of the hot liquid into the yogurt first to temper it, and then add the tempered yogurt back slowly to the liquid, stirring all the while. And, especially if you are using a lowfat version, you should stabilize it first by stirring a tablespoon of all-purpose flour or cornstarch into each 2 cups of yogurt; another method is to stir one egg white which has been lightly beaten with a pinch of salt into each 2 cups of yogurt. You may then safely add yogurt to a hot liquid, such as a soup or stew at the end of the cooking time, and let it simmer just a minute over a low heat, stirring constantly.

Butter

Butter is made by churning cream until it reaches a semisolid state. It takes about 9 quarts of milk to make 1 lb of butter, which by United States law, must contain at least 80 percent milk fat. Butter's taste and texture depend on the quality of milk, as well as the method used to make it.

U.S. butter is classified according to grades given by the United States Department of Agriculture, and these grades must be printed on the package. Starting with the highest, the grades and what they denote are: Grade AA, superior quality butter made from fresh cream, which must have a delicate sweet flavor, a fine pleasing aroma, a smooth and creamy texture, and should spread well; Grade A, very good butter made from fresh cream, must have a pleasing flavor, and a fairly smooth texture; and Grade B, standard butter, which is made from selected sour cream and has an acceptable flavor, but lacks the quality of the above grades. It is sold as an ingredient in processed foods, rather than as a product on its own. Grades AA and A are what you will find in U.S. supermarkets.

Butter is either lightly salted or unsalted, and it may be artificially colored with annatto. Unsalted butter is more perishable than salted butter, because the salt acts as a preservative.

I prefer to cook with unsalted butter as it has a clearer taste, and when melted, does not burn easily.

There is a new butter called Plugra with a high milk fat content being made in the U.S. As this book was being written, it was the only one of its type, and should be available in gourmet stores. It has an 82 percent milk fat content, as opposed to the 80 percent in regular butter. This allows you to use slightly less of it in a recipe, and it is also good in sauces, giving them a better sheen, texture, and color.

There are a number of margarines, butter spreads, vegetable oils, and lowfat or no-fat spreads sold as butter substitutes. I prefer the real thing and, when watching my diet, I would rather do without butter than resort to any of these.

To clarify butter

In order to get rid of the sediment when using butter in cooking, you can first clarify it. This turns the fat into pure butterfat with all the milk solids removed, so it can be heated to a higher temperature than whole butter without burning. Consequently, it is very useful for sautéeing or panfrying.

Clarified butter is easy to make yourself. Melt the butter over a low heat, and leave it to cook gently for a few minutes, making sure it does not turn brown. When it has separated, remove it from the heat, and let it stand for a few minutes. Then pour it through a strainer lined with dampened cheesecloth or white paper towel. It can then be heated to a very high temperature without burning, and will keep in the refrigerator for a couple of weeks.

Flavored Butters

Butter flavored with fresh herbs, ground spices, sugars, fruit purées, or other ingredients may be served with broiled or grilled meat or fish, muffins, or with hot desserts, such as crêpes or waffles. Best made with a slightly softened unsalted butter, flavored butters are easy to prepare and can be mixed up well in advance. This is an ideal way to take advantage of a glut of herbs in season: Use a single herb or combine several for an interesting flavor combination.

Spoon the butter mixture into the center of a sheet of aluminum foil; fold one long edge over the butter and roll and shape it into a log to store in the freezer for up to two months. Then, when you want to use the butter, you can simply slice off rounds.

Sauce Beurre Blanc

Best made with a good unsalted butter for a sweet creamy flavor, this classic French sauce is remarkably easy to make, provided you only beat the butter into the pan in small amounts and never let it get too hot or it will curdle.

SERVES 4

$\frac{1}{4}$ *cup finely chopped shallots*
3 tbsp dry white wine
2 tbsp white wine vinegar
1 stick unsalted butter, chilled
few drops of fresh lemon juice
salt and freshly ground white pepper

Put the shallots, wine, and vinegar into a small heavy-bottomed saucepan. Simmer over medium heat until reduced to about 1 tablespoon of syrupy liquid, being careful not to scorch.

Remove the pan from the heat while you cut the butter into small pieces, so the reduction has time to cool slightly.

Using a balloon whisk, start to whisk the pieces of butter into the liquid one at a time. Turn the heat down to low, return the pan to the heat, and continue adding and whisking in the butter until all the butter is incorporated and the sauce is frothy.

If the sauce looks like it is getting too hot, more than hand-hot, and the butter starts to melt into a clear liquid, simply remove the pan from the heat and continue whisking in the butter off the heat.

When all the butter is incorporated, add the lemon juice and season to taste with salt and pepper.

Serve immediately or keep warm off the heat in the top of a double boiler or in a bowl balanced over a saucepan filled with warm water. Alternatively, keep warm in a thermos bottle.

Lime Butter

SERVES 4

4 tbsp unsalted butter, slightly softened
grated zest and juice of 1 lime
coarse sea salt or kosher salt and freshly ground black pepper

Process the butter and lime zest in a food processor or blender until smooth.

With the machine still running, add the lime juice and season to taste with salt and pepper.

Turn the butter out onto the center of a sheet of foil and roll it into a log shape about 4-inches long, then wrap it up.

Store in the freezer up to 2 months, until required.

Variations

1 Make Chili Butter by replacing the lime zest and juice with a small pinch of Oriental chili paste, a pinch of cayenne, and 1 teaspoon of fresh lemon juice.
2 Make Mustard Butter by replacing the lime zest and juice with 1 tablespoon of grainy French mustard and the juice of $\frac{1}{2}$ lemon.
3 Make Herb Butter by adding a small bunch each of fresh flat-leaf parsley, chervil, and tarragon to the food processor, processing them until finely chopped, and then processing with the butter until smooth.
4 Make Sweet Butter by adding 1 tablespoon of superfine or granulated sugar, 1 or 2 soft, ripe strawberries, and 2 teaspoons of vodka to the butter.

Cheese

Turning milk into cheese has always struck me as one of the wonders of food production. That such a wide diversity of tastes, textures, shapes, and colors can be made from milk is nothing short of a miracle.

In fact, cheese-making dates back to the earliest days of European and Asian civilizations, when primitive farmers discovered an efficient means of preserving milk for those seasons when the animals were dry. Once the milk was collected, they would leave it to curdle in the sun, then beat it with branches and sprinkle it with salt. The cheese was finally matured by either further drying in the sun, or storing it in caves. Over the centuries, cheese-making has become very refined and sophisticated, and numerous techniques now exist.

To start at the beginning, nothing has such a strong influence on the cheese as the milk from which it is made. Most cheeses are made from cow, ewe, or goat milk, although in some parts of the world, mare, yak, reindeer, and buffalo milk (as for mozzarella) are used. The milk can either be whole, skim, or lowfat; it may also be fresh, raw, or pasteurized, and left to mature overnight or longer.

To explain the process of cheese-making as simply as possible, I have divided it into three basic stages.

First, the milk must be prepared, so a starter and rennet are added: The starter introduces the bacteria essential for the milk to ripen, and the rennet causes the milk to curdle so it separates out into curds and whey. The curds are what the cheese is made of, so the whey must be drained away. (Although a few cheeses, such as ricotta, are made from the whey.)

Then begin the processes specific to the actual making of cheese. These can include cutting, milling, or

The art of cheese-making, combined with individual local conditions, has produced an extraordinary variety of cheeses over the centuries.

kneading the curds, "cheddaring" them (a process specific to cheddar by which they are turned and stacked), heating them slightly, ladling them into molds, leaving them to drain naturally, salting them or leaving them to soak in brine for a saltier flavor, injecting them with mold for a blue cheese, or pressing them for a semihard or hard cheese.

Finally, there comes the process of ripening. Some cheeses are eaten fresh, within a day or so of being made; others may be aged for as long as three years. Again, depending on the cheese, the atmosphere in which it is matured may be damp or dry – in a cellar, cave, or drying room – and the cheese may be turned daily, or every two weeks or so to ensure that it ripens evenly. It may also be pierced, so a mold may develop within it; washed or brushed for a rind finish or for a bloom of mold to develop on its exterior; or even wrapped in a cloth or sealed in wax or fat.

Throughout the world, countless different cheeses are made. They may be loosely divided into the following categories:

FRESH-MILK or UNRIPENED SOFT CHEESES, such as fromage blanc (also sometimes called fromage frais), ricotta, Petit Suisse, pot cheese, cottage cheese, or cream cheese.

Fromage blanc, originally from France, is a soft, fresh cheese which is similar in consistency to sour cream. When made with whole milk, it has a minimum of 20 percent fat in the cheese, and is suitable for eating on its own, with fruit, or use in cooking. You may also find flavored versions in supermarkets, which make delicious snacks, similar to eating yogurt.

Cream cheese is a soft cheese made with a mixture of cow milk and heavy cream, and, by U.S. law, must contain at least 33 percent milk fat.

You can also find fresh goat milk cheeses, called CHÈVRE, sold as either individual cheeses, in small disks (often called crottins), pyramids, or logs, or the cheese may be cut from a larger log or packed into containers. The logs, disks, and pyramids may either be plain or rolled in ash to develop their flavor, rolled in pepper, or mixed with fresh chopped herbs. There are many excellent small goat cheese producers in the States (see mail order sources, page 250 and see page 59).

Then there are the creamy RIPENED SOFT CHEESES, covered with a downy rind (or, to put it more technically, coated with a bacteria culture). Camembert and brie are probably the most famous examples: Some people eat these while they are still quite hard and chalky; others prefer them melting and runny. If you are buying a cut piece, first check how ripe it is by looking at the inside; it will have a layer of soft creamy paste in the middle, sandwiched between two layers of firmer cheese — the width of the central band is an indication of the ripeness. For a whole cheese, press

Farmhouse cheddar must be matured for many months before being sold.

its sides gently: they should be soft and yielding. A good cheese should smell sweet with a hint of hay; if it has an ammonia odor, it is beyond its prime.

SOFT RIND-WASHED CHEESES have rinds which range in color from pale beige to a deep orange, a dense texture, and an earthy taste, as the surface has been washed with brine during ripening to give it a deeper flavor. Muenster, Pont l'Evêque, and Livarot are the best-known examples, and these are cheeses that should be served on a cheese board, but never used for cooking.

Although technically known as ripened soft and soft rind-washed cheeses, cheeses in the above two categories can also be called semisoft.

VEINED or BLUE CHEESES, on the other hand, can be used to great effect in soups (see page 62) and crackers (see page 62), as well as just being served sliced on top of a piece of steak for added piquancy or simply eaten with chunks of good bread or crackers. All blue cheeses are cultured with a particular bacteria to give

them their distinctive blue- or green-veined appearance, and their creamy, mellow-sharp flavor: The best include cow's milk Stilton and ewe's milk Roquefort.

HARD or PRESSED CHEESES, which have been pressed before maturation, include such famous examples as cheddar, Edam, and Parmesan. With hard cheese in particular, it is fair to say that you get what you pay for, as a handmade, well-matured cheese will cost a lot more. British Farmhouse Cheddar, made in the traditional way on the farm with its own milk, pressed with huge cheese presses into large wheels which are matured and turned regularly for a minimum of 14 months, is bound to taste better and more complex than blocks of cheese churned out of a highly industrialized and efficient creamery. What has been removed by industrialization is the craft element – the human contact of the expert who can tell so much by smell and feel that he or she is able to create a great cheese. Mass-produced cheeses are fine for cooking, but for eating on their own, I urge you to seek out a good farmhouse cheese which bears the stamp and flavor of its maker.

Excellent farmhouse cheddars are produced on a small scale in Vermont, New York State, and Wisconsin.

COOKED CHEESES are those made by the same process as hard cheeses, except that the curds are heated in the whey and "cooked" during the cutting stage. The result is a rubbery cheese, such as Gruyère or Emmentaler, which form long elastic strands when heated, and are delightful used in a fondue or a hot bowl of hearty soup.

Possibly the most used BRINED CHEESE is feta which originates from Greece, where it is made with ewe milk. A good feta should have a sharp, tangy, slightly salty flavor with a crumbly texture, neither too wet, nor too dry. It can be crumbled into salads or beaten into a soufflé mixture for extra pungency. It is also good on its own, enjoyed with a mound of olives.

Buying cheese

When choosing cheese, if possible, buy it at a store with a good stock and high turnover, and have it cut freshly, rather than buying prepacked slices from the supermarket. The chances are that the cheese will have been better matured, allowed to breathe, and ripen more naturally, and been kept at an ideal "cheese-friendly" temperature.

What is important when you are buying pieces cut from a whole cheese is to look for how firm and fresh the pieces are, and whether or not it is dried out and sweating, curling up at the edges, or showing signs of uneven ripeness. If in doubt, always ask for a taste, as any proud cheese purveyor will give you a sample.

To store cheese, wrap it loosely in plastic wrap and keep it in the refrigerator. Remember to take it out to let it breathe and come up to room temperature a good 30 minutes before serving time.

Farmhouse cheeses

British Farmhouse Cheddar has already been mentioned, but American farmhouse cheeses are excellent, as well. Maytag Blue Cheese, produced in Iowa, is a soft, creamy cheese, made almost entirely by hand. Bresse Bleu, made in Wisconsin, is a rich, triple-cream blue-veined cheese. Laura Chenel's Chèvre produces excellent fresh and aged goat cheeses, including Taupinière, which has a moist crumbly texture, and Tome, similar to Pecorino Romano, good for grating or serving as a table cheese. Little Rainbow Chèvre makes fresh and aged chèvres and a quite unusual smoked Chèvre de Ferme, which is smoked in grape vine trimmings. The Camembert produced by the Craigston Cheese Company is wonderfully rich. And Vella produces an aged Dry Jack cheese with pepper.

Unpasteurized cheeses

Many of the finest cheeses are made with raw (unpasteurized) milk, as most aficionados agree that if the milk is subjected to high temperatures, the inherent flavor and characteristics of that milk will be lost. The cheese will therefore not develop its full depth and complexity, and the resulting flavor is likely to be far more bland.

Unfortunately, very little raw-milk cheese is produced in the U.S., and if produced, it must age for 60 days. Also, by law, raw-milk cheeses may not be imported to the States unless they are aged 60 days as well, which causes a change in the taste and the texture.

Spinach, Ricotta, and Raisin Tart

SERVES 4–6

$\frac{1}{3}$ cup dark, seedless raisins

$1\frac{1}{2}$ tbsp dry sherry wine or dry white wine

4 tbsp butter, softened, plus extra for greasing

$\frac{1}{2}$ lb Basic Pie Pastry (see page 199)

1 lb fresh spinach, trimmed

grated zest of 1 orange

pinch of grated nutmeg

pinch of ground ginger

coarse sea salt or kosher salt and freshly ground black pepper

$1\frac{1}{2}$ tbsp superfine or granulated sugar

$\frac{3}{4}$ cup part-skim ricotta cheese

$\frac{2}{3}$ cup pine nuts

2 large eggs, lightly beaten

Soak the raisins in the sherry or wine about 30 minutes, or until they plump up. Preheat the oven to 375°F.

Generously butter an 8-inch tart or quiche pan with removeable bottom. Roll out the pastry to a thickness of about $\frac{1}{2}$ inch and use it to line the prepared pan. Let rest in the refrigerator about 15 minutes.

Prick the bottom of the pastry shell with a fork, cover it with a sheet of parchment paper weighted down with baking beans or rice, and bake it "blind" in the preheated oven 15 minutes. Let cool but leave the oven on. Remove the beans and parchment.

Meanwhile, wash the spinach, but do not drain it. Put it in a saucepan over medium heat, cover, and cook about 2 minutes or until it is wilted. (As long as it is still quite wet, it should not be necessary to add any water to the pan.)

Drain and, when cool enough to handle, using your hands, squeeze out all excess moisture, then coarsely chop the leaves. Put them in a bowl and add the orange zest, nutmeg, ginger, and salt and pepper to taste. Stir together, then spread the spinach mixture in the pastry shell, spreading it evenly.

In a clean bowl, cream the butter with the sugar until light and fluffy. Beat in the ricotta, and stir in the pine nuts and raisins in sherry. Stir the eggs into the mixture, then spread it evenly over the spinach.

Cover with a disk of parchment paper and bake about 15 minutes, then remove the paper, and bake 20 minutes longer, or until the filling has set and the top has turned golden brown.

Serve immediately.

SPINACH, RICOTTA, AND
RAISIN TART opposite.

Stilton Soup

When buying Stilton, make sure it is fresh and still creamy — the edges turn a deeper yellow. If it is not, ask for it well-matured.

SERVES 4

2 tbsp butter
1 onion, finely chopped
1 tbsp all-purpose flour
grated zest of ½ lemon
1 quart Chicken Stock (see pages 106–7)
¼ lb Stilton cheese
2 tbsp light cream (optional)
salt and freshly ground black pepper
small bunch of fresh chives, snipped

In a large saucepan over medium heat, melt the butter, add onion, and cook 5–7 minutes, until soft and golden. Sprinkle with the flour and cook 1–2 minutes, stirring frequently. Add the lemon zest and slowly stir the stock into the pan, and bring to a boil.

Chop the cheese or crumble it with your fingers. Stir it into the pan, turn down the heat, and simmer about 3 minutes until it has melted, stirring occasionally.

Remove the pan from the heat. If you like your soup really smooth, put it into a food processor and process.

Season with plenty of black pepper but, depending on the cheese, go easy on the salt. Serve with a swirl of cream, if you wish, and sprinkle with chives.

Blue Cheese Sablés

For this recipe you can choose any of the blue cheeses which can be crumbled. Roquefort gives the crackers a particular bite.

MAKES ABOUT 32

1 stick butter, plus extra for greasing
2 oz blue cheese, crumbled
2 oz sharp cheddar cheese, shredded
¾ cup self-rising flour
pinch of cayenne
pinch of salt
½ cup walnut pieces, crushed or coarsely chopped

Preheat the oven to 375°F and lightly butter a baking sheet.

Put the 2 cheeses, butter, flour, cayenne, and salt in a food processor. Process with on-and-off pulses until the mixture comes together to form a ball. (To mix by hand: Put all the dry ingredients into a bowl, melt the butter, and, using a wooden spoon, stir it into the mixture until it comes together to form a ball.)

Break off equal quantities of the dough with your fingers, about 1 scant tablespoon, and roll them into small balls about 1 inch in diameter with your hands.

Scatter the crushed walnuts on a lightly floured surface. Roll the balls in the nuts, pressing gently to make sure each ball is well coated with the nuts. Arrange the balls on the baking sheet, and press the balls down with a fork so they form a small, thick cracker.

Scatter any remaining nuts on top of the crackers, and bake about 15 minutes, or until the crackers are golden brown. Serve either straight from the oven or when cool, with cocktails.

Roquefort is salted before being taken to the caves where it matures left.
STILTON SOUP WITH BLUE CHEESE SABLÉS right.

Twice~baked Goat Cheese Soufflés

Goat cheese has a delightful earthy and gamy flavor. For this recipe, you can use a soft, semisoft, or pressed cheese. The harder and more aged the cheese, the stronger its flavor will be.

SERVES 4

1 tbsp unsalted butter, plus extra for greasing
2 tbsp hazelnuts (filberts)
$2\frac{1}{2}$ tbsp dry bread crumbs
$1\frac{1}{2}$ tbsp all-purpose flour
$\frac{1}{3}$ cup milk
1 egg yolk
$\frac{1}{4}$ lb goat cheese
salt and freshly ground white pepper
4 egg whites
$\frac{1}{2}$ tsp fresh lemon juice
vegetable oil, for greasing

Preheat the oven to 375°F and generously butter four 4-oz ramekins.

Scatter the hazelnuts on a baking sheet and toast them, stirring occasionally, in the oven 10–15 minutes, or until golden brown. While still warm, rub them in a dry cloth to remove the skins. Process in a food processor until finely ground, then mix with the bread crumbs in a small bowl. Turn the oven down to 350°F.

Spoon some of the nut-and-bread crumb mixture into each of the ramekins. Tilt and turn the ramekins around so the sides and bottom are thoroughly coated with the mixture. Tip out any excess and reserve.

Melt the butter in a small saucepan over low heat. Add the flour and, stirring constantly, cook for 2–3 minutes. Gradually pour in the milk, stirring constantly to prevent any lumps forming. Turn up the heat and bring to a boil, then simmer 1 minute, stirring.

Circular cheese molds, skimmers, and a ladle hang ready for use above.
TWICE-BAKED GOAT CHEESE SOUFFLÉ right.

Remove from the heat and beat in the egg yolk. Depending on whether you are using a hard or soft cheese, shred or mash it with a fork. Add three-quarters of the cheese to the milk-egg mixture. Season to taste.

In a clean bowl, beat the egg whites with a pinch of salt and the lemon juice until they form stiff peaks. Using a large metal spoon, carefully fold them into the cheese mixture.

Half fill the ramekins with the soufflé mixture, dividing equally. Sprinkle the rest of the goat cheese on top, then cover with the remaining soufflé mixture.

Using a spatula, smooth the surface. Scatter the remaining crumb mixture on top and run your thumb around the inside edge of each ramekin to create a little groove (this prevents the soufflés spilling over the edges).

Place the ramekins in a roasting pan, pour in enough boiling water to come about halfway up the ramekins, and bake 10 minutes, until lightly browned.

Remove the soufflés from the water bath, let them cool about 10 minutes, then unmold them onto a lightly oiled baking sheet. Leave the oven on.

For their second cooking, either return them to the oven for a further 5 minutes or place them under a hot broiler for 3–4 minutes until browned. Serve on a bed of salad greens dressed with a hazelnut vinaigrette.

The Rivers
And Seashores

*Rivers and lakes teem with countless freshwater fish,
delighting anglers and cooks alike; while from coastal waters
and deep-sea fishing grounds comes an even greater choice,
from huge halibut and cod to tiny cockles and shrimps.*

Freshwater Fish

Considering the number of rivers that flow through Britain and the United States and the thousands of anglers who patiently spend hour after hour on the banks with rod, line, or net in hand, it is surprising how few freshwater fish we actually eat.

Salmon and trout are both well-known and easily available; eel, even though it is a fish native to North American waters, is more widely accepted and available in Britain. Although not all fresh-water fish are worth the trouble, because they are too bony or their flesh too soft, or their flavor too coarse, there are several species, some less well-known than others, worth seeking out.

The best include CARP, a meaty fish, which is popular in the cooking of the Chinese and the East Europeans. CARP is essential for making gefilte fish and is superb baked and served with a sweet-and-sour sauce; CATFISH, very popular in the United States, is most often farm-raised and takes well to aggressive seasonings, breadings, and crumb coatings; PERCH, much favored by the landlocked Swiss and by those living in the Great Lakes region, is not unlike sole, and is best cooked in butter or lightly breaded and panfried; PIKE is a real treat baked in foil and served with a delicate beurre blanc sauce, or, if you cannot cope with the bones, turned into quenelles; SHAD, prized both for

Carp and eel are less commonly eaten freshwater fish.

the fish and its roe, signals the arrival of spring on the East Coast of the United States. The fish may be a bit difficult to bone, but is delicious broiled or sautéed and served with a light sauce. The roe is best when quickly sautéed in hot butter and served with crisp bacon and a sprinkling of chives; ZANDER (pike perch) in Britain, known in the States as WALLEYE or YELLOW PERCH, is less bony than pike and robust in flavor, needing no more elaborate preparation than a light coating of flour before being quickly sautéed in butter to bring out its flavor; WHITEFISH, found in lakes from New England west to Minnesota, and north into Canada, can weigh up to 20 lb and is excellent broiled, grilled and poached. This delicate fish is often smoked as well. Whitefish roe, golden in color, is considered a delicacy; STRIPED BASS, found mainly in the Northeast, is wonderful baked whole with fennel, or broiled or grilled, skin on, after being brushed with a seasoned oil.

Freshwater fish are at their best if caught from clear, clean rivers or lakes. When they come from the brackish waters of slow-running rivers or deep stagnant ponds, there is a danger of their tasting a little dank and muddy. If this is potentially a problem, clean them thoroughly and soak them for several hours in either ice cold water or water mixed with a dash of vinegar, changing it at least every couple of hours.

Salmon

The salmon is a curious fish in that it spends half its life in fresh water and half in the sea, but it counts as a freshwater fish as it is usually caught in rivers and streams.

The Atlantic salmon is rightly known as "the king of fish." In my mind, it is far superior to, and should never be confused with, the Pacific and Coho salmon; they are of a different genus, generally much smaller and with a far less interesting flavor. However, those living on the West Coast of the United States claim the Pacific King salmon, with its rich, complex flavor, is a superior fish. And more often than not, it is a wild fish.

The finest specimens of the Atlantic salmon, recognizable by the silver-blue, streamlined body lightly marked with black spots, are thought to come from the cool, clear waters of Scottish rivers. King salmon comes from the West Coast of the United States, from waters which run along the coast from Alaska south to California. Salmon migrate to the sea to feed and then return to the same river, eventually to spawn when mature. Most fish caught weigh anything from $3\frac{1}{2}$ lb to 10 lb, but older fish can be 60 lb.

As a mature salmon does not feed once it has come back to its river, it is at its best caught at the estuary or on a run upstream on its homeward journey. It is still plump and full of flavor from the rich feeding grounds at sea and has yet to exhaust itself by laying or fertilizing eggs.

A whole salmon should be stiff, with a sheen to its skin and blood-red gills. Both wild and farmed salmon are sold whole, in steaks, or in fillets. It is more difficult to tell if a steak or fillet is fresh, as you do not have the gills: The flesh should be firm and bright, and as in any fish, limpness and dull color is a sure sign of old age.

Salmon may be cooked in any number of ways: poached, broiled on its own or with butter, barbecued, steamed over a bed of vegetables, roasted, or baked. Despite its high oil content, it dries out rather quickly and does not take kindly to overcooking.

Poaching a whole salmon to serve cold

As salmon is quite a rich fish with compact meaty flesh, I generally allow a 5 lb fish for 8–10 people. Once the fish is cleaned and gutted, lay it flat in a fish poacher or a suitable pan with a lid which is large enough to hold the fish. Pour over it a mixture of three parts water to one part dry white wine, until the fish is completely submerged. Add the white parts of a couple of leeks, two sliced carrots, a couple of slices of lemon, a large bunch of parsley, a couple of peppercorns and a generous pinch of coarse sea salt or kosher salt. Very slowly bring it to a boil, then cover the fish poacher or pan and simmer for 6 minutes per pound. Leave the fish to cool in the liquid until just warm. When you lift the fish out you will find that it is cooked right through, but still moist and succulent. Refrigerate until required, then serve it with Mousseline Hollandaise (see page 128) or a Green Sauce (see page 45).

Wild or farmed salmon?

Over the last 10 years there has been a tremendous growth in salmon farming. This means that there is a constant supply of fresh salmon, and farmed salmon is far less expensive than wild salmon. While farmed salmon can be quite good, it lacks the full flavor of wild. Confined to pens, the fish are usually fattier due to lack of exercise.

Unfortunately, it is difficult to distinguish wild from farmed salmon just by looking at the fish. Because of the enormous difference in price, it must be a terrific temptation for an unscrupulous fish purveyor to sell inferior fish at the higher price. One way to discriminate, which I admit is not foolproof, is to look for a blunter-shaped head and a more-forked tail when buying a whole fish: farmed salmon heads have a more pronounced "V" shape and the tails are less defined. When it comes to buying steaks or fillets, examine the flesh closely: that of farmed salmon looks more ribbed and has thicker rings of fatty deposits.

Another way to be sure the fish is not farm-raised is to buy Alaskan salmon, which is always wild. It is also always frozen before shipping, but generally sold thawed. Check for signs of age or freezer burn, or ask for a frozen piece, so you can thaw it at home slowly in the refrigerator.

Tartare of Salmon with Cucumber Salad

This recipe is taken from Raymond Blanc's magical book, Recipes from Le Manoir aux Quat' Saisons. *Although he stipulates wild salmon, I think that as it is marinated it is an extravagance probably better suited to a deluxe restaurant than home cooking.*

As fillet of salmon is essential for this recipe and as it is also easier to make if you have a matching pair to lay one on top of the other, I suggest buying a whole tail and asking the fish purveyor to fillet and skin it for you.

SERVES 8

1 1-lb fresh salmon tail piece, filleted and skinned
1½ tbsp chopped fresh dill
grated zest and juice of 1 lemon
1 tbsp superfine or granulated sugar
coarse sea salt or kosher salt and freshly ground white pepper
½ tsp Dijon-style mustard

3 tbsp sour cream
½ cucumber, trimmed and peeled
1 tsp white wine vinegar
2 tbsp safflower oil
8 sprigs of fresh dill

Remove any stray pin bones from the salmon with a pair of tweezers, then lay the fillets flat on a plate. Mix 1 tablespoon of the chopped dill together with the lemon zest, sugar, and about 1 tablespoon of salt and rub the mixture all over both sides of the salmon. Place 1 fillet on top of the other, cover with foil, and let marinate in the refrigerator for 12 hours.

At the end of this time, unwrap the salmon and rinse it under cold running water to remove the salt. Drain it well, pat dry with paper towels, and cut it into thin strips about 1-inch long.

In a large bowl, mix the lemon juice with the mustard, 2 teaspoons of the sour cream, the remaining chopped dill, and a little pepper and stir in the salmon. Refrigerate for 1 hour.

Meanwhile, prepare the cucumber by cutting it in half lengthwise and scooping out the seeds with a teaspoon. Slice it finely, put it in a colander, sprinkle over about 1 teaspoon of salt, and let it stand for 30 minutes. Then rinse under cold running water, drain, and pat dry with paper towels. Put the cucumber slices in a small bowl, add the vinegar, oil, and a little pepper, and mix together thoroughly.

Raymond Blanc serves the salmon stunningly presented in individual molds – very effective but surprisingly simple. Using a 2-inch round cookie cutter as a mold, place it in the center of a plate and fill it almost up to the top with the salmon, pressing down gently with the back of a teaspoon to pack the fish firmly. Spread just under 1 teaspoon of sour cream on the top, smoothing it with a spatula, then carefully lift off the cookie cutter. Arrange slices of cucumber around the base and decorate the top with a sprig of dill. Repeat to make seven more.

Serve with slices of toasted Brioche (see page 196).

Fly-fishing for salmon left.
TARTARE OF SALMON WITH CUCUMBER SALAD below.

The Yellowstone River in Montana, known for its superb trout.

Eog Rhost, Roast Sea Trout or Sewin

to the sea and returning to the river to spawn, and can be cooked in exactly the same way; however, it is actually a trout.

Roasting "sewin" was a favorite practice of the Welsh fisherwives living by the banks of the Teifi and Tywi rivers. Although some true salmon are netted in these rivers, the catch usually consists mostly of SEWIN, or SEA TROUT.

The fishermen still fish from coracles, which are light, tub-like boats rowed with one oar. Traditionally made from horse- or ox-hide stretched over a framework of osiers, the coracle requires great skill just to keep it upright. Catching fish from one is even more difficult as two boats work together, rowing side by side with a net stretched between them.

Although they are two distinct species, sea trout is often confused with salmon. This is hardly surprising as sea trout looks and tastes like salmon, is a similar size, follows a similar life cycle of migrating

SERVES 6–8

1 stick + 2 tbsp cold butter, plus extra for greasing
1 fresh sea trout, weighing 4–5 lb,
cleaned and gutted
salt and freshly ground white pepper
large pinch of grated nutmeg
large pinch of ground ginger
2 bay leaves
sprig of fresh rosemary
2 whole cloves
2 tbsp dry white wine
grated zest of 1 orange
grated zest of 1 lemon

Preheat the oven to 350°F and butter a baking dish and a large piece of parchment paper.

Season the fish inside and out with salt and pepper to taste. Melt I stick of the butter, stir in the nutmeg and ginger, and, using a pastry brush, paint the fish all over with the mixture. Dip the bay leaves into the mixture and tuck them, along with the rosemary and cloves, inside the fish.

Place the trout in the dish and cover with the greased paper. Bake in the oven for $1-1\frac{1}{4}$ hours, allowing 15 minutes per pound, basting it occasionally with its juices. Transfer the cooked fish to a warmed serving dish and carefully peel off its skin.

Strain the cooking juices into a small saucepan and add the white wine and the orange and lemon zests. Bring to a boil and boil rapidly until the liquid is reduced by about half. Turn down the heat. Cut the remaining cold butter into small pieces and whisk it into the sauce, one piece at a time, without letting the sauce become more than hand hot, otherwise the sauce will become thin and curdled rather than frothy. Adjust the seasoning and pour the sauce over the fish.

Trout

The BROWN TROUT and the SEA or SALMON TROUT (see opposite) are the only wild trout species native to Britain. The brown trout lives in rivers, streams and lakes and, like all freshwater fish, has pale creamy gray flesh. Trout found in U.S. waters include the brown trout as well as BROOK, LAKE, and GOLDEN TROUT. These species, rarely seen on sale, are most often caught by anglers. Trout is delicately flavored and responds best to simple cooking methods, such as broiling or light sautéeing in butter.

The RAINBOW TROUT is the species you will generally find in your markets. It adapts well to confinement, and is therefore the choice for fish farming. Most American rainbow trout are farm-raised in Idaho; trout farming developed in Britain about 15 years ago.

Although the flesh of farmed rainbow trout is pink, do not be fooled into thinking that this is natural or that you are buying a sea trout. The color is achieved by adding a supplement to its feed. Available in a range of sizes from 1–5 lb, farmed rainbow trout has a coarser texture and a more robustly flavored flesh than its wild cousins.

Honeyed Trout

SERVES 6

4 tbsp butter, plus extra for greasing
3 onions, thinly sliced
2 tsp ground cumin
salt and freshly ground black pepper
2 tbsp honey
⅔ cup dry white wine
6 fresh trout, each weighing 8–10 oz,
cleaned and gutted
¼ lb button mushrooms, thinly sliced

Preheat the oven to 325°F and generously butter a baking dish.

Melt half the butter in a saucepan over a medium heat and soften the onions in it for 6–7 minutes. Stir in the cumin and season. Add the honey, 2 tablespoons of water, and the wine and simmer gently for 2–3 minutes.

Arrange the onions in a layer on the bottom of the prepared dish. Season the trout and place them on top. Scatter the mushrooms over, tucking a few inside the fish, and dot with the remaining butter. Cover and bake for 25 minutes, or until the fish flakes when tested.

Using a slotted spatula, transfer the fish and vegetables to a warmed serving dish, pour over the juices, and serve immediately.

Eels

The COMMON, FRESHWATER or AMERICAN EEL (*Anguilla anguilla*) is a wriggly wily snake-like fish, happy both in and out of water. It lives either swimming on the bottom of muddy rivers and ponds or slithering around on grassy river banks.

The best time to eat eel is in the autumn when the fat mature silver eel is plump and juicy and its flesh is rich and succulent, with plenty of texture. Eels are usually trapped in racks as they swim downstream, returning to the sea, making their mysterious and arduous journey to the Atlantic coast to spawn.

Check with the fish purveyor where your freshwater eel has been caught as, like some of the other freshwater fish, they are less able to discard any poisons from polluted rivers. If the source cannot be identified, you may prefer farmed eel. The dark-skinned seawater CONGER EEL also makes good eating, although its flesh is denser, with a more pungent flavor.

Eels in a Green Sauce

Always buy live eels: good fish purveyors often keep them in a tank. Insist that he or she does the really hard work: to kill, skin, and fillet the eel.

SERVES 4

2 tbsp butter

1 tbsp olive oil

1 lb eel fillets

$\frac{1}{4}$ lb fresh leaf spinach

2 oz fresh sorrel or watercress, chopped (1 cup)

grated zest and juice of $\frac{1}{2}$ lemon

2 tsp finely chopped fresh flat-leaf parsley

1 tsp finely chopped fresh tarragon

$\frac{3}{4}$ cup dry white wine

1 large egg yolk

1 tbsp heavy cream

salt and freshly ground black pepper

Melt the butter with the oil in a skillet over a medium heat and sauté the eel fillets in it for 3–4 minutes.

Add the spinach, sorrel, and lemon zest and simmer until the vegetables have softened into a purée, stirring occasionally. Add the parsley and tarragon, pour in the white wine and lemon juice, and simmer for 10 minutes longer, stirring occasionally.

In a bowl, beat the egg yolk with the cream and stir in a little of the hot sauce. Add this to the remaining sauce in the pan, season to taste, and stir gently over a very low heat until it starts to thicken. Adjust the seasoning. Carefully transfer the eel fillets with a slotted spatula to a warmed plate and serve covered with the sauce.

HONEYED TROUT far left.
Elvers, or baby eels, which are particularly delicious deep-fried (see page 79) left.

Sea fish

I am lucky enough to have friends living in France — in Barfleur, a pretty fishing port with rows of weathered stone houses crowding around a horseshoe-shaped harbor. As it is only 20 minutes from Cherbourg, I can catch the overnight ferry from Portsmouth, unpack, have my croissant and *café crème* and still be ready for market by 9 o'clock in the morning.

Friday is market day at nearby Valognes, and every time I go there, I reel with amazement at the difference crossing the English Channel makes. Valognes is a tiny town, but you can buy an amazing selection of fish and shellfish from at least six stalls. Even in the major fishing ports in Britain you never see the like; in fact, you are lucky to find one fish purveyor, and his range is bound to be limited.

What is also glorious about the fish in the markets of northern France is their freshness. Laid out on beds of crushed ice, they look as if they have been plucked straight out of the sea. Brilliantly colored fish glisten, their eyes shine and protrude with clear black pupils, their gills are full of bright red oxygenated blood, they

smell of airy sea breezes and they are still pert — or to use the correct technical term "stiff alive" — held rigid by rigor mortis.

Here, in my native Britain, you rarely find fish so fresh. In my travels in the States, I have been more encouraged by the fish markets, especially those in large coastal cities such as New York City and Seattle. However, some fish, even when sold as "fresh," may have been frozen and improperly thawed and may suffer from "freezer burn" when it has dried during cold storage, or a slight discoloration or dark glassy look if it has been frozen too slowly.

The signs that fish are not at their peak include: a certain slackness or flabbiness; a dull color; eyes sunken in their sockets; the blood in the gills a dark red; and a slight off smell which, at its most highly developed, will remind you of sour milk or stale cabbages. When buying fish, insist on examining them closely for the telltale signs; your fish purveyor will not mind if he or she has nothing to hide.

I have divided sea fish into three main groups: oily fish, in which the oil is dispersed throughout the flesh; white fish, in which the oil is concentrated in the liver (remember the cod liver oil capsules you were forced to take as a child?), and shellfish. Within these groups the fish are sometimes interchangeable for culinary purposes, and I give the substitutes when possible.

Oily fish

ANCHOVY, BLUEFISH, HERRING, MACKEREL, SARDINE, and TUNA are among the best-known oily fish. Because of their high oil content, these fish can be canned, salted, cured or smoked successfully, but are also good fresh.

Preparing the catch to take away left. Some fish are as attractive to look at as to eat — the blue-black stripes of mackerel, the orange spots of plaice, and the distinctive "thumb print" of John Dory are particularly striking right.

Broiled Mackerel with Gooseberry Sauce

A firm-textured fish, mackerel is in season all year round, and is an excellent value. Rich in vitamin A, its flesh is highly nutritious and has a meaty taste, slightly reminiscent of cold rare roast beef. Like all oily fish, mackerel is at its best plainly cooked by broiling or baking and served with a sharp sauce to cut its oiliness.

Use any fruit with a tart taste for the sauce, such as rhubarb, cranberries, tart apples, or, as here, gooseberries.

SERVES 4

4 small fresh mackerel, each weighing 6–8 oz, cleaned and gutted
coarse sea salt or kosher salt and freshly ground black pepper
1 lb (3 cups) gooseberries, trimmed
1 tsp fennel seeds
sprig of sweet cicely or a fennel frond
1 tbsp anise liqueur
2 tbsp cold butter, cut up

Preheat the broiler. With a sharp knife, slash the mackerel diagonally 3 times on each side so the heat can penetrate the flesh. Season with plenty of pepper and cook about 6 inches from the hot broiler for about 5 minutes on each side, or until the fish flakes when tested.

Meanwhile, make the sauce: Put the gooseberries, fennel seeds, and sweet cicely in a saucepan with enough water to cover. Bring to a boil over a medium heat and simmer, stirring occasionally, for 7–10 minutes or longer, until the fruit has softened to a pulp. Pass the fruit through a strainer, pressing hard to extract all the juices and then discard the solids. Alternatively, blend the whole fruit in a food processor until smooth, then strain.

Return the purée to the pan over a low heat, add the liqueur and beat in the butter, a few pieces at a time. Season and serve with the mackerel.

Herring Stuffed with Apple

The best time to eat herring is between May and December when they are at their most succulent. Frozen ones, however, are best avoided as they can be tough and dry with an unpleasant, slightly rancid taste.

In Holland, fresh herring are a delicacy and the start of the season causes great excitement. For the first few weeks, when the herring are still young, tender, and sweet, they are eaten raw — and chased down with a measure of genever, the local gin. The fish start to fatten up in June, and as they then swim down both the East and West coasts of Britain, they are caught for curing and smoking as kippers. If herring are unavailable, substitute the smallest whole mackerel you can find.

SERVES 6

olive oil
6 small fresh herring, each weighing 6–8 oz, cleaned and gutted
4 tbsp butter
1 small onion, finely chopped
1⅓ cups soft bread crumbs
1 tart apple, peeled, cored, and chopped
pinch of ground cinnamon
1 tsp granulated sugar
1 large egg, lightly beaten
salt and freshly ground black pepper

Preheat the oven to 375°F and generously oil an ovenproof dish.

With a sharp knife, score the herring diagonally twice on each side so the heat can penetrate the flesh.

Melt the butter in a skillet over a medium heat and cook the onion in it for 4–5 minutes until soft.

Meanwhile, mix the bread crumbs, apple, cinnamon, and sugar together in a bowl. Add the cooked onion, stir in the egg to bind the mixture, and season to taste.

Spoon this stuffing into the cleaned cavities of the

fish. Place the herring in the prepared dish on their sides. Brush them lightly with a little olive oil and bake for 20–30 minutes, or until the fish flakes when tested with a fork.

With a metal spatula, transfer to a heated serving dish. Serve with Mustard Butter (see page 55).

Deep-Fried Fish

Most small oily fish, such as anchovies, smelts, baby sardines, whitebait, and the small fry of herring, can be deep-fried and served with lemon wedges as a deliciously simple first course.

My particular favorite is ELVERS, or baby eels, which actually look more like transparent Chinese noodles than fish. A spring delicacy, they are caught any time between March and May in several of the European tidal rivers flowing into the Atlantic Ocean. If you can find them, they are well worth the exorbitant price you may have to pay for them.

Whatever fish you choose, it will not be necessary to gut them provided they are quite small. For deep-frying such baby fish, I always use seasoned flour rather than a batter as a coating; the result is a far lighter and crisper finish.

SERVES 4

6 tbsp all-purpose flour
1 tsp finely chopped fresh flat-leaf parsley
coarse sea salt or kosher salt and freshly ground black pepper
½ lb small fresh fish (see above), thoroughly rinsed and drained
oil, for deep-frying

to serve:
1 lemon, quartered
slices of brown bread and butter

In a plastic bag, mix the flour with the parsley, salt, and pepper to taste. Pat the fish dry with paper towels and place them in the bag, a handful at a time. Shake well so the fish are well coated with the seasoned flour.

Heat the oil until it reaches about 375°F. Test it by dropping in a small cube of dry bread: If it sizzles and starts to change color in about 30 seconds, the oil is at the right temperature. Deep-fry the fish in small batches, ensuring they have room enough to spread, for 2–3 minutes or until golden brown. Drain and turn out on paper towels. Keep warm and continue frying the fish in batches, until they are all cooked.

Sprinkle with sea salt and serve with lemon quarters and brown bread and butter.

DEEP-FRIED FISH left.

White Fish

For the purposes of cooking, white fish are generally divided into two groups: round and flat. The round fish which we eat in the greatest quantities is the meaty COD. A demersal fish which lives on the bottom of the sea or near the seabed, cod is fished in the North Atlantic all the way from Newfoundland to Norway. Most of what is on sale in Britain is deep-sea cod, caught in the trawlnets of boats which spend several weeks at sea. They obviously have to preserve their haul, so they clean, gut, and freeze the fish while still at sea. It is a pity, as really fresh cod that has never glimpsed a freezer is unbeatable.

Happily, in the States, most of the cod sold to the consumer is fresh. On the East Coast, you will often see SCROD, a small cod, which is very popular and good when broiled. We in Britain have small CODDLING for sale, which is a different species of fish, and quite delicious when very fresh.

A large fish can weigh anything up to 80 lb, but it is usually harvested at around 50 lb. Cod is sold whole and gutted, with or without the head, in fillets, skinned and not, and in steaks. Other members of the extensive cod family are COLEY, HADDOCK, HAKE, LINGCOD, and POLLACK. These vary widely in succulence and quality of flavor, but all are worth eating.

Other favorites include: GROUPER, a round fish which is excellent steamed over a bed of seaweed; SWORDFISH, a huge fish sold in steaks which are marvelous broiled with Herb Butter (see page 55); MONKFISH, the head of which is so ugly that it is always cut off prior to being put on display, but whose tail is rich and juicy and particularly fine roasted whole and served with a pungent Green Sauce (see page 45); RED SNAPPER, wonderful baked whole or filleted and broiled with olive oil and fresh thyme.

RED MULLET, eaten in Britain, is very tasty brushed with oil and baked in parchment paper. The mullet available in the States is a type of GRAY MULLET, a different fish in spite of the name, and needs strong flavors, such as ginger or fennel, to set it off. Gray mullet is primarily harvested for its roe (also called mullet milt) which is often dredged in flour or cornmeal and panfried.

ROCKFISH (sometimes passed off as red snapper on the West Coast of the U.S.) is a tasty fish in its own right, good marinated and grilled whole or steamed and served with julienne vegetables and a light herbed vinaigrette (see page 42).

Flat fish should be treated with care as they break up easily, and are generally best cooked simply, for example by broiling, poaching or dipping them in flour and panfrying them in butter. DOVER SOLE, having such a distinct flavor, needs nothing more elaborate to set it off. However, the distantly related LEMON SOLE and the rest of its family, which includes the ENGLISH SOLE, FLUKE, HALIBUT, GRAY SOLE, PACIFIC SANDAB, and PETRALE SOLE, are all more coarsely textured and flavored, and may be steamed, fried or stuffed and baked. The only acceptable way to cook SKATE is to panfry it, whereas TURBOT is superb poached or baked and served with a delicate Herb Butter (see page 55).

Poached Cod with Capers

The secret to poaching cod, or indeed all fish, is to use a well-flavored liquid, such as a court-bouillon (see below) or Fish Stock (see page 86). It is also important to simmer it over a very low heat so the liquid hardly trembles, with only the odd bubble rising to the surface. Poaching is a gentle means of cooking fish: If the heat is too fierce, you will toughen its texture.

For this recipe I like to use relatively chunky steaks, about 2 inches thick, otherwise they may fall apart while cooking.

SERVES 4

for the court-bouillon:
1 carrot, trimmed and thinly sliced
1 small onion, thinly sliced
1 celery stalk, trimmed and thinly sliced
1 sprig of fresh parsley
sprig of fresh thyme
$\frac{2}{3}$ cup dry white wine
$2\frac{1}{2}$ cups water
coarse sea salt or kosher salt and freshly ground black pepper
2 whole black peppercorns

4 cod steaks, each weighing 6–8 oz (see above)
$\frac{1}{3}$ cup pine nuts
$\frac{1}{3}$ cup extra-virgin olive oil
$2\frac{1}{2}$ tbsp capers, drained and rinsed
2 canned anchovy fillets, rinsed and chopped
4 sun-dried tomatoes, packed in oil, rinsed and chopped
bunch of flat-leaf parsley, chopped
1 garlic clove, chopped

Make the court-bouillon by putting the carrot, onion, celery, parsley, and thyme in a skillet large enough to hold all the cod steaks. Add the white wine and $2\frac{1}{2}$ cups of water. Add about 1 teaspoon of salt and the

POACHED COD WITH CAPERS

peppercorns. Bring the liquid to a boil, cover, reduce the heat, and simmer for 10 minutes.

Add the fish, turn down the heat to very low, and poach gently for 8–10 minutes or until the fish flesh turns an opaque white right through to the center, but is still quite firm. Using a slotted spoon, transfer the fish steaks to a serving dish. Strain the liquid, discarding the vegetables, and return it to the skillet. Bring it to a boil and boil rapidly to reduce it by about two-thirds.

Meanwhile, sauté the pine nuts in 1 teaspoon of the olive oil until golden. Mix them in a bowl with the capers, anchovies, tomatoes, parsley, and garlic. Stir in the rest of the oil and about $\frac{1}{3}$ cup of the poaching liquid. Season to taste and pour the sauce over the cod. Refrigerate for at least 1 hour to allow the flavors to seep into the fish. Serve chilled.

Fish Cakes

There are endless recipes for the wonderful fish cake, one of the great treats of British cooking. As I think that the perfect fish cake should be soft, buttery, and textured with shards of meaty fish, I use hake because it has a delightful creamy taste and performs well, especially if poached in one piece. This way you do not run the risk of drying out the fish, and it is a particularly good value if cut from the tail end as fish purveyors often sell these off cheap. You could use cod, haddock, or salmon or any other succulent fleshy fish that flakes well without falling apart.

Never overcook the fish, or the fish cakes will be far too dry. More importantly, never let it anywhere near a food processor as the fish will, more likely than not, be reduced to a mass of crumbs, resulting in a dense texture more like a hamburger than a light fish cake.

SERVES 4

$1\frac{1}{4}$ cups milk

1 small onion, sliced

2 whole black peppercorns

$\frac{3}{4}$ lb piece of fresh hake (see above)

$\frac{1}{2}$ lb russet or baking potatoes, peeled

2 tbsp butter

1 tbsp chopped fresh flat-leaf parsley

1 large egg, hard-boiled, shelled, and chopped

grated zest of $\frac{1}{2}$ lemon

pinch of cayenne

salt and freshly ground black pepper

1 large egg white, lightly beaten

1 tbsp all-purpose flour, or more as needed

corn oil, for frying

1 lemon, sliced, to serve

Put the milk, onion, and peppercorns in a saucepan and place over a medium heat until almost boiling. Turn the heat down, add the fish, cover, and poach very gently for 10–15 minutes, until the flesh just begins to break apart when tested with a fork. Strain the fish, reserving

the milk, then set aside; let cool.

Meanwhile, boil the potatoes until soft. Drain and mash them, adding the butter, parsley, and about 1 tablespoon of the poaching milk. You may find you need a little more milk: How much depends on the flouriness or dryness of the potatoes. However, do not overdo it: If the mash is too wet and sloppy, the fish cakes will not hold together while being fried.

Once the fish is cool enough to handle, skin it and flake the flesh into a bowl with your fingers, taking care to remove all bones. Then mash it lightly with a fork and stir in the hard-boiled egg, lemon zest, and cayenne, and season to taste. Gently fold the fish into the potatoes, adding the beaten egg white to bind the mixture. Let rest for about 30 minutes.

Divide the fish mixture into 8 equal portions and roll each into a ball between the palms of your hands. Press them gently to flatten them. Sprinkle the flour over a board and roll the fish cakes in it, until they are lightly covered.

Fry the fish cakes in fairly hot oil for a couple of minutes on each side, or until they start to turn a golden brown. Serve immediately with slices of lemon.

SALMON FISH CAKES

Whiting with Cottage Cheese

With a reputation of being an insipid but highly digestible fish, whiting was dismissed as invalid food in Victorian times. If caught in the deep seas, however, and sold when still pearly fresh with a shiny bloom, it is light and delicate with a smooth flesh and is an excellent value.

Whiting can weigh anything up to 4 lb. Although it is usually sold in fillets, if possible, buy a smaller whole fish and have it filleted, so you can see exactly how fresh it is. Like most of us, it grows tired and slack all too quickly; old whiting is very dull indeed.

SERVES 4

4 fresh whiting, hake, or haddock fillets, each weighing 6–8 oz
salt and freshly ground white pepper
juice of 1 lemon
butter, for greasing
1 cup small-curd cottage cheese
2 garlic cloves, finely chopped
small bunch of flat-leaf parsley, finely chopped
1 cup dry bread crumbs
½ cup freshly grated Parmesan cheese

Season the whiting fillets and put them in a shallow dish. Pour the lemon juice over the fish and let them marinate in the refrigerator for 1–2 hours, turning them over at least once.

Preheat the oven to 350°F and generously butter a gratin dish large enough to hold the fish in one layer.

Mash the cottage cheese with a fork until it is quite smooth, then beat in the garlic, parsley, bread crumbs, and season to taste with salt and pepper. Strain the juices from the fish and stir them into the mixture.

Spread a little of the cheese mixture thinly over the non-skin side of the fish, then fold the fillets over in half lengthwise and arrange them in the gratin dish. Spread the remaining cheese mixture over and around the fillets, and sprinkle with the Parmesan. Bake for 30–40 minutes, or until lightly browned on top and opaque white all the way through. Serve immediately.

Spiced Haddock

A smaller member of the cod family and easily recognizable by a distinctive thumb print and a black line running down its body, the haddock has firm-textured, white flesh and makes good eating.

In early spring in the Northeast of England and Scotland, you can often find whole tiny haddock, or "coble," named after the flat-floored inshore fishing boats from which they are caught. When fresh, these are amazingly sweet and are best simply fried or broiled with a little olive oil or butter. Most haddock on sale, however, weigh 2–5 lb and are sold in single fillets. If haddock is unavailable, cod or hake may be used instead.

SERVES 6–8

butter, for greasing
4 tbsp olive oil
2 onions, finely chopped
1 tsp peeled and finely grated fresh ginger
1 tsp granulated sugar
2 tsp ground cumin
2 tbsp ground coriander
pinch of garam masala (see page 251)
large pinch of cayenne
2 cups thick plain yogurt (see page 53)
2 tbsp fresh lemon juice
salt and freshly ground black pepper
2¼ lb fresh haddock fillets, cut into 3-inch pieces

Preheat the oven to 375°F and generously butter a shallow ovenproof dish.

Heat 1 tablespoon of the olive oil in a large, heavy-bottomed skillet over a medium heat and sauté the onions in it for 2–3 minutes.

Add the ginger, sugar, cumin, coriander, garam masala, and cayenne and stir for a few minutes until the onions are soft. Beat the yogurt in a bowl with the lemon juice and remaining oil. Season with about 1½ teaspoons of salt and black pepper to taste, then stir the onions into this mixture and give it a final beating.

Spread a little of this onion sauce on the bottom of the prepared dish. Arrange the pieces of haddock in a single layer on top, then spread the rest of the sauce over the fish in a thick layer so it completely covers the fish. Cover the dish with foil and bake for about 20 minutes, or until the fish flakes when tested with a fork. Serve immediately.

Fish Pie

A good fish pie depends on the mix, texture, and quality of the fish. Cod, hake, and haddock are all good white fish to use. If you are feeling a little extravagant, you could splash out on monkfish or John Dory. Flatfish tend to be rather expensive and are too delicately flavored or totally unsuited to baking in a pie. Oily fish are best avoided as their flavors are too overpowering.

SERVES 4–6

1½ lb mixed white fish (see above)
4 sprigs of fresh flat-leaf parsley
1 bay leaf
2 whole black peppercorns
salt and freshly ground black pepper
3 tbsp white vermouth
1 stick butter, plus extra for greasing
3 tbsp all-purpose flour
pinch of saffron threads
1¼ cups milk
2 lb all-purpose potatoes, peeled and quartered

¼ lb peeled cooked small shrimp
1 onion, finely chopped
2 large hard-boiled eggs, shelled and sliced

Put the fish in a large skillet with 2 sprigs of parsley, the bay leaf, peppercorns, a large pinch of salt, and 2 tablespoons of the vermouth. Add just enough water to cover, bring to a boil, lower the heat, and poach gently for about 15 minutes. Drain the fish, reserving the cooking liquid and discarding the solids.

Preheat the oven to 400°F and generously butter a deep, 3-quart baking dish.

To make a white sauce: Melt 2 tablespoons of the butter in a saucepan over a low heat, stir in the flour and saffron and cook gently for 1 minute. Measure ⅔ cup of the cooking liquid, mix it with the same volume of the milk, and pour this into the saucepan, a little at a time, stirring continuously and vigorously. Once all this liquid has been added, simmer for about 5 minutes, stirring occasionally, until the sauce thickens. Season.

Meanwhile, boil the potatoes until soft. Drain and mash them, adding the remaining butter and milk. Season to taste.

Once the fish is cool enough to handle, skin and flake it coarsely with your fingers, taking care to remove all bones. Put the fish in the prepared baking dish. Scatter the shrimp, onion, hard-boiled eggs and remaining parsley, chopped, over the fish. Sprinkle with the rest of the vermouth. Pour over the white sauce, then cover with the mashed potatoes, spreading evenly.

Bake in the oven for about 30 minutes, or until the top is a golden brown and the pie is heated through.

Fish Soup

A good fish soup depends on two things: a good stock and a wide variety of fish.

Never make fish stock with a bouillon cube, it just does not taste right. Unless you can buy fresh stock, there is nothing for it but to make your own. It is actually incredibly easy and, as you are going to buy various fish, your fish purveyor will certainly oblige you with a selection of trimmings. The fish stock can be made a day or two ahead and refrigerated, or frozen for up to six months.

As for the fish, choose firm fish which do not break apart and which have gutsy flavors. The most appropriate include hake, monkfish, cod, and gray or red snapper. I usually buy a mixture of whatever is available. There is no need to go for prime white flatfish: they work out far too expensive. Equally, avoid oily fish, such as herring, mackerel, sardines, or tuna, as their strong flavors upset the balance of the soup.

SERVES 8–10

for the stock:
2 lb fresh fish trimmings, such as bones, skin, head, etc.
1 onion, sliced
1 carrot, sliced
1 leek, sliced
1 bay leaf
piece of lemon peel

blade of mace or $\frac{1}{2}$ tsp ground mace
8 whole black peppercorns
$\frac{2}{3}$ cup dry white wine
for the soup:
3 tbsp olive oil
2 carrots, trimmed and sliced
1 leek, trimmed and sliced
2 onions, sliced
1 fennel bulb, trimmed of its feathery tops and sliced
2 garlic cloves, minced
$1\frac{1}{2}$ lb fresh fish (see above), cut into $\frac{1}{2}$-inch cubes
$1\frac{1}{4}$ quarts fish stock (see above)
1 cup dry white wine
1 bay leaf
2 sprigs of fresh thyme
2 sprigs of fresh flat-leaf parsley
2 sprigs of fresh lemon balm or 1 piece of lemon peel
salt and freshly ground black pepper
1 lb ripe tomatoes, peeled, seeded, and chopped
pinch of granulated sugar
1 tbsp anise liqueur

To make the stock: Put all the ingredients into a large pot, along with the trimmings from the fennel for the soup, and cover with $7\frac{1}{2}$ cups of water. Bring to a boil, skim off the foam, and simmer for about 15 minutes.

Strain through a cheesecloth-lined strainer.

To make the soup: In another large pot, heat the oil over a medium heat. Add the carrots, leek, onions, fennel, and garlic and sauté gently for about 5 minutes.

Tie the herbs in a cheesecloth bag. Add the stock, wine, the herb bag, salt, and pepper to taste. Cover and simmer for 10 minutes. Add the prepared fish and simmer for 5 minutes longer. Then add the tomatoes and sugar and simmer for 5 minutes longer. Stir in the liqueur, discard the herb bag, and adjust the seasoning.

Skate with Onions and Raisins

Usually you only see the "wings" of the large skate or ray on sale. Some cooks think the meat from large skates should be refrigerated for a day or two to tenderize it. This may result in a faint smell of ammonia, which can be counteracted by adding a little vinegar to the poaching liquid.

The best size of wings to buy weigh 1–3 lb and are sold skinned, sometimes on one side, sometimes on both. When larger, they tend to become a little coarse. Although you can find smaller wings, they are not really worth the trouble; they are a bit skimpy or sparsely fleshed and lack the fullness and gelatinous qualities that make eating skate such a pleasure.

SERVES 4

24 pearl onions, peeled
1¼ cups hard or sparkling cider
1 bay leaf
8–10 whole black peppercorns, crushed
2 skate wings, each weighing about 1½ lb, cut into 2 pieces
1½ sticks butter
1 small onion, sliced
3 tbsp raisins, soaked in warm water until plump
1 tsp granulated sugar
2 tbsp white wine vinegar
coarse sea salt or kosher salt and freshly ground black pepper

Put the pearl onions, cider, bay leaf, crushed peppercorns, and 1¼ cups water in a skillet over a high heat and bring to a boil. Cover and boil for 5 minutes.

Reduce the heat, add the skate wings to the skillet, and simmer gently for 7–10 minutes. With skate you can easily tell when the fish is cooked as the flesh starts to detach itself from the bone in shards. Using a slotted spoon, transfer the fish to a warmed serving dish and remove the pearl onions and reserve. Discard the cooking liquid.

Melt the butter in the same skillet over a high heat until it just begins to turn brown. Add the sliced onion, the reserved pearl onions, raisins, and sugar and stir together. Then add the vinegar, season to taste, turn up the heat, and stir and scrape any browned bits from the skillet until the sauce begins to foam. Pour it over the skate and serve immediately.

Making a gill net, which traps fish as they swim into a mesh.

Turbot in Rock Salt

Distinctively diamond-shaped with knobby, sludge-brown, spotted skin, turbot is the most delicious and delicate of flatfish. Unfortunately, it is also the most expensive.

Mainly fished from the Baltic Sea, the English Channel, and the Atlantic waters off France and northern Spain, it is not unusual to land huge turbots weighing 40 lb. A "chicken" turbot is a far more manageable proposition: It has all the qualities of the larger fish, but only hits the scales at $2\frac{1}{4}$–5 lb. If a chicken turbot is not available, halibut is a good substitute.

The traditional way of preparing turbot is to poach it, then serve it with a Hollandaise Sauce (see page 128). For a change, I have used a method common in northern Spain, whereby a whole fish is baked buried in salt. The salt does not overpower the fish: It hardens into a thick crust and, when you break this, the turbot emerges superbly tender.

PREPARING TURBOT IN ROCK SALT

SERVES 4–6

butter, for greasing
2 tbsp milk
2 whole black peppercorns
1 bay leaf
1 chicken turbot, weighing $2\frac{1}{4}$–$3\frac{1}{2}$ lb
(see above)
$2\frac{1}{4}$ lb (3 cups) rock salt

for the sauce:
$1\frac{1}{4}$ cups heavy cream
grated zest and juice of 1 lime
$1\frac{1}{2}$ tsp grated fresh horseradish or 1 tsp prepared horseradish
pinch of granulated sugar
salt and freshly ground white pepper

Preheat the oven to 375°F and generously butter an ovenproof dish just large enough to hold the turbot.

Put the milk in a small saucepan with the peppercorns and bay leaf. Bring to just below a boil over a low heat, then remove from the heat and let the milk infuse and cool.

Brush the fish all over with the cooled milk and place it in the prepared dish. Dampen the salt slightly with water and pack the dish tightly with it, tucking it in around the edges of the fish so the turbot is completely enclosed. Bake in the preheated oven for about 20 minutes. Remove and let cool for 30 minutes.

Meanwhile, prepare the sauce: Put the cream and lime zest in a saucepan and bring it to a boil over a medium heat. Stir in the horseradish, sugar, and lime juice, then lower the heat and simmer for a couple of minutes. Season to taste.

Break open the salt crust by crushing it with a rolling pin. The skin of the fish sticks to the salt, so lift off the pieces of salt peeling away the skin as you go. Serve the turbot cut into fillets, with the sauce served separately.

Terrine of Lemon Sole with Shrimp

This recipe comes from Richard Stein's English Seafood Cookery, *based on his experience running one of England's best seafood restaurants in Cornwall. He suggests you use lemon sole, and advises that you should first chill the ingredients for a light, airy terrine. He also warns that this terrine "hovers on the edge of being difficult to handle."*

SERVES 8–10

$\frac{1}{2}$ *lb raw medium shrimp in their shells*
1 tsp tomato paste
1 small celery stalk, trimmed and finely chopped
2 small shallots, finely chopped
butter, for greasing
$\frac{1}{2}$ *lb fresh lemon sole fillets, skinned, cut into pieces, and chilled*

1 large egg, chilled
2 tsp fresh lemon juice
coarse sea salt or kosher salt and freshly ground white pepper
6 sprigs of fresh flat-leaf parsley
6 sprigs of fresh chervil
small bunch of fresh chives
1$\frac{1}{4}$ cups heavy cream, chilled
pinch of cayenne

Peel the shrimp and chill in the refrigerator, reserving the shells.

Start making the sauce: Put the shrimp shells in a saucepan with the tomato paste, celery, and half of the shallots. Add just enough water to cover and bring to a boil, then reduce the heat and simmer for 25 minutes.

Preheat the oven to 350°F and butter a 1-quart terrine or mold and a piece of foil for covering the top.

Put the sole, egg, remaining shallot, half the lemon juice, and a large pinch of salt into a food processor, and process to a smooth purée. Add the parsley, chervil, and chives and, with the machine still running, slowly pour in 1 cup of cream until well blended. Season to taste and chill the mixture for about 15 minutes.

Fold the peeled shrimp into the chilled mixture and carefully spoon into the terrine. Cover loosely with the buttered foil, put it in a roasting pan, and add enough hot water to come half way up the side of the terrine. Transfer to the preheated oven and bake for about 40 minutes. To test if it is cooked, pierce it to the center with a skewer or thin knife; if it comes clean, the terrine is ready. Remove it from the oven and let stand for about 10 minutes before carefully unmolding it.

To finish the sauce: Place the shrimp stock with the shells in a food processor, process and then strain into a small saucepan. Discard the solids. Add the rest of the cream, bring it to a boil and boil the sauce to reduce it until it is thick enough to coat the back of a spoon. Stir in the remaining lemon juice and the cayenne.

Serve the terrine in slices on a bed of the sauce.

Shellfish

The British coast is rich in shellfish, as are the East and West Coasts of the United States.

I think the LOBSTERS from the clear cold waters of the Minch, off the Scottish coast, are amongst the best in the world, but those caught off the coast of Maine, a different species, are truly excellent as well. They should be simply cooked, broiled or poached and served with hot melted butter.

The CRAWFISH with its firm creamy white tail meat is superb eaten cold with mayonnaise. Although it looks rather like a lobster, it is diminutive in size and has small front claws.

There are numerous SHRIMP, both brown and pink, swimming around coastal shores. Almost all of the shrimp sold in fish markets have been previously frozen. In Britain, we have Cornish or Cromer brown CRABS; in the States, you will find blue crabs on the East Coast and Dungeness and Alaskan King crabs on the West Coast. SCALLOPS and MUSSELS are meatier and fuller-flavored in the winter months. Sea scallops are the largest of the scallops available in the U.S., calico scallops are next in size, and bay scallops are the smallest and sweetest of all. Mussels either grow wild in beds in coastal shallows or attached to rocks, or they are artificially bred and grown on ropes and stakes or "sown" in beds, and then transplanted into deeper waters to fatten up.

Excellent OYSTERS may be found along both coasts of the United States. On the East Coast, try Apalachicola, Blue Point, Box, Chincoteague and Maine-raised Belon. On the West Coast, I recommend the Olympia, Golden Mantle, Kumamoto, Malapeque, Pacific, and Wilipa Bay varieties.

Probably the best of all native British shellfish are our oysters. The round, crinkly shelled Native oyster can only be eaten when there is an "r" in the month. However, with its silky gray flesh and slightly salty juice, it is well worth waiting for.

Oysters should really never be cooked as they taste so good as they are that it seems a travesty to heat them or drown them in some sauce or other. My favorite way to enjoy them is simply dressed with lemon juice or a dash of Tabasco sauce, accompanied with slices of brown bread spread with a good unsalted butter. However, you need to make sure they are from open, unrestricted waters, so buy them from a reputable source and discard those that are not live. Because of the small, but possible threat of illness from consuming raw shellfish, they should not be eaten by persons with damaged immune systems, the very young, or the

Making a lobster pot left. Cooked and uncooked shellfish right.

An oyster farm uses an old-fashioned means of transport to bring oysters in from the beds.

elderly. But they are perfectly safe if cooked.

Keep oysters well chilled until ready to use them. Stack them in a baking pan in the refrigerator with the larger part of the shell facing down and cover them with a damp towel. They should be kept no longer than a week before consuming. Before shucking, scrub the shells thoroughly with a stiff brush to remove all traces of sand and bacteria.

Shrimp Bisque

The fish trade in Britain and the States seem to differentiate rather haphazardly between shrimp and prawns, but in most cases, prawns are larger than shrimp. There is no need to peel the shrimp at any stage of this recipe, as their shells are broken by the food processor and the pieces removed by straining.

Make the fish stock using a mixture of fish and as many shellfish trimmings as your fish purveyor will give you.

SERVES 8

3 tbsp olive oil
2 leeks, trimmed and chopped
2 onions, chopped
$1\frac{1}{2}$ lb raw shrimp in their shells (see above)
$1\frac{1}{2}$ lb ripe tomatoes
small bunch of fresh flat-leaf parsley
sprig of fresh lemon thyme or thyme
few strands of saffron
1 cup dry white wine
$1\frac{1}{2}$ quarts Fish Stock (see page 86)
$1\frac{1}{4}$ cups heavy cream
2 tbsp brandy
salt and freshly ground white pepper

Heat the olive oil in a large saucepan over a moderate heat, add the leeks and onions, and sauté for 5 minutes until soft. Stir in the shrimp (reserving a few for garnish, if wished), tomatoes, parsley, lemon thyme, saffron, wine, and fish stock. Cover and simmer for about 30 minutes over a medium heat.

Process the shrimp mixture in a food processor until puréed. Pass this through a fine strainer, pressing down hard to extract all the juices, and return the strained soup to the pan, discarding the solids.

Pour in the cream and brandy and bring to just below a boil over a low heat. Adjust the seasoning and serve hot with croûtons and garnished with a few whole shelled shrimp.

Crab and Saffron Quiche

For the freshest possible crab meat, buy a live crab and cook it yourself. Everyone has their own way of killing crab and lobsters in the kindest way: mine is to put them in a large pot of boiled water which has been allowed to cool and then bring it back to a boil. As the water has been deoxygenated, the crab or lobster swiftly "drowns."

A medium-size crab will probably need about 15 minutes simmering, by which time it should have turned bright pink, then it should be drained and left to cool. Once it is cool enough to handle, twist off the legs and claws and crack them open to extract the meat. Turn the crab over and, with your thumbs, force the shell and body apart. Scoop the meat out of the shell and throw away the gills or "dead men's fingers" attached to the body, then cut it in half and extract the rest of the meat.

If you cannot buy a live crab, buy fresh crab meat from a good fish market and use the same quantity.

SERVES 4

pastry dough for an 8-inch pan (see page 199)
$6\frac{1}{2}$ oz ($1\frac{1}{2}$ cups) freshly cooked meat from 1 crab
$\frac{2}{3}$ cup heavy cream
1 large egg + 2 large egg yolks
small bunch of fresh chives
few strands of saffron
juice of $\frac{1}{2}$ lemon
2 tbsp dry sherry wine
pinch of cayenne
salt and freshly ground white pepper

Preheat the oven to 375°F.

Roll out the pastry dough on a lightly floured board to a thickness of about $\frac{1}{2}$ inch and line an 8-inch quiche pan with it. Let rest in the refrigerator for about 15 minutes, then line, weight, and bake it blind (see page 242) for 15 minutes. Let it cool in its pan.

Cook the crab (see above) and flake the crab meat. Spread the crab meat in an even layer on the bottom of the pastry shell and chill. Put the cream, egg and egg yolks, chives, saffron, lemon juice, and sherry in a food processor and process until smooth. Season to taste with the cayenne, salt and pepper, then pour the mixture on top of the crab meat in the pastry shell.

Bake the tart uncovered in the preheated oven for 25–30 minutes, until the filling turns a golden brown and is just set.

Mussels with Garlic, White Wine, and Bacon

Mussels are native to U.S. shores, yet they are often neglected in favor of clams and oysters. The mussel is at its plumpest and tastiest during the cold winter months.

"Farmed" mussels are sold in packs, scrubbed, scraped, and de-bearded, which saves you a lot of work. Once you get them home, let them soak in cold water for 2–3 hours and throw away any that float to the top or remain open even after you have given the shell a quick firm tap.

SERVES 4

2 tbsp butter

1 tbsp olive oil

$\frac{1}{4}$ lb thick-sliced bacon, finely chopped

$\frac{1}{4}$ lb shallots, finely chopped

2 garlic cloves, finely chopped

1 lb tomatoes, peeled, seeded and chopped

3 sprigs of fresh oregano or marjoram

pinch of granulated sugar

1 cup dry white wine

$2\frac{1}{4}$ quarts fresh mussels, scrubbed

1 tbsp finely chopped fresh flat-leaf parsley

salt and freshly ground black pepper

MUSSELS WITH GARLIC, WHITE WINE, AND BACON

In a large Dutch oven with a tight-fitting lid, melt the butter with the olive oil over a medium heat. Sauté the bacon, shallots, and garlic for about 5 minutes or until soft. Add the tomatoes, oregano, sugar, and white wine and bring to a boil.

Put the mussels in the pan, cover, and cook for 5–7 minutes, or until they have opened. Using a slotted spoon, lift the mussels out of the pan and remove most of them from their shells, leaving just a few in their shells for effect, and keep warm in a 200°F oven. Discard any unopened shells.

Turn up the heat and bring the sauce to a boil. Boil rapidly for 2–3 minutes to reduce the quantity of liquid by about half.

Stir in the parsley, adjust the seasoning, and pour the sauce over the mussels. Serve either on its own or with freshly cooked pasta.

Steamed Scallops with Leeks and Orange Butter

Try to buy scallops in the shell when possible and ask the fish purveyor to open them for you. All you then have to do is lift them out of their shells and separate the muscle (the white meaty chunk) and the coral (the bright orange crescent) from the frilly "skirt" which is only useful for a stock. Unfortunately, in the U.S. you are most likely to find scallops sold out of their shells and without their coral, but this dish is still well worth making.

SERVES 4

2 sticks cold butter
4 leeks, trimmed and cut into fine shreds
grated zest and juice of 3 large oranges
⅔ cup dry white wine
12 fresh scallops
salt and freshly ground white pepper
6–8 sprigs of fresh chervil or flat-leaf parsley

In a wide-bottomed skillet with a tight-fitting lid, melt 4 tablespoons of the butter over a medium heat and sweat the leeks with the orange zest, covered, for 2–3 minutes until soft. Stir in the orange juice and white wine and slowly bring almost to a boil.

Season the scallops lightly, then place them in a single layer on top of the leeks. Cover and steam-boil for 3–4 minutes, until just cooked. With a slotted spoon, transfer the scallops and leeks to a warm serving dish, arranging the scallops on a bed of the leeks.

Turn up the heat and reduce the liquid by about one-third. Reduce the heat and cut the remaining butter into small cubes. Whisk them, one at a time, into the sauce without letting it become more than hand-hot, otherwise the sauce will be thin and curdled, rather than frothy. At the last minute when all the butter has been added, stir in the chervil. Pour the sauce over the scallops and serve.

Mixed Poached Seafood with Salicornia

Salicornia, also called samphire, or glasswort, is a sea plant which grows wild on the "saltings" or mudflats around the coast of Britain and France. Traditionally said to be ready for eating on the longest day in the year, its season is short, from July to August, and during this time you can either pick it yourself or buy it from a good fish purveyor. Salicornia does not keep very well, so make sure you wash it thoroughly and eat it within a couple of days. With its salty flavor and crunchy texture, it is particularly good in a mixed fish stew.

In the United States, fresh seaweed is often available through some fish purveyors and health food stores.

MIXED POACHED SEAFOOD WITH
SALICORNIA overleaf

SERVES 4–6

18–20 mussels, scrubbed
⅔ cup Fish Stock (see page 86)
6 oz monkfish tail, cut into 1-inch slices
6 oz red mullet or red snapper fillet, cut into 2-inch slices
10 raw jumbo shrimp, shelled
4–6 fresh scallops
2 tbsp unsalted butter
white of 1 leek, thinly sliced
1 shallot, thinly sliced
1 small carrot, trimmed and thinly sliced
⅔ cup dry white wine
1 fresh flat-leaf parsley stem
1¼ cups heavy cream
2 oz salicornia, washed and drained
salt and freshly ground white pepper

Put the mussels with the fish stock in a large heavy-bottomed skillet over a medium heat. Cover and simmer for 5–7 minutes, or until the mussels have opened. Transfer to a warm dish, discarding any mussels with shells that remain shut.

Put the pieces of monkfish into the same skillet and poach gently for 2–3 minutes. Add the red mullet or snapper and shrimp and cook for 1 more minute. Slice the scallops in half horizontally and add them to the skillet. Poach for 1 more minute. Transfer the fish, shrimp, and scallops to the dish with the mussels, reserving the cooking liquid.

In a separate saucepan, melt the butter and soften the leek, shallot, and carrot. Add the wine and parsley and boil to reduce by half. Add ⅓ cup of the reserved cooking liquid and again reduce by half. Stir in the cream and simmer for 5 minutes.

Pass the sauce through a fine strainer into a clean pan; discard the solids. Add the salicornia and poach for a couple of minutes, or until tender. Add the mussels, still in their shells, and the rest of the seafood. Reheat for about 1 minute. Adjust the seasoning.

Smoked Fish

Long before refrigeration was even thought of, food was usually preserved by smoking, drying, salting, brining or pickling. Now smoking is merely a means of adding flavor and, unfortunately in these times of processed food, a misguided fashion exists for smoking just about anything that stays still long enough. From eggs, nuts, cheese and chicken to shrimp, nothing escapes, and the processors would be best to leave well enough alone. Most of the time they are ruining perfectly good raw ingredients, drowning their inherent taste in the flavor of smoke.

Smoking is a subtle craft and only certain ingredients, principally some fish and meat, are suitable. Salmon, eel, mackerel, cod, whitefish, herring, trout, and haddock are obvious candidates as they have robust flavors that are not in danger of being overpowered. Moreover, as their flesh is firm textured and succulent, with a reasonably high oil content, there is no risk of it drying out.

Before smoking, the fish must be cured first. This may either be done in a dry salt cure or in brine. Other flavoring ingredients, such as whiskey, sugar or herbs, are sometimes added to the cure. Once cured, the fish may either be hot-smoked at a fairly high temperature for a relatively short burst of time to "cook" it; or cold smoked, a longer, more gentle process. See page 250 for mail-order smoked fish sources.

If you are buying Scottish SMOKED SALMON, the best quality is sold with the Scottish Salmon Smokers Association golden label on the pack; this guarantees that the smoked salmon within is from a fresh Scottish salmon, as opposed to a frozen foreign import which is then just smoked in Scotland.

The fishing fleet in Stornoway harbor, on the Isle of Lewis in Scotland left. Sides of freshly smoked salmon right.

The richest SMOKED EEL is made from mature freshwater silver eel. These fat eels take anything up to 12 years to mature and are caught during the autumn when they are at their plumpest, on their descent downstream to the sea. Hot-smoked over beech mixed with a little applewood for sweetness, they are a great delicacy of southwest England, but are difficult to come by in the States.

SMOKED WHITEFISH is a specialty of Jewish delicatessens in the States. You can buy pieces of a large fish, or the whole fish. You will also find smaller whitefish that are smoked, and they are called CHUBS.

SMOKED SABLEFISH, or sable, is sold sliced or in whole sides, called plates. Another specialty of Jewish delicatessens, this is cold-smoked from Pacific black cod, very rich and oily.

British specialties include the versatile herring, which is left whole and ungutted, then lightly salted and cold-smoked to make BLOATERS; red herrings are beheaded, gutted and hot-smoked as BUCKLING, or split down the middle, gutted, salted and smoked as KIPPERS. The best kippers come from Loch Fyne or Craster in Northumberland, made from the fat summer herring, and can be broiled or "jugged" (simply stood in a jug or pitcher of hot water for a few minutes) and eaten with melted butter. SMOKED COD ROE is sensational when served thinly sliced with lemon juice, a few drops of virgin olive oil and a little ground black pepper; or you can easily make your own *taramasalata* by processing it in a food processor with some bread soaked in milk, lemon juice, garlic and olive oil.

Arbroath smokies and Finnan (or Findon) haddie are both types of SMOKED HADDOCK. The former are gutted, beheaded, dry-salted, tied by the tails into pairs and briefly hot-smoked; the latter are gutted, cleaned, beheaded and split open. They are then lightly brined, hung on "speats" (metal rods) and cold-smoked.

It goes without saying that the best smoked fish are never colored either artificially or with annatto, which gives smoked haddock a bright yellow color.

Cream of Horseradish Sauce

The best and simplest way of eating smoked eel and mackerel is to fillet them and eat them with slices of a good country bread (see page 191) and a creamy, but sharp, sauce.

SERVES 4–6

1 shallot, finely chopped
2 tsp prepared horseradish
1 tbsp finely chopped fresh dill
$\frac{1}{3}$ cup sour cream
salt and freshly ground black pepper
1 tsp fresh lemon juice

Mix all the ingredients together, except the lemon juice. Season to taste but remember to be sparing with the salt, depending on the saltiness of the fish.

Let stand for 30 minutes, to allow the flavors to infuse. Taste and, if you do not think the sauce is sharp enough, add the lemon juice.

Kedgeree

Arbroath smokies are hot-smoked over oak or beech for up to two hours.

Kedgeree is only worth making with good-quality finnan haddie. Choose cold-smoked haddock with its rich, slightly nutty flavor, its pale honey color, and its springy texture. Once poached, it will flake easily into satisfying chunks and hold together well when mixed into the rice mixture.

SERVES 6–8

$\frac{1}{2}$ lb finnan haddie

1 small onion, sliced

3 whole black peppercorns

1 bay leaf

$1\frac{1}{4}$ cups milk

$1\frac{1}{3}$ cups white rice

1 stick butter, melted

3 tbsp heavy cream

3 large hard-boiled eggs, peeled and chopped

3 tbsp finely chopped fresh flat-leaf parsley

salt and freshly ground black pepper

pinch of cayenne

Put the finnan haddie in a saucepan along with the onion, peppercorns, bay leaf, and milk. Place over a medium heat and bring almost to a boil. Turn down the heat and simmer gently for 5–7 minutes, until the fish is cooked. Drain the fish, discarding the onion, bay leaf, and peppercorns. Reserve the milk and let the fish cool. Meanwhile, cook the rice in boiling water according to package directions and then drain thoroughly if all the water hasn't been absorbed.

When the fish is cool enough to handle, remove the skin and any bones and flake it gently into sizable chunks with your hands; do not be too rough or break the fish down into small pieces as it will disintegrate when you stir it into the rice.

In a clean pan, melt the butter, add the cream, a couple of tablespoons of the reserved milk, and the rice, and stir until the rice is thoroughly coated with the mixture. Carefully fold in the fish, the hard-boiled eggs and parsley and cook over a low heat for 1 minute. Adjust the seasoning and serve sprinkled with cayenne.

The Farmyard

The farmyard has always been home to chickens and turkeys, ducks and geese, often as valued for their eggs as for their meat. Quail and guinea fowl, originally game birds, are now more frequently found alongside them.

Poultry

In the sixteenth century, Henri IV of France wrote that he wanted no peasant in his kingdom to be so poor that he could not have a chicken in his pot every Sunday. His ambition was never realized for, although most farms did keep poultry, the birds were usually fattened for market rather than for the farmers' own tables.

Poultry, domestic fowl or birds kept for eggs or meat, including chicken, turkey, goose, duck, guinea fowl, and occasionally quail, were generally the domain of the farmer's wife until recently. It was she who would feed and tend them and collect their eggs. During the day, the birds would waddle contentedly around the farmyard, scratching for food and were only locked up at night. This, however, was for their own safety and to keep out marauding foxes or any other greedy predators rather than for the purely commercial considerations of today's producers.

Times have changed, and the rearing of poultry has become an intensive and lucrative industry in which few birds ever see the light of day. I think the result of this type of raising compromises the chicken's flavor, texture, and health.

Chicken

The price of chicken may nowadays be remarkably low but, ironically, this has been achieved at great cost, as the eating quality and the health and welfare of the birds have been sacrificed. Chicken in modern farms may be prone to various diseases, so for safety's sake, cook chicken thoroughly. If stuffing, cook the bird immediately after stuffing it to kill any bacteria.

The alternative to buying a mass-produced bird is to opt for FREE-RANGE chicken. Unlike mass-produced chickens, they are produced under more humane

Traditionally, most country women kept fowl, deriving extra income from the eggs.

conditions. They are not subjected to constant artificial light and consequently grow at a slower rate. They also have space to move around and some get to go outside.

There is no doubt in my mind that a free-range chicken actually does taste better. Several factors affect eating quality: breed, feed, housing, and age. If a bird is fed with a cheaper feed, its flesh may be less flavorful; or if it has been forced to grow too fast without any exercise, the flesh may be vapid and probably covered with an excess of fat.

Obviously the more stringent the specifications for a bird, the more it costs to rear and the more we, the customers, will have to pay for these better products. However, when you try them I think you will agree that a fully flavored chicken is really worth the expense.

What sizes or types of chicken are there? ROCK CORNISH GAME HEN weighs not more than 1–2 lb, so you will generally allow one bird per person. They are very tender, but sometimes just too young to have developed full flavor. A BROILER or FRYER is the chicken we most commonly find, usually $6\frac{1}{2}$ weeks old and weighing from $2\frac{1}{2}$–$4\frac{1}{2}$ lb. A ROASTER is larger, from 6–8 lb and 8 to 9 weeks old. A CAPON, a neutered male chicken, is generally under 10 to 12 weeks old and weighs 6–10 lb. These may be roasted, braised, or poached to develop their full dense taste. A HEAVY HEN (also called a stewing or baking hen, or a fowl) is over 1 year old, a rather tough bird, weighing $4\frac{1}{2}$–6 lb, which is just the ticket for soups, stocks, or poaching. However, never roast one, as its meat will be far too stringy and dry.

Most mass-produced chicken in the U.S. is sold fresh. Chicken is most commonly chill-packed, which keeps it at a temperature between 28° and 32°F. This tends to freeze parts of the chicken, like the wings or drumsticks, and it also may leave ice crystals on the skin. Another way of shipping chicken is to pack it in ice. Chill-packing, like freezing, tends to alter the flavor, whereas ice packing has no effect on the taste.

When choosing a bird, look for a plump breast, and a smooth, dry, unbroken skin which is free of blotches. As a rough guide, allow about 12 oz of chicken on the bone per person: so a $3\frac{1}{2}$ lb bird should feed 4 people.

What is free-range?

As of this date there are no legal definitions in the United States for free-range chickens, or for any other free-range or organically raised animals or products. There is, however, legislation pending that will standardize the code of practice. The organic farming industry is very enthusiastic that measures will be adopted and certifications set in place by the year 1993.

What you should expect from a chicken labeled free-range is: that it has been fed organic grains; that it has not received any medications (except for vaccinations); that it has been kept uncaged in a large house and raised in a much less confined manner than a mass-produced chicken; that it may have had the chance to go outside.

Free-range chickens are available frozen by mail order (see page 250 for sources), and at some butcher shops.

The chicken (and any other products making free-range or organic claims) should carry some type of certification sticker or a stamp. There are numerous local and state-wide organizations that certify organically raised animals and products. Some of the names which may appear, generally in initials, are: O.F.P.A.N.A., O.C.I.A., and N.O.F.A. If the chicken or the farm stand itself is not labeled with the approval of such an organisation, or it just says "organic," ask how the chicken was raised.

To roast a chicken

Roast the bird in an oven preheated to 425°F for about 15 minutes. Then turn the oven down to 350°F and allow about a further 15 minutes per pound. Do not forget to baste the chicken with the pan juices every so often. The one certain way of being sure that the bird is thoroughly cooked is to prick the thickest part of the thigh with a skewer; the juices that ooze out must be clear, without any trace of pink. If you are worried about the breast drying out, cook the bird breast down for the first 30 minutes.

Another interesting way of adding flavor to a bird, which also has the added benefit of keeping the breast really moist, is to loosen the skin over the breast and stuff it with a flavored butter (see page 54). Finish by rubbing the skin all over with a little more of the butter and sprinkling over a pinch of coarse sea or kosher salt.

Because of the current risk of contamination, you may prefer not to stuff chickens with a traditional dressing. Instead, put into the cavity a chunk of butter, a whole scrubbed lemon, which has been pierced all over with a skewer, a couple of cloves of garlic, or even a handful of fresh herbs, such as tarragon or rosemary.

To make stock, clarified fat, and consommé

The recipe for chicken soup which follows is also a master recipe for a chicken stock, or indeed any stock from poultry. You can make stock with a whole bird; a raw carcass stripped of its meat; a roasted carcass after carving; or even just the giblets, such as the heart, liver, gizzard, and neck.

To remove the fat from the stock after simmering, strain it and put it in the refrigerator to chill until the fat rises to the surface and forms a thick layer on the top. This can then be removed with a spoon or metal skimmer or by using some white paper towel like blotting paper, patting it over the surface so it soaks up the fat. This fat may then be clarified by heating it gently and passing it through a strainer lined with dampened cheesecloth or a tea towel. Clarified fat will keep for several weeks in the refrigerator in a covered jar or it may be frozen. It is very useful for cooking.

To turn any poultry stock into a sparklingly clear consommé, it must also be clarified after skimming off the fat. The stock is heated gently and a couple of lightly beaten egg whites are then whisked in. The liquid is whisked until it comes to a boil and the heat is then turned down to allow it to simmer gently for about 10 minutes. The stock is then ladled through a strainer lined with a dampened cheesecloth or a tea towel.

A solitary chicken rules the roost.

Jewish Chicken Soup with Matzo Balls

For this deep and richly flavored soup, use a boiling or stewing chicken and simmer it for hours. Although a roaster would cook in half the time, it would only have half the flavor. Some people might say it is rather extravagant to use a whole bird just for a soup, but once you have tasted it . . . .

Not for nothing is this soup called "Jewish Penicillin": it is so wholesome that it cures all ills. Traditionally a Jewish-style chicken soup is never skimmed or clarified and so comes streaked with fat.

SERVES 6–8

for chicken stock:
1 heavy hen or stewing chicken, including neck and gizzard
1 large onion, cut up
2 carrots, trimmed and cut up
2 celery stalks, trimmed and cut up
2 leeks, trimmed, cleaned and cut up
large bunch of fresh flat-leaf parsley
6 whole black peppercorns
salt

for the matzo balls:
1 large egg
1 tbsp clarified chicken fat, melted (see opposite), or vegetable oil
5 whole blanched almonds, finely ground
large pinch of ground ginger
salt and freshly ground white pepper
$\frac{2}{3}$ cup matzo meal

Make the stock: Put the chicken in a large pot with the vegetables, parsley, peppercorns, some salt, and about $2\frac{1}{2}$ quarts of water. Slowly bring to a boil over medium heat, occasionally skimming off the foam as it rises to the surface, using a metal skimmer.

Simmer gently, partially covered, for about 2 hours or until the chicken is tender and the meat actually starts to fall away from the bones.

Lift the bird with large slotted spoons out of the pot, draining carefully, and let cool slightly. Remove and discard the skin, strip the meat off the bones, and set it aside. (Although the meat will not have much taste, you can chop and dress it in Green Sauce (see page 45) or use it in sandwiches or salads.) Put the bones back into the pot and simmer for 1 hour longer.

Meanwhile, make the matzo balls: In a large bowl, lightly beat the egg with the chicken fat or vegetable oil, 2 tablespoons of the chicken soup, the ground almonds, and ginger. Season with a generous pinch of salt and some pepper to taste and stir in the matzo meal to make a soft, almost runny mixture. The meal absorbs plenty of liquid, so if it is still too dry add a little more soup. Cover and let rest in a cool place for about 1 hour.

When the soup has simmered for the hour, strain it to remove the vegetables and bones and discard the solids. Return the liquid to a clean pot and bring to a boil again over a medium heat.

Wet your hands with cold water, take a small amount of the matzo mixture about the size of a walnut, and roll it into a ball between your palms. Do this until all the mixture has been used up. When the soup has reached a good rolling boil, drop in the balls, cover, and simmer for about 5 minutes. Adjust the seasoning and serve immediately with the soup.

As the matzo balls soak up a fair amount of the soup while cooking, you may prefer to cook them in a pan of lightly salted boiling water rather than in the soup.

Liver Mousse with a Basil and Tomato Sauce

Chicken livers are wonderfully economical. Usually sold frozen in tubs, they can be used in pasta sauces, pâtés, and mousses. Once thawed, cut away any discolored bits tainted with the bile. Rinse and drain the livers thoroughly to get rid of the bloody liquid, the taste of which can overpower the delicate flavor of the meat. Also, trim away any connective tissue, especially when planning to purée them smoothly as here.

SERVES 4

$\frac{1}{4}$ *lb chicken livers, trimmed*
$\frac{1}{2}$ *garlic clove*
salt and freshly ground white pepper
1 large egg
$\frac{1}{4}$ *cup port wine*
$\frac{2}{3}$ *cup heavy cream*
4 large Swiss chard leaves or fresh spinach leaves
butter, for greasing

for the sauce:
$\frac{2}{3}$ *cup dry white wine*
4 tbsp cold unsalted butter, cut up
2 ripe tomatoes, peeled, seeded and diced
12–14 fresh basil leaves, finely chopped

Preheat the oven to 375°F.

Put the chicken livers and garlic in a food processor and season generously. Process until smooth, then add the egg and port wine and, with the machine running, slowly pour in the cream. Pass the mixture through a fine strainer, forcing the mixture through with a rubber scraper. Refrigerate for 15 minutes.

Meanwhile, tear off and discard the stems from the chard leaves, then blanch the whole leaves for a few seconds in boiling water. Refresh them immediately in ice water and pat dry with paper towels.

Have ready 4 lightly buttered round or oval $\frac{1}{2}$-cup molds, such as ramekins, and 4 matching circles of buttered parchment paper. Line each mold with 1

LIVER MOUSSE WITH A BASIL AND TOMATO SAUCE

chard leaf, pressing it down so it takes on the shape of the mold, but letting it hang over the edges. Spoon the liver mixture into the molds, smoothing each top, and fold the overhanging leaf over to enclose the top. Cover with the circles of parchment paper.

Place the molds in a roasting pan and fill the pan with boiling water until it comes to about halfway up the sides of the molds. Bake in the oven for 15 minutes, or until set.

Meanwhile, make the sauce: In a saucepan, bring the white wine to a boil over a medium heat and boil rapidly until it has reduced by half. Turn down the heat to low and whisk in the butter, a piece at a time, without letting the sauce become more than hand hot. Stir in the tomatoes and the basil and remove from the heat.

To unmold the mousses, peel off the circles of parchment paper. Place a warmed plate on top of each mold, turn them over together, give the mold a quick sharp shake, and then carefully lift it off. Serve warm with a little sauce spooned over the mousses.

Chicken Breasts with Orange

Boned and skinned chicken breast halves, sometimes called cutlets, are sold pre-packed in supermarkets and are very useful. My butcher also sells chicken "suprêmes," a French cut consisting of the breast half complete with the upper wing, trimmed of its tip, left attached. Both are ideal for this recipe as the delicate flavor marries well with that of the fruit.

SERVES 4

4 skinless, boneless chicken breast halves
3 tbsp unsalted butter
grated zest and juice of 1 lemon
½ cup heavy cream

for the marinade:
grated zest and juice of 2 oranges
3 celery stalks with their leaves, trimmed and chopped
4 scallions, trimmed and chopped
salt and freshly ground white pepper

Make the marinade: Mix the juice of one of the oranges with a few of the chopped celery leaves and the chopped green tops of the scallions, then season.

Put the chicken breasts in a glass or stainless steel dish suitable for marinating, pour the marinade over the chicken, and refrigerate, covered, for at least 1 hour, turning the breasts over once or twice.

In a skillet over a low heat, melt the butter and soften the celery and remaining scallions in it for a couple of minutes. Turn down the heat to very low, cover the pan, and cook for 10 minutes, stirring occasionally. As the vegetables should not color, add a couple of tablespoons of vegetable stock or water to the pan if they start to brown. If the lid is not very tight fitting, cover the vegetables with a sheet of buttered parchment paper, then replace the lid.

Lift the chicken pieces out of the marinade and scrape off the pieces of vegetable. Place the chicken in the skillet on top of the vegetables and cook them for about 2 minutes on each side. Strain the marinade, pour it over the chicken, and cook for 5 minutes longer, or until the chicken is cooked through. Using a slotted spoon, transfer the chicken breasts and vegetables to a warmed dish and keep warm.

Add the orange and lemon zests and the remaining fruit juices to the skillet. Turn up the heat and simmer for 1 minute. Pour in the cream and mix together thoroughly. Simmer for 1–2 minutes.

Return the chicken and vegetables to the skillet with any juices, season, and simmer for a couple of minutes to allow the flavors to blend. Adjust the seasoning and arrange the chicken pieces on a warmed serving dish with the sauce and vegetables spooned over them.

Chicken Drumsticks with Red Pepper Sauce

One of the major growth areas in the chicken industry is the sale of fresh and frozen chicken parts, such as breast halves, drumsticks, wings, and thighs — and very convenient they are, too! However, my aversion to frozen chicken extends to such pieces, as these seem to lack both flavor and texture. Moreover, no matter how carefully they are thawed, the skin is always flabby. Freshly prepared pieces, especially after a spell in a judicious marinade, are much more acceptable. Trimmed drumsticks or thighs are best grilled or broiled and served with a robust sauce. Depending on their size and thickness, they can be cooked in a remarkably short time.

SERVES 4–6

8 chicken drumsticks or thigh portions

for the marinade:
$\frac{1}{3}$ cup olive oil
juice of 1 lemon
1 tsp harissa paste
1 garlic clove, minced
salt and freshly ground black pepper

for the sauce:
2 sweet red bell peppers
2 garlic cloves, unpeeled
$\frac{1}{3}$ cup virgin or extra-virgin olive oil
salt and freshly ground black pepper

To prepare the chicken: Using a sharp knife, slash the skin of the drumsticks or thighs diagonally a couple of times on each side and put them in a glass or stainless steel dish suitable for marinating.

Mix all the marinade ingredients together and pour this over the chicken. Refrigerate, covered, for at least one hour, turning the chicken pieces over once or twice.

To make the sauce: Preheat the broiler and brush the red peppers and garlic with a little of the oil. Put them on a broiler rack and broil about 6 inches from the heat, turning them occasionally, for 12–15 minutes, or until the peppers are slightly charred and have softened. Transfer them, with the garlic, to a plate.

To make them easy to peel, cover them with plastic wrap and let cool for about 10 minutes, then peel off the skins. Using a spoon, scoop out and discard the seeds and ribs.

Slit the skin of the garlic cloves with a knife and press the cloves gently to extract the cooked pulp. Put this into a food processor with the peppers and process until smooth. With the machine still running, slowly add the remaining oil in a steady stream to make a smooth bright-red sauce.

Heat the broiler again. Take the pieces of chicken out of the marinade and broil them for 12–15 minutes, or until they are a deep brown and cooked right through. Turn them and baste occasionally with the marinade during cooking.

Serve the chicken pieces with the sauce on the side, or to dip into, and with a large green salad.

CHICKEN DRUMSTICKS WITH RED PEPPER SAUCE

Poulet Sorges

For a really authentic flavor, use a capon for this dish. However, as these are not always available, a large fat hen can be used instead.

SERVES 8

2 slices of thick-sliced bacon, cut up
2 garlic cloves, peeled
2 shallots
3 scallions, trimmed
2½ cups soft bread crumbs
small bunch of fresh flat-leaf parsley
½ tsp freshly grated nutmeg
10 oz chicken livers, trimmed and finely chopped
1 large egg yolk
salt and freshly ground black pepper
1 8-lb capon-style bird (see above)
2 tbsp clarified chicken or goose fat (see page 106)
3 carrots, trimmed and cut into 2-inch pieces
2 turnips, peeled and cut into quarters
3 leeks, cleaned, trimmed and cut into 2-inch pieces
3 celery stalks, trimmed and cut into 2-inch pieces
1 large onion
1 whole clove
1 lb Swiss chard leaves, or spinach leaves, tied in a bunch

for the sauce:
1 tsp Dijon-style mustard
⅔ cup extra-virgin olive oil
2 tbsp white wine vinegar
small bunch of fresh flat-leaf parsley, chopped
2 scallions, trimmed and chopped
1 shallot, finely chopped
2 large eggs

Put the bacon in a food processor with the garlic, shallots, scallions, bread crumbs, parsley, and nutmeg. Process until the ingredients are well chopped.

Add the chicken livers and egg yolk and process to mix together. Season the mixture to taste and spoon into both the neck and vent of the chicken, securing the skin flaps tightly so the stuffing cannot escape.

In a large pot or Dutch oven, melt the chicken or goose fat over a medium heat and brown the chicken all over. Pour over enough boiling water to submerge the bird completely. Add the carrots, turnips, leeks, celery, onion stuck with the clove, and the Swiss chard, along with a generous teaspoon of salt and plenty of pepper. Cover and simmer gently for about 1½ hours.

Make the sauce toward the end of that cooking time: Beat the mustard with the olive oil and vinegar and stir in the parsley, scallions, and shallot. Soft-boil the eggs for 3 minutes, lift them out of the pan with a slotted spoon, and put them under cold running water. When they are cool enough to handle, carefully crack the shells, spoon out the yolks, and whisk them into the vinaigrette.

Pour 3–4 tablespoons of the stock from the chicken into a clean saucepan and bring it to a boil. Carefully shell the egg whites, add them to the pan, and cook for about 3 minutes or until the whites are quite firm. If the whites are still very runny, you can always cook them first and remove the shell afterward. Drain off the liquid, chop the whites finely, and stir them into the sauce. Season.

When the chicken is cooked, lift it out of the pot and then serve surrounded by the vegetables, with some of the chicken stock as a gravy and the sauce handed separately.

Chicken in a Loaf

You really must use a free-range chicken for this recipe, as you need a meaty full-flavored bird to complement the richness of the sauce.

The idea of presenting chicken inside a whole loaf of bread like this comes from southern Italy, where it is served cut in thick slices. In those distant days long before anyone dreamed of the food processor, the nuts and bread were pounded painstakingly by hand to obtain a smooth texture.

SERVES 6–8

$\frac{1}{3}$ *cup olive oil*

1 3-lb chicken, cut into pieces

2 cups Chicken Stock (see pages 106–7)

salt and freshly ground black pepper

1 8-inch round crusty loaf of white bread

3 tbsp shelled almonds, toasted

$\frac{1}{4}$ *cup shelled pistachios*

2 large eggs

juice of 1 lemon

$\frac{1}{4}$ *cup capers, drained*

bunch of fresh flat-leaf parsley, chopped

Using a heavy-bottomed skillet which has a tight-fitting lid, heat 3 tablespoons of the oil over a medium heat, add the chicken pieces, and brown on all sides.

Pour in 1 cup of the stock. Season to taste, cover, and simmer for 15–20 minutes, or until the chicken is tender, adding more stock if the mixture looks in danger of drying out. Drain the chicken and let it cool, reserving the stock.

Preheat the oven to 350°F.

Prepare the bread "dish" and "lid" by cutting the loaf horizontally in two, about one-third down from the top. Hollow it out carefully so as not to tear the crust, reserving the soft bread from the center. Brush the crust all over, both inside and out, with the remaining olive oil.

Put the almonds and pistachios together in a food processor along with the bread from inside the loaf and process until the texture is like fine crumbs. With the machine still running, slowly add the rest of the stock, followed by the eggs and lemon juice. As the mixture should be quite runny, be prepared to add an extra tablespoon or two of stock if necessary.

When the chicken is cool enough to handle, skin it and remove the meat from the bones. Cut the meat into small pieces and stir in the capers, parsley, and the nut sauce. Season and spoon this mixture into the prepared bread crust. Cover with the "lid" and place on a baking sheet. Bake in the oven for about 20 minutes or until golden. Serve either hot or cold, spooning out the filling, then cutting the bread into slices.

Although it is traditional Thanksgiving fare, turkey makes good eating all year round.

Turkey

Like chicken, the best-tasting turkey is always fresh and never frozen. I prefer free-range turkeys, those which have matured at a natural rate and have been given space to move around in. I also prefer a turkey which has been hung (aged) for at least four days to develop a more gamy flavor. However, this process is not done in the States; butchers with whom I spoke told me that most people are not fond of the gamy flavor.

Most of the turkeys raised, processed and sold both in Britain and the United States are Broadbreasted White Turkeys, a commercially developed variety which has the advantage of a buxom breast with plenty of meat. In Britain, I can sometimes find old-fashioned breeds, such as the Cambridge Bronze and the Norfolk Black, which have a far gamier taste. Despite their superior flavor, they are all too often passed over because their breasts yield comparatively little meat, and their skin is stubbly. Some customers actually will not buy them because they prefer a pale, smooth skin. In the States, you may be able to find Bronze turkeys, raised by some smaller growers. Also, you can ask a good butcher to special-order a wild or a free-range turkey for you.

Mail order is another source for free-range turkeys (see page 250), but these birds are often frozen. You can also seek out a store which sells fresh-killed poultry; it may not be free-range, but you can't find a fresher bird.

One word of warning! When you are choosing a turkey, do not be taken in by claims such as "free-range" or "organic" unless it can be backed up by a certification sticker. As with chicken, there is no legal definition yet for these terms. However, there are generally accepted standards. The best way to insure that these standards have been followed is if the turkey has been certified by an organic growers' organization.

In the States, turkeys appear at the dinner table most often as a part of a traditional Thanksgiving feast. But turkey consumption is on the way up. You now can buy turkey throughout the year in a variety of ways other than a whole bird: thin-sliced breast cutlets; breast tenderloins; whole breasts on the bone or boned; breast halves; thighs; wings; drumsticks; and ground. These convenient parts are nearly always sold fresh. The majority of whole turkeys are sold frozen or have been previously frozen, but a fresh turkey, especially around Thanksgiving, is quite easy to obtain.

For the best of all birds, look for a free-range turkey; lacking that, one that hasn't been frozen. It may cost more, but the taste and texture will be worth it.

To roast a turkey

The simplest and most effective way to cook a whole bird is to put it breast down in the hot oven (see below), turning it over for the last hour. This gives a crisp golden finish without dried-up breast meat.

If your bird is too large to safely turn over, or will not balance on its breast, leave it breast side up and protect it with cheesecloth soaked in melted butter. This will baste it continuously but still allow it to crisp.

I prefer not to stuff a turkey before roasting, and cook the stuffing separately (see page 150 for a sausage meat recipe). Instead, I fill the cavities with any, or a mixture, of the following, fresh sage, cored tart-sweet apples, onions studded with cloves, scrubbed whole oranges, raisins or prunes soaked in brandy, walnuts or chestnuts moistened in white wine. If you must stuff the bird, do it only just before popping it into the oven.

Roasting times for a turkey:

(oven temperature is 325°F)

	Unstuffed	Stuffed
6–8 lb	$2\frac{1}{4}$–$3\frac{1}{4}$ hrs	3–$3\frac{1}{2}$ hrs
8–12 lb	$3\frac{1}{4}$–4 hrs	$3\frac{1}{2}$–$4\frac{1}{2}$ hrs
12–16 lb	4–$4\frac{1}{2}$ hrs	$4\frac{1}{2}$–$5\frac{1}{2}$ hrs
16–20 lb	$4\frac{1}{2}$–5 hrs	$5\frac{1}{2}$–$6\frac{1}{2}$ hrs

Source: The America Turkey Federation

When the bird is cooked, a meat thermometer inserted in the thickest part of the thigh next to the body, not touching bone, should register 180–185°F. Let stand 15–30 minutes before carving.

To make a gravy, boil the giblets with a cut-up onion, carrot and fresh parsley in water to cover for about an hour. When cooked, remove the bird from the pan and leave it to one side, covered, to rest. Drain off most of the fat from the pan, pour in the strained stock from the giblets and a glass of dry white wine, and then set it over a high heat. Stir up all the delicious sticky bits on the bottom of the pan, then simmer.

Turkey Breasts with Ginger and Sherry

This recipe makes good use of the economical and now widely available turkey-breast cutlets. As they can be a little bland, they are best cooked with a spicy sauce. You can also make this dish with turkey steaks, which are larger and thicker, about $\frac{3}{4}$-inch and weigh about 12 oz apiece. These steaks cook better if flattened first: Simply place each between two sheets of plastic wrap and then roll them out with a rolling pin using plenty of pressure, then cut them to size.

SERVES 4

2 tbsp safflower oil
salt and freshly ground white pepper
4 thin-sliced turkey-breast cutlets, each weighing 4–6 oz
3 scallions, trimmed and finely chopped
2 garlic cloves, finely chopped
1 oz fresh lemon grass, finely chopped
1 tbsp peeled and finely chopped fresh ginger
$\frac{1}{3}$ cup medium sherry wine
$\frac{1}{2}$ cup Chicken Stock (see pages 106–7)
3 tbsp cold unsalted butter, cut up

In a heavy-bottomed skillet, heat the oil. Season the turkey breasts and sauté them for about 5 minutes on each side, or until cooked through. (If they are quite thin they will cook a lot quicker.) Using a slotted spoon, transfer them to a serving dish and keep warm.

In the same skillet, sauté the scallions, garlic, lemon grass, and ginger for about 5 minutes, or until soft. Add the sherry wine and stock and turn up the heat to bring to a boil. Boil rapidly until the liquid has reduced by one-third. Turn the heat right down and beat in the butter, one piece at a time, until it is all incorporated and the sauce has a rich shiny texture. The sauce should never become more than hand hot, or it will separate. Pour the sauce over the turkey breasts and serve.

Goose

In season from September to December, geese were once very popular in Britain. All over the country, farmers would drive their geese to market to sell them at goose fairs. A green goose, the young tender bird fed on grass or "stubbings" from the recently harvested fields, was traditionally eaten at Michaelmas (the feast of St. Michael) on September 29th; whereas older fatter birds were the usual fare on Christmas Day.

In Britain, most geese nowadays are bred from the Legarth variety, with a good meat-to-bone ratio. However, you can still find some Toulouse or Embden Cross birds which, although less plump, are juicier and more gamy. In the States, 90 percent of the geese raised commercially are of the Embden breed, which came over with the Pilgrims from Embden, England. These geese have been selectively bred to be heavier, with a wider, deeper breast. On a small scale, some producers raise Toulouse, White, and Brown Chinese geese and these may be mail ordered (see page 250) or found at a specialty butcher.

Again a fresh, rather than frozen goose, is a far better buy. However, fresh geese are rather difficult to come by in the States. If you do find a goose labeled "fresh," it may have been previously frozen and thawed. When choosing a fresh goose, look for a plump breast, with firm meat that is resilient to the touch.

As a general rule, allow over one pound per person, so a 10–12 lb goose should feed eight people.

The products of the goose, particularly its fat, are not only useful in cooking below. Formerly, goose fat was used as a medicinal ointment. Today, goose feathers continue to be used as down for comfortable bedding. ROAST GOOSE STUFFED WITH APPLES right.

pound plus 15 minutes extra. Turn it breast side up for the last 1½ hours of cooking to crisp the skin. When done, the legs will feel quite tender, and a meat thermometer inserted in the thickest part of the thigh, not touching bone, should register 180°–185°F.

To cut the fattiness of the bird, serve it with Onion Marmalade (see page 23), Spiced Crab Apples (see page 224) or a tart applesauce made with peeled, cored and quartered apples simmered in hard cider or apple juice flavored with grated orange and lemon zests and generous pinches of ground cloves, sugar and salt. As with turkey, I prefer to bake the stuffing separately and either prepare a traditional sage, bread crumb, and onion stuffing enriched with the goose liver, or a more-unusual mixture of chopped fennel mixed with brandy-soaked prunes, slices of lemon and bread crumbs.

To roast a goose

Goose is a rich meat with a very high fat content and is therefore best roasted standing on a rack in a roasting pan so the fat can drain off. Never throw the fat away as, once it has been clarified (see page 106), it keeps for months, ideal for cooking potatoes (see page 21) or browning poultry (see Poulet Sorges, page 112).

Rub the breast with salt and, if you wish, prick the skin all over to let the fat run out. Stuff the bird with peeled and quartered apples and onions soaked in hard cider or Calvados and sprinkled with ground cinnamon, salt, and pepper. Set the bird, breast down, on a rack and either slow-roast in an oven preheated to 350°F, allowing 20 minutes per pound plus 20 minutes extra, or fast-roast it at 400°F for 15 minutes per

Duck

Farmyard ducks are milder flavored, far fattier and a good deal larger than ducks found in the wild.

A good duck should be neither too fatty, nor too bony. In Britain, the breeds with the best eating qualities are the Rouen, with its fine-flavored flesh; the large, fat Aylesbury, with its buttery meat; the more delicately flavored Pekin; the Nantes, a small strongly flavored duck with a good layer of fat; and the Muscovy, with a full breast, meaty legs and an almost smoky flavor.

In the States, the duck you will most commonly find is the white Pekin duck, usually sold frozen in supermarkets and butcher shops, weighing 3–5 lb. Long Island ducks, found most commonly on the East Coast, are, in fact, Pekin ducks raised on Long Island, New York. A 5-lb duck will serve four, but it might be a better idea to roast two smaller ducks. As you can now buy duck breasts, or sometimes legs, duck has become a more convenient buy. The only disadvantage is that you no longer have a whole carcass to boil up for a stock or soup, or the liver to transform into a rich pâté or stuffing.

To roast a duck

First stuff the bird with a couple of cored and quartered apples soaked in brandy, or peeled and quartered oranges, or a traditional sage-and-onion stuffing. Rub the skin all over with salt. If it is very fatty, prick it with a fork. Roast it on a rack in a roasting pan in an oven preheated to 400°F, allowing about 15 minutes per pound plus an extra 15 minutes. If the legs are still bloody, they may need extra cooking: in which case, detach them and return them to the oven for an extra 10 minutes. Like most roasts, a duck should be given time to rest before being carved.

Quail, guinea fowl, duck right. *Ducks enjoy a ride home from market* opposite.

Duck Legs Braised with Onions and Cabbage

In traditional French country cooking, succulent duck legs were sometimes turned into confit, *one of the oldest ways of preserving meat. They were salted, slowly cooked in their own fat, then sealed and stored in the same fat.*

This recipe, taken from Chez Panisse Cooking *by Paul Bertolli with Alice Waters, is based on this old-fashioned method. However, as you might expect from these Californian cooks, it has been cunningly adapted so that although the meat is still meltingly soft, it has a lighter, cleaner flavor and none of the cloying quality which can result from too much duck fat.*

SERVES 4

1 tbsp finely chopped fresh thyme

1 tbsp freshly ground black pepper

2 tbsp coarse sea salt or kosher salt

4 duck legs, each weighing about 5 oz

3 large red onions, sliced

$\frac{3}{4}$ lb Savoy cabbage, cut in thick slices

3 tbsp balsamic vinegar

salt and freshly ground black pepper

2 cups Chicken Stock (see pages 106–7)

$\frac{3}{4}$ lb ripe tomatoes, peeled, quartered, and seeded

large pinch of superfine or granulated sugar

4 sprigs of fresh thyme, to garnish

Make a dry marinade by mixing together the thyme and the measured amounts of black pepper and sea salt. For this recipe you really must use coarse sea salt or kosher salt, otherwise the taste is far too harsh.

Using a sharp knife, slash the duck skins to make a couple of thin cuts about $1\frac{1}{2}$ inches long. Rub the mixture into the duck legs all over and let marinate in the refrigerator for $1\frac{1}{2}$ hours, by which time the duck will have absorbed a fair amount of the salt.

Preheat the oven to 350°F.

Using a damp cloth, wipe the duck legs free of the dry marinade and place them, skin side down, in a Dutch oven over a low heat. Cook them very gently, turning occasionally, for 20 minutes, or until golden brown. (If the heat is low enough, you do not need any oil or butter as the legs give off so much fat there is no risk of them burning. Sometimes they give off so much fat that you should remove some of it with a spoon during cooking and reserve it.) Transfer the duck legs to a warm plate and keep warm. Reserve the duck fat.

Rinse the pot, warm 3 tablespoons of the duck fat in it over a medium heat, add the onions, and cook gently for 5–7 minutes, or until soft. Stir in the cabbage and vinegar, season, and simmer, stirring occasionally, for about 3 minutes, or until the cabbage is wilted.

Arrange the duck legs on top of the cabbage and add the stock. Sprinkle the tomatoes with the sugar and scatter them over the duck legs. Cover the pot and bake in the oven for $1\frac{1}{2}$ hours, or until the legs are tender. Using a slotted spoon, transfer them to a serving dish with the vegetables and keep warm.

Make a simple sauce by straining the cooking liquid into a saucepan and boiling it vigorously to reduce it until only about 1 cup remains. Season and serve the duck legs on the bed of vegetables, garnished with the thyme sprigs. Serve the sauce separately.

Duck Breasts with Pears

A few years ago, magrets de canard, *boneless duck breast halves, were all the rage with top chefs, and there was no end to the sweet, sharp, or sour sauces dreamed up to serve with them. As a result, duck breasts are now available in some top-quality butcher shops for the home cook. You may need to special-order them from your butcher; alternatively, they are available by mail order (see page 250 for sources).*

Magret is traditionally from the French Barbary duck and comes with its skin and underlying layer of fat intact. It is sold in pieces weighing about 6 oz, from the female duck, or around 11 oz from the male duck. One large magret *will easily feed two people, so cut it diagonally across in half before cooking to divide it into two individual portions.*

Duck breasts in the States are usually from the Long Island (Pekin) duck, although, sometimes, breasts from Moulard and Muscovy ducks are available; these are smaller, so you need to allow one breast half per person.

SERVES 6

6 boneless duck breast halves, each weighing about 6 oz or 3 large
magrets, *each weighing about 11 oz, cut in half diagonally*
(see above)
salt and freshly ground black pepper
6 firm Comice pears, peeled, cored, and quartered
1 cinnamon stick
2 tbsp butter
1 tbsp olive oil
1 tbsp honey
2 onions, sliced
1 tbsp five-spice powder
2 ripe tomatoes, peeled, seeded, and chopped
pinch of granulated sugar
2 tbsp sherry vinegar
½ cup dry sherry wine
1¼ cups chicken or duck stock (see pages 106–7)

Preheat the oven to 425°F. Season the duck breasts with salt and pepper to taste.

In a saucepan, combine the pears, cinnamon stick, and enough water to cover. Bring to just below a boil and simmer for 8–10 minutes, or until the pears are just tender. Drain the pears, reserving the cooking liquid and discarding the cinnamon stick.

Meanwhile, melt the butter with the oil in a heavy-bottomed ovenproof skillet over a medium heat. Fry the duck breasts skin side down for 6–8 minutes. This not only seals them but also allows the fat to infuse the meat. Drain off the fat, keeping it for later use, turn the breasts over, brush the skins with the honey, and bake them in the oven for 15 minutes, or a little longer if you do not like the meat pink.

Meanwhile, heat 3 tablespoons of the duck fat in another heavy-bottomed skillet over a medium heat and fry the pear quarters until just golden, turning occasionally. Using a slotted spoon, transfer them to a plate and keep warm. Sprinkle the onions with the five-spice powder and sauté them in the same skillet, along with the tomatoes and sugar for about 10 minutes, or until soft. Pour in the sherry vinegar and sauté for another 5 minutes.

Remove the duck from the oven and keep warm. Carefully pour the fat from the skillet into the onions. Turn up the heat, add the sherry, stock, and about 1¼ cups of the drained cooking liquid from the pears. Bring to a boil and cook rapidly, uncovered, for about 10 minutes so that it reduces by about two-thirds.

Transfer the contents of the skillet to a food processor and process until smooth. Return the sauce to the skillet, stir in any juices from the cooked breasts, and adjust the seasoning. Arrange the duck breasts in the skillet with the pears on top and heat gently for a couple of minutes. Serve immediately.

DUCK BREASTS WITH PEARS

Quail

Quail are an extremely popular game bird in the States. Farm-raised quail are available year-round from a good butcher, a local game farm, or by mail order (see page 250). They weigh from 4–5 oz, with jumbo quails weighing 8 oz. Sold fresh and frozen, either they may be braised or casseroled whole, or spatchcocked (see page 168) and then grilled, broiled, or roasted.

It is also a good idea to stuff the birds for roasting, in which case you could buy semi boned-out quails, or you can stuff them unboned. Sometimes quails are sold with their livers; chop these up, sauté them in oil or butter for a few minutes and then add them to the stuffing.

As quails are quite lean, the breast can readily dry out when roasting. To prevent this, cover with a slice of bacon, or salt pork, or, as in the following recipe, with grape leaves.

Quails with Lemon and Coriander

If you grow a grape vine, you can use your own leaves for wrapping the quails provided you blanch them first for a few seconds in boiling water; otherwise buy leaves in brine and rinse and dry them.

SERVES 6

1 tbsp olive oil, plus extra for brushing
1 cup uncooked long-grain white rice
¾ cup pine nuts, toasted
grated zest and juice of 2 lemons
6 tbsp finely chopped fresh flat-leaf parsley
6 tbsp finely chopped fresh coriander leaves (cilantro)
salt and freshly ground black pepper
12 small fresh quails, whole or boned (see above)
12 grape leaves (see above)

½ cup extra-virgin olive oil
3 shallots, finely chopped
1¼ cups dry white wine

Preheat the oven to 400°F and generously oil a baking dish. Cook the rice in a saucepan of salted water until soft, according to the directions on the package. Drain it thoroughly and put it into a large mixing bowl. Stir in the pine nuts, lemon zest, half the lemon juice, half each of the parsley and coriander and season to taste.

While the rice is cooking, wipe the quails all over with a damp cloth, both inside and out. If the livers are available, remove them from their cavities and chop them finely. Heat 1 tablespoon of the olive oil in a skillet over a medium heat and sauté the quail livers for a couple of minutes, until they have changed color. Stir the livers into the rice.

Spoon the rice stuffing into the cleaned cavities of the quails, packing it in quite firmly but not too tightly otherwise the birds will burst when cooking. Secure the opening of each with a wooden toothpick. Using a pastry brush, paint the birds with some olive oil, place a grape leaf over each breast, tucking it into the wings, and brush again with olive oil.

Place the quails in the prepared baking dish and bake in the oven for about 25 minutes.

Meanwhile, in a pan, heat 2 tablespoons of the extra-virgin olive oil. Add the shallots and sauté them until soft. Add the wine and boil, uncovered, for 5–7 minutes, or until the wine has reduced by half.

When the quails are cooked, transfer them with a slotted spoon to a warmed serving dish and keep warm. Strain any juices from the baking dish into the saucepan and simmer for 1 minute. Turn down the heat and stir in the remaining parsley, coriander, and lemon juice. Slowly trickle in the remaining extra-virgin olive oil, stirring constantly. Season and serve immediately.

QUAILS WITH LEMON AND CORIANDER opposite.

Guinea Fowl

The French rave about the guinea fowl or guinea hen, deeming it a superior alternative to chicken, although I am not completely convinced. Originally a game bird, guinea fowl is now farmed like chicken. It has a mild gamy taste which reveals its origins, with slightly fibrous meat that tends to dry out unless cooked very carefully. Order guinea fowl from a butcher that sells a lot of poultry, or mail-order it (see page 250).

Because the meat has little fat covering, I prefer to buy a whole bird and use its leg meat in a pâté, its carcass for stock and then to bone the breasts, leaving the upper wings attached (this cut is called a suprême). I then panfry the suprêmes separately, as in the following recipe.

Breasts of Guinea Fowl with Lentils

I am indebted for this recipe to the excellent chef Ian McAndrew, whose book On Poultry and Game *remains one of my favorites. If guinea fowl suprêmes are unavailable, substitute duck or chicken suprêmes or cutlets.*

SERVES 4

1 tbsp unsalted butter
2 tsp olive oil
4 guinea fowl suprêmes (see above)
salt and freshly ground black pepper
2 oz thick-sliced bacon, diced
1 onion, chopped
1 carrot, trimmed and thinly sliced
$\frac{1}{2}$ cup dry white wine
$1\frac{1}{2}$ cups Chicken Stock (see pages 106–7)

$\frac{1}{3}$ cup red lentils, rinsed and drained
1 ripe tomato, peeled, seeded, and diced
1 tbsp chopped fresh thyme leaves

Melt the butter with the oil in a skillet over a medium heat. Season the suprêmes to taste and sauté them, skin side down, for about 5 minutes, or until they are golden brown. Turn them over and cook the other side in the same way. Using a slotted spoon, transfer them to a warmed serving dish and keep warm.

Strain off all but 1 teaspoon of the fat from the skillet. Heat this over a medium heat and sauté the bacon in it for 2–3 minutes. Add the onion and carrot and cook for 4–5 minutes, or until golden brown.

Pour in the white wine, scraping up any browned bits from the bottom of the skillet, turn up the heat and simmer until it has reduced by half. Then add the chicken stock, bring to a boil, and stir in the lentils. Reduce the heat, cover, and simmer for 15 minutes or until tender, adding the tomato and thyme leaves after 10 minutes. Adjust the seasoning.

Serve the guinea fowl on a bed of the lentils.

Eggs

Not only are eggs nutritious, as they contain 15% of our recommended daily protein requirement, vitamins A, B, and D, and minerals such as iron, calcium, and iodine, but they are also incredibly versatile as you can boil, poach, bake, scramble, and fry them.

CHICKEN EGGS are the most commonly used and they are invaluable in cooking, in areas as diverse as making sauces (see Hollandaise Sauce, page 128) and setting and enriching terrines (see Terrine of Lemon Sole with Shrimp, page 89). Whipped egg whites are also the most common means of aerating and lightening mixtures (see Soufflé Omelet, page 131).

Commercially sold eggs come in cartons showing the grade and the size and, if inspected by the USDA, the date the eggs were packed and usually, an expiration date, beyond which the eggs cannot be sold. They are graded AA, A, and B. Grade is determined by the quality of the egg and its shell, although there is no difference in nutritional value between the grades. Sizes are Jumbo, Extra Large, Large, Medium, Small, and Peewee. The size is determined by the average weight of the eggs per dozen.

There are only two breeds of hens laying eggs commercially in the United States. Leghorn Whites, which lay white-shelled eggs, and Rhode Island Reds, which lay brown-shelled eggs. Contrary to what you might think, there is no inherent difference in the flavor between a brown- or white-shelled egg.

I prefer to buy "real" farm or organic eggs directly from a farm stand or a good health food store. These, if properly certified, will be from hens which are reared more humanely, which are free to scratch about on grass and, if organic, are fed on organically grown feed. If fresh, these should be superb. In Britain, instead of buying eggs from modern hybrids, which have been developed primarily for their laying efficiency, I am sometimes lucky enough to find eggs from such old-fashioned breeds as the Silky, Maran, Aracuna or Wellsummer hens. These really do taste better.

Of course, chicken's eggs are not the only eggs we eat. During the spring and early summer months you may be able to buy enormous GOOSE EGGS for baking. One goose egg is the equivalent of two large chicken eggs. DUCK EGGS make excellent omelets, although as some people are wary of their safety, they must always be thoroughly cooked. TURKEY EGGS are very delicately flavored and take a good 15 minutes to hard-boil; whereas tiny, speckled QUAIL EGGS cook in a matter of minutes and are superb soft-boiled and tossed into a salad, or hard-boiled and served with salt spiced with cayenne.

Egg safety

Because of the small, but very real chance of salmonella contamination from raw or soft-boiled eggs, you may wish to avoid serving dishes with raw or soft-boiled eggs to children and the elderly. It is important to follow certain safeguards:

Refrigerate eggs in their carton as soon as you bring them home from the market;

Do not use eggs with cracked shells for dishes which are not thoroughly cooked, like scrambled or soft-boiled eggs, or for mayonnaise. However, cracked eggs may be safely used in baked goods, such as cakes, and for hard-boiled eggs;

Refrigerate egg-rich dishes, such as custards, soon after baking or serving. Keep mayonnaise well chilled, and serve Hollandaise sauce directly after it's made.

Separating eggs

Eggs separate more easily when cold and beat to a greater volume when at room temperature. Use three bowls if you need more than one white; one for the egg being separated, one for the whites, and one for yolks. Crack the egg and pull apart, letting the white run out of the shell. Tip the yolk from one half of the shell to the other, dripping the white into the bowl; put the yolk in another bowl. Inspect the white carefully: Any yolk will keep the whites from beating to a proper volume. Tip the white into the mixing bowl and continue.

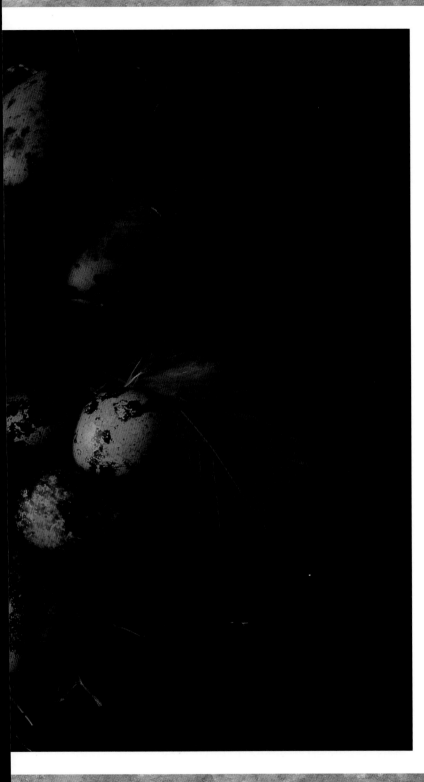

Mirror Eggs

An excellent appetizer or brunch entrée, this dish is William Verrall's version of the French classic. Master of the White Hart Inn in Lewes, England, in the first half of the eighteenth century, Verrall had served his apprenticeship under St Clouet, the Duke of Northumberland's renowned French chef.

SERVES 4–6

2 tbsp butter, for greasing
10–12 scallions, trimmed and finely chopped
3 tbsp finely chopped fresh flat-leaf parsley
1 tbsp finely chopped fresh tarragon
grated zest of 1 and juice of 3 oranges
6 large eggs
1¼ cups heavy cream
juice of 2 lemons
salt and freshly ground white pepper

Preheat the oven to 375°F and generously butter a baking dish or other shallow, ovenproof dish.

Sprinkle the scallions, parsley, tarragon, and orange zest into the prepared baking dish. Carefully break 1 egg into a small bowl and slide into the baking dish. Repeat with the remaining eggs.

Mix the cream with the orange and lemon juices, season, and pour over the eggs. Bake for about 20 minutes, or until the eggs are just set. Serve immediately.

Eggs range in size and color from the huge creamy white goose egg to tiny brown-speckled quail eggs. Eggs from traditional English breeds, such as the speckled dark brown egg of the Wellsummer hen, look much more interesting than those of modern hybrid hens.

Basic Hollandaise Sauce

MAKES ABOUT 1½ CUPS

6–8 whole black peppercorns, coarsely crushed
⅔ cup dry white wine
½ cup white wine vinegar
4 large egg yolks
2 sticks unsalted butter, cut up
salt and freshly ground black pepper

Combine the peppercorns, wine, and vinegar in a saucepan over a moderate heat and bring to a boil. Boil rapidly to reduce the liquid until only about 1 tablespoon remains.

Meanwhile, slowly heat some water in the bottom of a double boiler. If you don't have a double boiler, balance a lined copper, stainless steel, or glass bowl in a saucepan half filled with water so it does not touch the water. Keep the water at the barest simmer.

Strain the reduction into the top of the double boiler to get rid of the peppercorns, and whisk in the egg yolks until they are thick and warm, taking care not to let them over-heat or they will start to scramble.

Slowly beat in the butter, one piece at a time, to make a thick, smooth sauce. If it does curdle, try stirring in one tablespoon of hot water or an ice cube. Or put 1 teaspoon of vinegar in a clean bowl and start all over again, beating the curdled mixture into the bowl a drop at a time.

When all the butter has been added, season the sauce lightly. If the taste is a little too sharp, add a little more butter. Keep warm in the double boiler, covered, or in the bowl over the saucepan of water, for a short time, until ready to serve.

Variations

1 To make a Maltaise Sauce, add the grated zest and juice of ½ orange once all the butter is added.

2 To make a Lemon Hollandaise, add the grated zest and juice of ½ lemon once all the butter is added.

3 To make a Mousseline Hollandaise, fold in 4 heaping tablespoons of lightly whipped cream once all the butter is added.

4 To make a Béarnaise Sauce, add 1 chopped shallot and a couple of sprigs of fresh tarragon to the vinegar while it is being boiled and reduced. Then stir 1 tablespoon each of chopped fresh tarragon and chervil into the finished sauce.

Basic Sabayon Sauce

Serve this on its own or with fresh seasonal fruit, or as a sauce with slices of sweet cake.

SERVES 4–6

4 large egg yolks
⅓ cup superfine or granulated sugar
1 cup dry white wine

In a lined copper, stainless steel, or glass bowl, beat together the egg yolks and sugar until thick and creamy. Add the wine and continue beating until the mixture is light, airy, and very frothy.

Balance the bowl in a saucepan half filled with boiling water, so it is just over the water without touching it. Beat the mixture continuously until the sauce thickens to the texture of lightly whipped cream. Serve immediately.

Variations

1 Replace the white wine with Champagne.

2 Replace the white wine with Marsala to make Italian-style Zabaglione.

ROULADE WITH ASPARAGUS right.

Roulade with Asparagus

A roulade only works if the eggs are very fresh, otherwise the whites cannot be properly aerated, or beaten into stiff peaks, and will collapse quickly, producing an unfortunate flat roll with a heavy texture, rather than the light fluffiness of a proper roulade.

SERVES 4

1 tbsp butter, melted, plus a little more for greasing
4 extra-large eggs, separated
salt and freshly ground black pepper
1 lb fresh asparagus, trimmed
1¼ cups Maltaise Sauce (see opposite page)

Preheat the oven to 400°F. Line a jelly-roll pan lined with a piece of parchment paper and lightly butter it.

Beat the egg yolks until thick, pour in the melted butter, and season to taste. Beat the egg whites in a separate bowl until they form stiff, but not dry, peaks. Then using a large, clean metal spoon, carefully fold them into the yolks. Season.

Spread the mixture in the prepared pan and bake for about 10 minutes, or until just set.

Meanwhile, tie the asparagus into a bundle and cook upright in a pan of lightly salted boiling water, with the tips standing up out of the water, or cook in a steamer, for about 10 minutes, until just tender. Drain and cut the asparagus into 2-inch pieces. Keep these warm.

Make the Maltaise sauce and keep warm.

Remove the roulade from the oven and unmold it onto a warm serving plate covered with a damp dish towel. Carefully peel off the parchment, and spread the roulade evenly with some of the Maltaise sauce. Arrange the asparagus on the sauce in rows and cover with the remaining sauce. Gently pull up on the corners of one end of the towel to roll up the roulade. Transfer to a serving plate. Serve immediately.

Soufflé Omelet with Sorrel and Crème Fraîche

One of the tips I learned when working in the kitchens of Oswald Mair, the fiercely tyrannical chef of the London Hilton, was always to beat egg whites in a copper bowl and to fold them into a mixture with a metal spoon to ensure that they are light and keep in the air — it does work!

SERVES 2

4 extra-large eggs, separated
salt and freshly ground black pepper
2 tbsp butter
½ lb fresh sorrel, trimmed and chopped
small bunch of fresh flat-leaf parsley, finely chopped
small bunch of fresh chervil, finely chopped
2 tbsp crème fraîche

Preheat the oven to 400°F.

In a bowl, beat 3 of the egg yolks and 2 of the egg whites until light and frothy, then season to taste. In a separate bowl, beat the remaining egg whites until they form stiff, but not dry, peaks. Using a metal spoon, carefully fold them into the yolk mixture.

Melt half of the butter and pour it into a shallow ovenproof dish, about 13- × 9- × 2-inches. Swirl it around to coat the bottom, pour in the egg mixture, and bake it for about 10 minutes, or until it is just set.

Meanwhile, melt the remaining butter in a saucepan over a low heat, add the sorrel, parsley, and chervil, and cook for about 5 minutes, or until soft, stirring occasionally. Remove the pan from the heat, and stir in the crème fraîche and the remaining egg yolk. Season to taste, return the pan to the low heat, and cook, stirring constantly, until the mixture thickens, about 1–2 minutes. Take care not to let the mixture get too hot or it will scramble. When the omelet is ready, spread this filling over one half of it and then gently fold over the other half. Serve immediately, cutting into 2 servings.

Scrambled Eggs

Scrambled eggs are the ultimate in nursery food. Warm, soft, and comforting, they are what I long for whenever I am feeling old, sad, or tired. Proper scrambled eggs are meltingly creamy and slowly cooked, although I cannot help thinking that Molly Keane, in her Nursery Cooking, *slightly overdid it when the eggs were "sighed over for twenty minutes in a bain-marie."*

SERVES 2

4 tbsp unsalted butter
5 large eggs
1 tbsp heavy cream
salt and freshly ground black pepper
2 slices of whole-wheat toast, cut into triangles, to serve

In a heavy-bottomed saucepan over a low heat, melt half the butter. Beat the eggs until light and frothy. Cut up the remaining butter into small pieces and stir them into the eggs.

Whisk the mixture into the saucepan and remove from the heat. Carry on whisking while counting slowly to 10, then return the pan to low heat and, using a wooden spoon, stir the eggs until they start to scramble.

The eggs will carry on cooking even when they are no longer in contact with the heat. So, when they look just done, remove them from the heat, immediately stir in the cream and season to taste. This will lower their temperature and stop the cooking. Spoon the eggs over the toast and serve immediately.

SOUFFLÉ OMELET WITH SORREL AND CRÈME FRAÎCHE
opposite.

The Pastures

According to geography and climate, meat-eating habits vary considerably from country to country. Lush pastures are suited to rearing beef cattle; sheep thrive in harsher conditions; while that invaluable domestic animal, the pig, is to be found in countless areas.

Fresh meat

In the early days, beef cattle and sheep were grazed freely on vast ranges in the western United States, or on pastureland on farms. They moved about as they wished, and then were driven in large herds to market. Today, directly after weaning, most livestock is sent to feedlots to be fattened intensively before going to market. In these feedlots, animals are kept confined and fed aggressively so they gain weight as quickly and cheaply as possible.

The production of quality meat depends on many factors, such as breed, feed, age, housing conditions, aging, and butchering, and they all affect the meat's eating quality. However, because of the switch of emphasis in farming, with efficiency rather than taste as the motivating factor, the farmers' and ranchers' energies have been directed to producing meat at as low a price as possible. Short-cuts have been taken – often, I feel, at the expense of consumers' taste buds – and the eating quality of meat has been compromised.

Breeds are selected to mature faster, and the animals are fed on concentrates and kept indoors so they do not waste valuable energy by exercizing. They are brought to market at an earlier age than in previous times, and the carcasses are aged for only a few days to ensure as little weight loss as possible.

However, all is not lost! In response to both the taste and welfare issues, "alternative" methods of production have recently gained support with the discerning public, producing "organic," "grass-fed," "free-range," and/or "naturally raised" meat. But, as these methods are less cost-effective, you have to pay more for them.

There is obviously a demand for meat raised by alternative methods, as some supermarkets and butcher shops have introduced this meat to their shelves. Alternatively raised meat may also be found in large health-food stores, at farmers' markets, through small producers, and by mail order from ranchers and farmers, or organic-foods catalogues (see page 250).

Another trend is afoot in the United States and in Britain, and that is to produce leaner beef, pork, and lamb. Through selective breeding, and through changes in feeding practices, the fat-to-lean ratio has changed, so meat has less fat covering and less marbling (the small veins of fat which run through the meat, especially in beef), than it did in times past. Meat is also trimmed much closer than it used to be. The beef sold today generally has an external fat layer of no more, and

What is "organic" meat?

If meat is labeled "organic" or "free-range," it should carry a certification sticker from an organic food producers' association.

If labeled "organic," you can assume that the animal ate only certified organic feed and was treated medically only as needed. If labeled "hormone-free," the animal should have received no growth hormones or stimulants. If labeled "free-range," or "naturally raised," it was naturally weaned from its mother, allowed to roam about with few restrictions on its movement, and was not put in a feedlot to be fattened, but instead, allowed to gain weight at a normal rate.

Some people remain sceptical as to whether the meat actually does taste better. However, I think any animal reared at a natural pace on a cereal and grass diet will develop a fuller flavor; if it is allowed to exercise it must have a better texture, and if slaughtered humanely it will show fewer signs of stress. Therefore it follows that the meat that finally reaches the consumer will be superior in its taste and texture.

Various breeds, including a creamy beige Charolais, graze on Scottish pastures.

usually less, than ⅛ inch. These changes in fat content came about because of consumers' concerns about fat and cholesterol in their diets. However, fat has flavor and it makes meat juicy and tender. Leaner meat requires more careful cooking so it does not dry out and, excepting stews and some braises, beef and lamb are more tender, more flavorful, and retain more moisture when cooked rare to medium-rare, and pork is more succulent when cooked to a medium doneness. Stews and braises are more successful if made with cuts with a sufficient content of fat. If you want to avoid extra fat in your diet, cook such dishes in advance, refrigerate overnight, and skim off the fat that has risen to the top before reheating the dish.

Beef

In my country, for the finest-tasting beef, nothing beats pure-bred, grass-fed Aberdeen Angus, with Hereford coming in a close second. Because of the trend for larger, leaner carcasses, however, most of our beef now comes from Continental breeds. Most of the breeds of beef cattle in the United States, however, are derived from breeds that originated in Britain. Through inbreeding, cross-breeding, and linebreeding with cattle brought from other European countries and later from Africa and India, U.S. breeds have been developed that are hardy enough for ranches in the western ranges.

As with all meat, there are many factors affecting the eating quality of beef. It is particularly important that beef be well aged, as aging improves the tenderness and allows the flavor to develop and mature. Aging is especially important for the expensive cuts that are cooked by dry heat methods, such as roasting or broiling. Most retailers are, however, reluctant to age beef, which involves storing it at 34–38°F for at least 10 days, because of the inevitable weight loss and because it takes up valuable space and time. Only the top grade of beef, Prime, is aged, and, if labeled "aged beef," the meat will have been stored for 2–3 weeks.

Although most people think the color of the flesh should be cherry red, it is not necessarily a sign of good quality. Some of the best beef I have ever bought has been of a much darker hue, a sign that it has been well aged. Look, instead, for a firm, slightly moist piece of meat with a clean aroma and a layer of glossy fat, the color of which can vary from a milky white to yellow.

For a roast, choose a cut from the rib or loin (tenderloin or the sirloin). Although top and bottom round, cut from the inside of the hind leg, are often sold for roasting, I find they are a little dry and are usually better in a pot roast or a braise. Shank, from the foreleg, is also excellent for braising and stewing, as is meat from the chuck, or shoulder area.

In the States, ground beef is either labeled by the cut from which it is made (round, chuck, or sirloin), or labeled as ground beef, or it is labeled by the percentage of fat to lean. I prefer to grind my own beef so I know where it comes from: I buy a lean chuck or round steak and grind it in the food processor.

To roast beef

Allow 20 minutes per pound plus an extra 20 minutes at 400°F, for a roast on the bone; 25 minutes per pound plus an extra 25 minutes for a boneless roast. For rare meat allow only 15 minutes per pound. If using a meat thermometer, rare will register 125–130°F; medium, 140°F; medium-to-well-done, 150°F. Let the roast stand for 10–15 minutes before carving.

Daube of Beef

For this glorious, robustly flavored, and slowly cooked dish, it really is a waste of money buying an expensive cut of beef. A piece of shank, with its connective tissue running through the meat, is ideal as it will give the rich gelatinous quality essential for this dish. Buy a whole piece or cross-cut beef shanks, bone it (or have the butcher do this for you), then trim away some of the fat, and cut the meat into cubes.

Two ideas for adding extra flavor are to place a piece of pork skin, skin side down, or strips of bacon on top of the daube while it cooks (this also prevents evaporation), and to stir in a gremolada (traditionally an accompaniment to risotto or osso bucco) at the last moment for extra piquancy.

SERVES 6

$\frac{1}{3}$ cup olive oil
3 lb boned cross-cut beef shanks, cut into 1-inch cubes
$\frac{1}{2}$ lb salt pork or fresh side pork or unsmoked slab bacon, cubed
2 large onions, sliced

10 garlic cloves, chopped
3 cups dry red wine
$1\frac{1}{2}$ lb ripe tomatoes, skinned, seeded and chopped (3 cups)
1 tbsp allspice berries
1 tbsp chopped fresh flat-leaf parsley
1 tbsp chopped fresh thyme
1 tbsp chopped fresh marjoram
salt and freshly ground black pepper
large piece of pork skin (optional)
1 cup pitted ripe olives, halved

for the gremolada:
3 garlic cloves, finely chopped
grated zest of 2 large oranges
bunch of fresh flat-leaf parsley, finely chopped

In a Dutch oven with a tight-fitting lid, heat the oil over a medium heat, and lightly brown the beef cubes. (If the pot is not large enough to hold the meat in a single layer, brown it in batches.) Remove the browned beef from the pot with a slotted spoon and reserve.

In the same pot, sauté the pork or bacon for 2–3 minutes, then add the onions and garlic and cook 2–3 minutes longer. Add the wine, tomatoes, allspice, parsley, thyme, and marjoram. Turn up the heat and bring the liquid to a boil.

Turn the heat down to low, return the beef to the pot, and season to taste. Place the piece of pork skin on top, fat-side up. (If you cannot find pork skin, a piece of parchment paper can be used instead, although it will obviously not give the same rich flavor.) Cover and simmer very gently about $2\frac{1}{2}$ hours. Remove the pork skin, stir in the olives, and simmer 30 minutes longer, or until the beef is meltingly tender.

To make the gremolada, mix the garlic with the orange zest and parsley. Just before serving, sprinkle it over the top of the daube.

DAUBE OF BEEF

Simmered Beef Tenderloin

Although this may seem an extravagance, simmering beef tenderloin results in a delicate and subtle dish that is quite superb. For this recipe, buy a whole tenderloin and ask the butcher to trim and tie it into a neat shape.

SERVES 2

1 tbsp olive oil

salt and freshly ground black pepper

1 10-oz beef tenderloin (see above)

1 cup Chicken Stock (see pages 106–7)

1 carrot, trimmed and sliced

1 celery stalk, trimmed and sliced

1 leek, trimmed, cleaned and sliced

2 scallions, trimmed and sliced

6–8 small new potatoes

2–3 whole black peppercorns

1 tbsp grated fresh horseradish or 2 tsp prepared horseradish

$\frac{1}{3}$ cup heavy cream

In a skillet which has a tight-fitting lid, heat the olive oil over a high heat. Season the meat to taste, and brown the tenderloin on all sides in the oil for 2–3 minutes.

Pour in the stock and add the carrot, celery, leek, scallions, potatoes, peppercorns, and a pinch of salt. Turn down the heat, cover, and simmer 10–12 minutes, until the meat is tender. Using a slotted spoon, transfer the meat and vegetables to a dish; keep warm.

To make the sauce, strain $\frac{1}{2}$ cup of the cooking liquid into a separate saucepan. Skim off any fat. Bring it to a boil and boil rapidly to reduce by half. Stir in the horseradish and cream, then turn down the heat and simmer for 2–3 minutes. Adjust the seasoning.

Serve the beef, cut into thin slices, surrounded by the vegetables, with the sauce poured over the top.

Oxtail with Grapes

This is one of my favorite Elizabeth David recipes. It is one she found cooked by the wine growers in France when the grapes are ripe during the vendage. I particularly love to cook it in October, when the rich, sweet, juicy muscat grapes are in season, as they give the sauce great body.

A meaty oxtail will serve three or four people, and can either be bought ready-trimmed or whole, in which case, ask your butcher to cut it into slices. The ideal thickness for these slices is about 2 inches, as you can then simmer them slowly for ages to extract all the flavor, without worrying about the meat becoming tough or dry.

SERVES 6–8

$\frac{1}{4}$ lb salt pork or unsmoked slab bacon, cubed

2 large onions, chopped

4 large carrots, trimmed and diced

2 garlic cloves, minced

2 oxtails, each weighing 3–4 lb, cut into 2-inch pieces

coarse sea salt or kosher salt and freshly ground black pepper

2 bay leaves

sprig of fresh flat-leaf parsley

sprig of fresh thyme

pinch of ground mace

2 lb green grapes

Preheat the oven to 300°F.

Put the pork or bacon, onions, carrots, and garlic in a Dutch oven, which has a tight-fitting lid. Cook gently over a low heat, stirring occasionally, without adding any oil, for about 10 minutes, or until the fat starts to run. Season the oxtails, then add to the pot with the bay leaves, parsley, and thyme, tied together in a bunch, and the mace. Cover and simmer for 20 minutes.

Pick the grapes off their stems, lightly crush them in a bowl, and add them to the pot along with any of their juice. Line the lid of the pot with a sheet of parchment paper and bake for a minimum of $3\frac{1}{2}$ hours, or until the meat is so tender that it is falling off the bones.

Using a slotted spoon, transfer the oxtails and some of the bacon to a warmed serving dish and keep warm. Remove the herbs and discard. Ladle the sauce into a food processor and process until smooth. Then pass it through a strainer to get rid of the grape seeds and skin. Season the sauce and pour over the oxtail.

If you prefer a lighter sauce, leave the oxtail to cool in the gravy overnight, then skim off the fat, process the sauce in the food processor, strain, and then thoroughly reheat the whole dish before serving.

Broiled Calves' Liver Kabobs with Lettuce Sauce

One advantage of buying a piece of the more expensive calves' liver is that it is easier to see exactly how fresh it is. It should be firm and a deep reddish-brown in color, with a slight sheen and an unmottled surface. Ask the butcher to slice the liver, or, when cutting the slices, use a very sharp knife and cut against the grain to make sure it will not shrink during cooking.

SERVES 4

1 $1\frac{1}{2}$-lb piece of calves' liver
small bunch of fresh marjoram, finely chopped
1 garlic clove, finely chopped
juice of $\frac{1}{2}$ lemon
coarse sea salt or kosher salt and freshly ground black pepper
$\frac{1}{2}$ lb thick-sliced bacon
$\frac{1}{4}$ cup olive oil
4 tbsp unsalted butter
small bunch of scallions, trimmed and chopped
1 small head of romaine lettuce, chopped
2 tbsp crème fraîche

Preheat the broiler.

Trim the calves' liver to remove any sinew or connective tissue and, using a sharp knife, cut it across the grain into pieces about 1 inch wide and $\frac{1}{4}$ inch thick. Mix the liver in a bowl with the marjoram, garlic, and lemon juice, then season, and let stand for about 10 minutes, stirring occasionally.

Cut the bacon into pieces the same size as the liver. Thread the liver and bacon alternately onto 8 metal skewers. Pour the oil into a flat dish and roll the skewers in it.

Broil the kabobs about 6 inches from the heat for about 5 minutes, turning them over once and brushing them lightly with the oil during cooking.

Meanwhile, melt the butter in a skillet over a low heat and sweat the scallions in it, covered, for 2–3 minutes. Add the lettuce and stir until coated in the butter, then cover the skillet and simmer for 5–7 minutes, or until the lettuce has softened.

Transfer the kabobs to a warm serving dish and keep warm. Pour the cooking juices from the bottom of the broiler pan into the lettuce. Put the lettuce mixture into a food processor and process until smooth. With the machine still running, pour in the crème fraîche. Season to taste and serve with the kabobs.

Lamb

Strictly speaking, in the States, lamb is meat from a sheep less than a year old. If labeled "spring" lamb, it was processed between the first Monday in March through the first Monday in October. This labeling is less important than it used to be; years ago, lamb production was at its peak in the springtime, and the meat available at other times of the year was generally frozen. Nowadays, lamb is sold fresh year-round. Lamb is a popular meat in England, but less so in the U.S., which is a shame, because when it is properly cooked, it has a soft, subtle flavor, and the meat is juicy and succulent.

Age, feed, and breed all make a difference to the taste of lamb. BABY LAMB are produced year-round and are sent to market at 6–10 weeks of age, before they are weaned. They are an Easter tradition for many, and have pale-colored, soft and buttery meat with a gentle flavor. However, they are difficult to find both in Britain and the States, with much of the baby lamb going to restaurants. But in France and Spain, they are rightly considered a treat.

YEARLING is meat from a sheep between one and two years of age and again, is not widely found in markets. MUTTON is from a sheep over two years of age, and has a dark, dense meat with a strong, almost cloying, flavor which can be so rich that it needs a sharp vinegar- or wine-based sauce to set it off to advantage. While mutton is much enjoyed in Britain, the stronger flavor is not well appreciated in the States.

Most of our British lamb is fed on grass, which gives it a well-rounded flavor. Sometimes, however, you can

Hardy breeds of sheep can survive harsh winter conditions.

buy Shetland lamb which has a diet consisting predominantly of heather, or Romney Marsh lamb which graze on fields occasionally flooded by the sea, giving them a more pronounced taste.

My favorite lamb of all is the *pré-salé*, or the salt-marsh lambs of Normandy and Brittany. These animals graze right down to the sea and eat copious amounts of seaweed, resulting in a gently iodized meat that is quite unlike any other lamb.

Sheep are produced in every state in the U.S., with most of the production in the West. However, most of the sheep raised for lamb meat, instead of for wool, come from the Midwest. There are more than 30 different breeds of sheep raised across the United States, and most of them are of British origin.

All lambs are allowed to graze, and in the States much of their diet consists of grass, brush, clover, and alfalfa. Some are also fed grain, and they often eat hay in the winter when little grazing ground is available.

It is possible to buy organic, or naturally raised lambs; and you can assume, if properly certified, that the animal has been given feed, and/or grazed on land that was not treated with herbicides or pesticides. Also, the animal will have been naturally weaned, and treated medically no more than necessary. Organic lamb is available at farmers' markets, from small producers, or by mail order (see page 250).

Both British and American lamb have become leaner over the years and most cuts should have a thin layer of clean, whitish fat. The color of the meat can range from a pearly pink to a deeper red with a fine-grained texture. Whether or not lamb should be aged for any significant length of time is a subject of much debate. Julia Child, in her useful and explicit *Mastering the Art of French Cooking*, recommends wrapping a leg of lamb in brown paper and refrigerating it for three to four days to age it. Following her instructions, I had a robustly flavored, but meltingly tender piece of meat. But it might perhaps have been a good idea to have asked the butcher first how long he had allowed the meat to mature before it was sold.

Almost every cut of lamb can be roasted: The leg, saddle, rack or rib, loin, and crown roast are the finest cuts, but a shoulder or even the fattier breast are also fine for roasting.

For braises and stews, use the boned shoulder, the neck, or shoulder-blade chops. Noisettes or medallions, cut from the rib or loin, are superb panfried, and chops, from the rib, loin, and sirloin may be broiled, barbecued, or panfried.

To roast lamb

If you prefer lamb cooked right through, allow 25 minutes per pound in a 350°F oven, plus an extra 20 minutes. If you prefer lamb very pink, or rare, allow 15 minutes per pound. Rare meat will register 130–135°F on a meat thermometer; medium-rare 140°F; medium 160°F. Let the meat rest 15 minutes before carving. Depending on the size of the roast, the temperature will rise 5–10 degrees.

A good way of cooking a large leg is to put it in a 425°F oven for 10 minutes to sear it, then reduce the temperature to 350°F and allow 12 minutes per pound; it will be crisp outside, juicy and pink inside.

Lamb Shanks with Flageolets and Garlic

A lamb shank, the lower section of the foreleg, is excellent for slow braising as this method of cooking tenderizes the meat beautifully. Depending on the size of the lamb, a shank can weigh anything from 12 oz to 2 lb, or even more.

A shank has a lot of bone and fat, so a small one is perfect for one hungry person, while a large shank will feed two generously. I like to buy smaller shanks, one per serving, as they look so good on the plate. You could also try this recipe with a lean, boned and rolled lamb shoulder roast instead, but allow about 15 minutes per pound cooking time.

SERVES 4

4 small lamb shanks, each weighing about 12 oz, trimmed of excess fat
4 garlic cloves, thinly sliced
salt and freshly ground black pepper
2 tbsp olive oil
1 onion, finely chopped
$\frac{3}{4}$ lb (2 cups) dried flageolet or baby lima beans, soaked for 6—8 hours and drained
14- to 16-oz can Italian tomatoes
$\frac{1}{4}$ tsp granulated sugar
1 tbsp tomato paste
$\frac{2}{3}$ cup dry red wine
bunch of fresh flat-leaf parsley, chopped
Béarnaise Sauce (see page 128)

Using the point of a sharp knife, cut 3 or 4 thin slits in each shank and push a slice of garlic into each slit. Season the shanks to taste.

In a Dutch oven with a tight-fitting lid, heat the oil over a medium heat and brown the shanks on all sides. Remove them from the pot.

Add the onion and remaining garlic to the pot and sauté about 5 minutes, until soft. Add the beans and stir until they are coated with oil. Add the canned tomatoes with their juice, breaking them up with a wooden spoon. Stir in the sugar, tomato paste, and red wine. Bring the liquid to a boil. Return the shanks to the pot, cover, lower the heat, and simmer I—I$\frac{1}{2}$ hours, or until the meat and beans are tender. Stir in the parsley at the last moment, and serve with the Béarnaise Sauce.

Grazing on rich grass gives lamb a well-rounded flavor left. LAMB SHANKS WITH FLAGEOLETS AND GARLIC *right.*

Lambs' Kidneys with Mustard Sauce

Lambs' kidneys have a good rounded flavor, neither too strong nor too insipid, and fresh ones are a rich brown color, faintly tinged with red, quite soft to the touch and with a mild smell.

For the freshest possible kidneys, buy them still in the suet, their protective coat of fat, rather than loose. A simple, if rather rich, way of cooking these is to split them in half, open them up, and roast them still encased in their suet in an oven preheated to 375°F for about 25 minutes.

To prepare the kidneys for other methods of cooking, all you need do is cut through the suet, peel it off, peel off the membrane from the kidneys, cut them in half, and trim away their central core.

SERVES 4

1 stick butter, at room temperature
8 lambs' kidneys, each weighing about 3 oz,
halved and trimmed (see above)
2 shallots, finely chopped
⅔ cup dry white wine
2 tbsp grainy mustard
1 tsp fresh lemon juice
3 tbsp finely chopped fresh flat-leaf parsley
salt and freshly ground black pepper

Preheat the oven to 325°F.

In a heavy-bottomed ovenproof skillet, melt 4 tablespoons of the butter over a medium heat, then sauté the kidneys gently for about 2 minutes on each side.

Put the skillet in the preheated oven and roast the kidneys for 5 minutes, then remove the skillet from the oven. Using a slotted spoon, transfer the kidneys to a warm serving dish and keep warm.

LAMBS' KIDNEYS WITH MUSTARD SAUCE

Sauté the shallots in the skillet over a medium heat for 3–5 minutes, or until just soft. Pour in the wine, scraping the bottom of the pan to loosen any browned bits. Turn up the heat and boil rapidly to reduce the liquid by about two-thirds.

Meanwhile, combine the mustard, the remaining butter, and the lemon juice in a bowl. Remove the skillet from the heat and beat in this mixture, a little at a time, to make a creamy sauce. Stir in the parsley, season to taste, and pour the sauce over the kidneys.

Navarin of Lamb

One of the joys of spring is a navarin, *the sophisticated French version of English hotchpotch. It must be made with spring lamb, using any lean and trimmed cut from the shoulder or loin — although I find small lamb steaks or loin chops look very attractive, which is what I use here. The spring vegetables should also be small, tender, and sweet, assuring a succulent lamb stew which will remind you that all the good things of summer are just around the corner.*

SERVES 4–6

2 tbsp olive oil
2½ lb lamb loin chops
1 onion, sliced
pinch of granulated sugar
6 tbsp all-purpose flour
2½ cups Vegetable Stock (see page 12)
coarse sea salt or kosher salt and freshly ground black pepper
1 cup chopped canned tomatoes
2 garlic cloves, chopped
1 bay leaf
sprig of fresh rosemary
½ lb small new potatoes
½ lb pearl onions
½ lb baby turnips

½ lb baby carrots
½ lb (1½ cups) shelled fresh green peas
½ lb (1½ cups) shelled fresh young fava or lima beans
small bunch of fresh flat-leaf parsley, chopped

In a large Dutch oven with a tight-fitting lid, heat the olive oil over a medium heat. Brown the chops in it for 3–4 minutes on each side to seal them. Remove the chops from the pot.

Add the onion to the pot and sauté it for 6–8 minutes, or until soft. Stir in the sugar and flour and cook for 1–2 minutes longer, just to brown the flour slightly.

Pour in the stock and stir until smooth. Return the meat to the pot, season, and add the tomatoes, garlic, bay leaf, and rosemary. Cover with the lid lined with parchment paper, turn down the heat, and simmer for about 20 minutes. Add the potatoes, pearl onions, and turnips. Cover, and simmer for 20 minutes longer. Add the carrots and cook for 10 minutes longer. Add the peas and fava or lima beans and cook for 5–7 minutes, or until the vegetables are tender.

If the sauce looks a little thin, turn up the heat to medium and remove the pan lid for the last few minutes. Adjust the seasoning and serve sprinkled with the chopped parsley.

Pork

The pig is the most efficient of our domesticated animals, as not one jot of it goes to waste – even its bristles are used for brushes. Traditionally, pigs were reared on farms where cheese was made, as they were fed on whey, a by-product of cheesemaking, resulting in a meat with a creamy, pearly finish.

Most of the pork we eat nowadays in Britain comes from the modern Landrace, Large White, or Duroc pure breeds or crossbreeds. When they are brought to market, at four to five months, their flesh is a pale pink, firm and smooth, and their thin layer of fat is a creamy white. Pork in the States is bred today to be much leaner, 50% leaner than the pork of the 1950s and 60s. The breeds most commonly found, either pure bred or crossbred are, the Berkshire, Duroc, Hampshire, Poland China, Spot, Landrace, Yorkshire, and Chester White. They are brought to market at between $4\frac{1}{2}$–$6\frac{1}{2}$ months, with the average pig weighing 240 lb.

Pork today also tends to have a milder flavor. This is to a great extent due to the lower fat content. As with beef, fat carries flavor and makes pork juicy and tender. Nevertheless, the leaner pork is probably healthier to eat, although it needs more careful cooking.

Certified organically raised pork has a richer, finer, stronger flavor and firmer texture than the meat that is found in supermarkets. Organic pigs are fed first on their mother's milk, then on organically grown feed (usually corn), and given no medications unless they become ill. Free-range animals (and it does not follow that all organically raised pigs are free-range), are raised according to the above conditions; plus, they are not confined in pens, they are naturally weaned, and they are allowed to dig about in the soil, gaining nutrients from the roots of plants. Pigs raised in an organic and/ or free-range manner take longer to fatten because they grow more naturally and are not placed in feedlots before being sent to market. You may be able to find organic pork at a good butcher shop, a large health-food store, or by mail order (see page 250).

When shopping, look for meat which is finely grained, pale in color without any blemishes, and neither too dry nor too wet. Pork is perishable, so refrigerate and keep it for no more than three days.

The cut you choose will depend on how you want to cook the meat. For roasting, if you are expecting a crowd, a whole leg, also known as a fresh ham, which usually weighs about 10 lb, should serve your purposes; you can either buy the whole leg bone-in, a boneless rolled fresh ham, or the shank portion of a fresh leg. Pork leg cutlets, cut from the top of the leg, are excellent panfried, grilled, broiled, or braised. The loin also roasts well, either on or off the bone, but always ask the butcher to saw the chine bone, or crack the bones of a bone-in roast for easier carving. Pork tenderloin, a long, thin piece of meat taken from the inside of the loin, is the most tender cut of pork, and is fine roasted, grilled, broiled, or sliced into medallions and sautéed.

The leanest and most tender chops are from the rib or loin. There is a trend today in the States to cut chops very thin, about $\frac{1}{2}$-inch or so; and these are tender and very quick cooking, delicious panfried and served with sautéed apples. You can also buy much thicker chops, which are suitable for stuffing and roasting, or they may be marinated and barbecued or broiled. Blade pork chops, from the shoulder or the shoulder-end of the loin, although they have a thicker covering of fat, are a good buy, and delicious gently sautéed or broiled and seasoned with rosemary. A pork butt (also called a blade roast or Boston roast), may come bone-in or boned and tied, and is an excellent cut for braising or roasting. Spareribs and side pork come from the belly. Ribs may also come from the bones of the loin called back ribs. Meatier country-style ribs come from the blade end of the loin. All ribs are excellent barbecued and served with a spicy sauce.

However you cook pork, do not use too fierce a heat as this makes the meat tough and fibrous. Pork today may be cooked to medium, so that it is slightly pink and retains its juices. But rare pork is rather unpleasant.

To roast pork

Roast pork in a 350°F oven, allowing 30 minutes per pound, until a meat thermometer inserted in the thickest part reads 150–155°F. Let the meat stand 10–15 minutes before carving. The temperature will rise 5–10 degrees, depending on the thickness, to the desired temperature which for medium is 160°F.

Braised Pork with Wild Mushrooms and Juniper Berries

Although some butchers sell pork stew meat for slow braises or stews, I prefer to buy a whole piece and then cut it up myself. Use one of the cheaper cuts from the forequarter, such as a fresh boneless pork shoulder or boneless butt roast.

Surprisingly, you can often pick up a package of dried wild mushrooms reasonably cheaply from a specialty store. Porcini *(see page 178) are a good buy as they hold together well in a stew and infuse the gravy with their rich flavor.*

SERVES 4

1 oz dried wild mushrooms, such as porcini or cèpes
⅓ cup olive oil
1 small onion, chopped
1½ lb boneless pork (see above), cut into 1-inch cubes
½ cup dry white wine
2 tbsp white wine vinegar
3 anchovy fillets, drained and chopped
1 tsp finely chopped fresh marjoram
1 bay leaf
20 juniper berries, crushed
salt and freshly ground black pepper

Soak the mushrooms for 30 minutes in 1½ cups of lukewarm water. Using a slotted spoon, lift them out of the water and reserve it. As they can sometimes be full of grit, rinse them thoroughly under cold running water, drain, remove any tough stems and discard, and roughly chop the mushrooms. Let the soaking water settle, so any grit sinks to the bottom, then strain it through a paper-towel-lined strainer and reserve.

In a Dutch oven with a tight-fitting lid, heat the olive oil over a medium heat and soften the onion in it, 2–3 minutes. Add the pork, turn up the heat slightly, and brown the meat on all sides. Pour in the wine and vinegar, and raise the heat again slightly. Cook for 1–2 minutes, stirring constantly. Stir in the mushrooms, the water in which they have been soaked, the anchovies, marjoram, bay leaf, and crushed juniper berries. Season with plenty of black pepper, but go easy with the salt.

Turn the heat down to low, cover the pot with the lid lined with a sheet of parchment paper, and simmer for 1½–2 hours, or until tender. Occasionally check the meat, and if it becomes too dry, add a little more water. Remove the bay leaf before serving.

Roast Loin of Pork Studded with Ham

This Spanish recipe uses ham from Serrano in the Sierra Nevada mountains, a mild, dry-cured, and air-dried ham. You can also use the similarly flavored Italian prosciutto instead.

Choose a lean loin, either middle or long loin from the rear, and ask the butcher to bone, skin, and trim the fat. Keep the bones, as they make a useful rack for setting the meat on during cooking.

SERVES 6

1 2¼-lb boned and skinned loin of pork, with
bones reserved
2 oz raw cured Serrano or prosciutto ham, cut into thin strips
salt and freshly ground black pepper
24 pearl onions
1 cup dry sherry wine
3 tbsp Chicken Stock (see pages 106–7)
⅔ cup heavy cream

A Gloucester Old Spot pig in a traditional pen below. *ROAST LOIN OF PORK STUDDED WITH HAM* right.

Preheat the oven to 375°F.

Lay the loin of pork out flat, fat side downward. Using a larding needle, lard the meat with the strips of ham until it is studded with them. Rub in a little ground pepper, then roll up the meat so the fat faces outward and tie it securely every 2 inches with string.

Arrange the bones in the bottom of a roasting pan so they form a rack, place the pork on top, scatter the onions around it, and season. Pour ⅔ cup of the sherry wine and all the stock over the pork. Roast, basting occasionally, for about 1 hour, then raise the oven temperature to 400°F and roast for 15 minutes longer to allow the onions to caramelize.

Using a slotted spoon, transfer the meat and onions to a warm platter and let it rest. Discard the bones and most of the fat from the pan, reserving about 1 tablespoon along with the pan juices. Heat the pan over a medium heat, and scrape up the browned bits from the bottom with a wooden spoon.

Pour in the remaining sherry wine, turn up the heat, and stir to deglaze the pan. Add the cream, simmer for a few minutes, then strain the sauce and season to taste. Carve the meat in thin slices and serve surrounded by the onions, with the sauce handed separately.

Sausages

Unlike the rest of Europe, with its cured sausages like salami, *chorizo*, and *rohwurst*, the British sausage is made with fresh meat, primarily pork but sometimes beef or lamb, or a mixture of all three.

Some good butchers do make their own sausages which are free of preservatives and are lower in fat, with a good high meat content, and these are well worth seeking out. In the States, I have enjoyed fresh, handmade Italian sausages from small, family-run butcher shops. These can be mildly spiced and redolent of fennel seed and garlic, referred to as sweet sausage, or fiery hot with red pepper flakes, and are especially good when panfried or broiled.

If you neither like nor trust store-bought sausages, don't have access to a butcher who makes his or her own, or you prefer to eat sausages without too much fat, the alternative is to make your own. This really is remarkably easy, provided you do not bother with the fiddly and hard part of stuffing them into skins or searching out caul fat in which to wrap them. How, you are probably wondering, do they hold together? Very simply, the meat is chopped in a food processor, kneaded lightly with your hands and rolled into sausage shapes which are wrapped in aluminum foil and lightly poached before being grilled, broiled, or fried.

Homemade Sausages

Sausages are traditionally made from the cheaper, fattier cuts, and I use either shoulder or fresh pork side or belly. The proportions I work to are 4 to 1: so for every 4 oz of lean meat, I add 1 oz of fatback. This gives a good juicy mixture and allows for some of the fat to boil away while the sausages are simmering. (This is inevitable, as no matter how tightly you wrap the sausages, some of the water will seep in.) If you think the mixture is still too fatty, just cut down on the amount of added fat.

MAKES 6 SAUSAGES

1 lb lean boneless shoulder, fresh pork side or belly of pork (see above)
$\frac{1}{4}$ lb fatback
1 garlic clove
bunch of fresh flat-leaf parsley
large pinch of coarse sea salt or kosher salt
small pinch of ground cloves
small pinch of ground ginger
small pinch of grated nutmeg
$\frac{1}{3}$ cup soft bread crumbs
freshly ground black pepper

Roughly cut the pork and fat into pieces of a size that the food processor can handle. Working in batches, put them in the food processor with the garlic, parsley, salt, cloves, ginger, nutmeg, bread crumbs, and a generous amount of black pepper. Process, until all the ingredients are mixed together and reduced to the texture of fairly coarse bread crumbs. You do not want to over-process the meat as this will make the sausages far too dense; on the other hand, if you do not process them enough, they will not hold together.

Place the meat in a bowl and divide it into 6 portions, each weighing 3–4 oz. Using your fingers, knead each portion lightly to make sure it sticks together, then roll it between your palms into a sausage shape about 4 inches long. Wrap each sausage in a piece of aluminum foil and secure each end by twisting the foil tightly and tying it with string.

Have ready a large, deep saucepan filled with gently simmering water. Drop in the sausages and simmer them for about 10 minutes.

Using a slotted spoon, lift out and put them in a colander. As soon as they are cool enough to handle, unwrap 1 to make sure it is cooked through. Unwrap the remaining sausages and drain well.

Finish by browning the sausages, either by brushing them lightly with olive oil and broiling or grilling them,

or by frying them in a little olive oil or butter in a skillet over a moderate heat. Serve with Onion Marmalade (see page 23).

Variations
1 Add a shallot and I teaspoon of tomato paste to the mixture in the food processor.
2 Replace the cloves and ginger with I teaspoon of fennel seeds.

SKINLESS HOMEMADE SAUSAGES, WITH COARSE-GRAIN MUSTARD (SEE PAGE 159) AND ONION MARMALADE (SEE PAGE 23).

3 Replace the parsley, nutmeg, and cloves with $\frac{1}{4}$ cup of shelled pistachio nuts.

Ham

Ham is the cured hind leg of the pig. A good ham is one of the great delicacies: subtle and glorious, well balanced with a yielding texture but a biting edge. Producing a quality ham demands great skill as there are many stages and factors involved, all of which affect the ham's final taste and texture.

First, you must start with a well-reared, firm-textured pig with well-developed hind legs. Two styles of curing are used: dry-salting (or dry-curing) and brining. The former is the old-fashioned way of rubbing salt mixed with nitrates, nitrites, and dry seasonings into a ham and curing it for weeks, sometimes even months. Brining (or pickling) is a more modern method in which the ham is immersed in (or more often injected with) a wet cure, usually a solution of salt, nitrates, nitrites, and often, sugar or honey. This results in a milder-flavored, less-assertive ham. To confuse the issue, however, some hams are even cured using a mixture of both techniques: dry-cured for a few days and then wet-cured, or pickled, for a longer period. The hams most widely sold in the States are brined and then fully cooked, sometimes called "city" hams, and they may be eaten cold, or reheated.

There are several traditional cured hams in Britain and the better-known ones include: Bradenham ham and Suffolk ham, both cured in molasses; dry-salted York ham; Wiltshire ham, which is cured in sweet pickle; Devonshire ham, which is cured in treacle, often with added vinegar; and Cumbrian ham, which is briefly dry-salted and then cured in an ale-flavored pickle mixture.

Hams may also be smoked, and this greatly affects both their taste and texture. Sometimes smoking does no more than set and deepen the cure; it may, however, add a completely new dimension of taste, a mustiness of mellow flavor tinged with a rich, woody haze.

Finally, the maturation or aging process for hams can last anything from days to years. Maturing hams is like ripening cheese; an expert can tell by touch and smell when they are ready. Italian prosciutto hams or Spanish Serrano hams are left unsmoked and then air-dried. Most British hams are cured, smoked, and then aged. They usually require cooking before eating.

Excellent hams called "country" hams are found in the southeastern United States, and they are dry-cured, usually smoked, and then aged. The most famous of these is the Smithfield ham, a lean, rich, salty ham, coated with black pepper, which must be cured and processed in the area of Smithfield, Virginia. Country hams may sometimes be eaten raw like prosciutto, but more usually they are cooked.

When choosing a whole uncooked ham, look for a well-rounded shape with plenty of meat and an even, but not too thick, layer of fat. The color of the meat will depend on the cure, and can vary from a dusky rose-pink to a deep burnt brown. Country hams are sold in cloth bags and sometimes have a coating of mold and pepper that must be removed with a stiff brush before soaking and cooking. Don't be alarmed by this mold, which grows naturally during maturation and does not mean the ham is spoiled. If buying sliced ham, have it freshly cut from a whole ham, preferably from one on the bone, as you will probably get a better deal in terms of taste, even if it is more costly.

Air-drying Parma hams left. Slices of British and Continental cured hams right.

CHAPTER FIVE

To boil an uncooked ham

Depending on its cure, you may first need to soak the ham overnight in several changes of water to remove the saltiness. Check with your supplier. This is always the case with country hams. Then, to cook it, simply place the ham in a large pot and cover it with enough water so it is well and truly submerged. Add an onion studded with a couple of cloves, a couple of cut-up carrots, a handful of parsley stems, a bay leaf, and a few peppercorns and slowly bring it to a boil. Once the water has started bubbling, let it simmer gently for about 1 hour, then turn off the heat and leave it in the pot until the liquid is quite cold. Because it continues cooking in its own liquid while it cools, no matter the size of the ham, provided it is well covered with water, it will be cooked through while remaining moist and succulent. All you then need to do is skin it with a sharp knife, trim the fat to an even layer, and then glaze and finish it as described in Ham in a Huff (see overleaf).

Jambon Persillé

For this recipe, use the shank portion of ham. If you buy it on the bone, allow extra for the weight of the bone and make sure you skin it before cooking.

As jambon persillé should have quite a meaty — but not too overpowering—flavor, it is a good idea to start off by boiling the ham, throwing away the water, and starting again. This way you are certain of getting rid of any excess saltiness.

If you do not have a terrine, you can always make this in a large mixing bowl. The only disadvantage to this is that you will not be able to cut it into neat rectangular slices for serving. I daresay, if it tastes as good as it should, no one will mind.

JAMBON PERSILLÉ

SERVES 8

1 1½-lb ham shank (see above)
11 whole black peppercorns
2 bay leaves
1 calf's foot (optional)
1 small veal shank (or 2 if not using calf's foot)
few sprigs of fresh chervil
few sprigs of fresh tarragon
few sprigs of fresh thyme
few sprigs of fresh flat-leaf parsley
2 cups dry white wine
2 tsp white wine vinegar
large bunch of fresh curly parsley, finely chopped

Put the ham in a deep saucepan, add just enough water to cover, and bring to a boil over a medium heat. Just as the water starts to bubble, remove the pan from the heat, pour off the water, rinse the pan, and start again. This time, add 3 peppercorns and 1 of the bay leaves and simmer the ham gently for 25 minutes.

Lift the ham out of the water and, when it is cool enough to handle, trim away the fat and cut the meat into sizable chunks.

Meanwhile, in a clean saucepan, combine the calf's foot, veal shank, the herb sprigs tied together in a bunch, the remaining bay leaf and peppercorns, and about 5 cups water. Bring to a boil over a low heat, skimming off the fat as it rises. Lower the heat, cover and simmer gently for about 1½ hours. Pour in the wine and add the cubes of ham, then simmer for 30 minutes longer, or until the meat is very tender.

Using a slotted spoon, transfer the ham to a terrine or large bowl and flake it with a fork. Strain the liquid into a bowl through a strainer lined with cheesecloth. Add the vinegar and let it stand until slightly set. Then stir in the chopped parsley and pour it over the ham. Refrigerate overnight to set. To serve, unmold onto a serving dish and cut into slices.

Ham in a Huff

The most satisfactory way of baking a ham is first to wrap it up in a huff, a flour and water paste, as this seals in all the juices and stops the ham from drying out.

SERVES 20

9 cups all-purpose flour
12- to 14-lb uncooked ham
about 30 whole cloves

for the glaze:
1 tbsp honey
grated zest and juice of 2 lemons
$\frac{1}{3}$ cup fine-cut orange marmalade
1 tbsp Scotch whisky
1 tsp Dijon-style mustard

Preheat the oven to 350°F.

Mix the flour in a bowl with 3–3$\frac{1}{2}$ cups water to make a stiff paste, turn it out on a flat surface, and roll it out into a rectangle large enough to enclose the ham. Wrap it around the ham, pinching the edges together tightly and sealing them with a little water.

Bake the ham on a rack in a roasting pan, allowing about 25 minutes per pound. Remove the ham from the oven and let it cool for about 15 minutes, otherwise you may be scalded by the steam when you break the huff. Break the huff with a sharp knife, lift out the ham, and let cool for 15 minutes longer.

Peel off any skin (it will usually just pull away easily while it is still warm). Trim the fat to a layer $\frac{1}{2}$ inch thick. Using a sharp knife, score the fat across into a diamond lattice pattern and stud the center of each diamond with a clove.

Turn up the oven to 375°F.

To make the glaze: Heat the honey with the lemon zest in a saucepan over a medium heat. Stir in the lemon juice, marmalade, and whisky, then beat in the mustard and cook for 2–3 minutes, until the glaze just starts to bubble.

Remove the saucepan from the heat and, using a pastry brush, paint the ham all over with the glaze. Roast for 30 minutes to set the glaze. If there is any glaze left over, brush occasionally while roasting.

If you are serving the ham hot, let it rest for about 15 minutes before carving; otherwise let stand on a wire rack to cool.

Bacon

Bacon is commonly the boneless side or underside of the pig's belly which has been cured and possibly smoked. It can also be from the pig's back. Finding an excellent quality bacon with a good ratio of fat to lean is not easy. Like a ham, it can either be dry-cured or brined; but regrettably, bacon is most commonly injected with the curing solution rather than being immersed in brine, to speed the curing process. Although this may result in an exceptionally light cure which some people prefer, it does cause the bacon to absorb more water ("bulk up" is the technical term). You may, therefore, actually be getting less for your money. When you cook this sort of bacon it tends to splutter and shrink in the skillet.

Depending on your taste and on the requirements of the recipe, you can choose between a mild or sweet cure or a smokier flavor. Bacon available in the States is most often sliced, about $\frac{1}{16}$-inch thick, and apart from being eaten on its own, it is useful for lining pâté pans and adding flavor to soups and stews. You can also buy unsliced slab bacon to cut into lardons. Slab bacon has a thick outer rind which can be sliced off before or after the bacon is cooked. Another choice is country-style bacon, which is cut into thick slices.

Ouillade

For this hearty soup I use a small, fresh pork hock. Based on a French recipe, this country-style soup is finished by crumbling in a chunk of Roquefort. This may not be to your taste, so if you prefer, the cheese can be omitted.

SERVES 8

*1 fresh pork hock, weighing about 2 lb
2½ cups dried navy beans, soaked overnight in water
2 tbsp olive oil
1 large onion, chopped
1 small head of green cabbage, finely sliced
3 boiling potatoes, sliced
1 turnip, sliced*

to finish:
*3 garlic cloves, finely chopped
2 tbsp finely chopped fresh flat-leaf parsley
1 small onion, finely chopped
freshly ground black pepper
2 oz Roquefort or other blue cheese, crumbled (optional)*

Put the pork hock in a deep saucepan, add 5 cups water or just enough to cover, and bring to a boil over a medium heat. Cover and simmer for about 45 minutes, then remove from the heat and let cool.

Meanwhile, drain the beans and put them in a saucepan. Add 2½ cups water and bring to a boil over medium heat. Reduce the heat, cover and simmer for about 1 hour, or until the beans are tender. Drain, reserving ⅓ cup of their cooking liquid.

In another saucepan, heat the oil over a medium heat and cook the onion and cabbage until soft. Lift the hock out of its liquid and set aside. Strain the liquid into the pan with the cabbage. Add the potatoes and turnip and simmer for about 15 minutes, or until the vegetables are tender.

Meanwhile, skin the hock, trim off the fat, and chop the meat into bite-sized chunks. Add these to the soup once the vegetables are cooked, along with the beans and their reserved liquid. Simmer for 5 minutes to reheat the beans and meat.

To finish: Mix the garlic, parsley, and onion together in a bowl, then add this to the soup off the heat. Add plenty of black pepper and, if you think you will like it, stir in the cheese, a little at a time, and then taste, just to be on the safe side. Serve immediately.

Fields of mustard plants turn golden in June.

Mustards

COARSE-GRAIN MUSTARD has been made for cen-turies in Britain by milling or lightly crushing a mixture of white and black mustard seeds and mixing them with vinegar, water, wine, or cider, and any number of spices and flavorings. Its strength depends on the quantity of white seeds, how finely they are ground (the finer you grind the seeds the stronger the bite), the quality of the vinegar, and the blend of spices.

ENGLISH MUSTARD is made by a technique supposed to have been invented in 1720, by a Mrs. Clements of Durham, England. She pounded a mixture of white and black seeds very firmly and then sifted the powder to remove the husks. Her mustard flour became all the rage, because of its smooth texture and fierce flavor. Today, English mustard, is still made along similar lines.

French mustard is also divided into two similar types. The grainy *L'ANCIENNE* types of mustard, of which *Moutarde de Meaux* is probably the best known, differ from English coarse-grain mustard in that they are made from a mixture of brown and black mustard seeds and the seeds are soaked first either in verjuice or wine vinegar before being gently crushed. This mixture gives the mustard a more tranquil nose, and the pre-soaking ensures a far creamier texture. DIJON MUS-TARD, is a velvety textured, creamy condiment with a subtle aroma and deep beige-brown color. It is made from a blend of presoaked brown and black seeds, which are wet-ground, then spun in a drum to separate out the husks which are then discarded.

American-style BALL PARK mustard is prepared from white mustard seeds, vinegar, sugar, and turmeric, which provides the distinctive bright-yellow hue. It is quite mild in flavor, and very popular, but not an acceptable choice for recipes. DELI-STYLE mustard, is usually made from a mixture of black and white seeds, vinegar, and spices, and it has more bite than ball park mustards.

Whatever mustard you choose will obviously depend on your particular palate and the food with which it is being served.

Making homemade mustards is really very simple. Mustard seed can be bought from health-food stores or Oriental and Indian specialty shops. (Never buy seeds sold for sowing, as they have usually been treated with chemicals.) When first made, a mustard tastes rather harsh and needs to be stored in a clean, sealed jar in the refrigerator for at least two weeks for flavors to mellow.

As well as being condiments, mustards may be used to flavor butters (see page 55), in glazing hams (see page 156), or simply spread over a piece of lamb or beef, prior to roasting, to give it a pungent crust.

Coarse-grain Mustard

1 oz white mustard seeds
2 oz black mustard seeds
lukewarm water
1 shallot, finely chopped
½ cup white wine vinegar
1 tbsp coarse sea salt or kosher salt

In a glass bowl, cover the mustard seeds with lukewarm water and let them soak overnight at room temperature.

Drain the seeds and crush them lightly in a mortar, then stir in the shallot, wine vinegar, about 4 tablespoons of water, and the salt. Mix the ingredients thoroughly and then pack the mixture into an airtight, sterilized jar. Let stand for 14 days at cool room temperature or in the refrigerator before use.

Tarragon Mustard

3 oz black mustard seeds
1 oz yellow mustard seeds
small bunch of fresh tarragon, chopped
½ cup dry white wine
1 tbsp white wine vinegar
1 tbsp coarse sea salt or kosher salt

Grind the mustard seeds in a coffee grinder, but remember that the finer you grind them, the fiercer the mustard will be.

Transfer the ground seeds into a bowl, stir in 3 tablespoons of water, and let the mixture stand for about 10 minutes.

Stir in the tarragon, white wine, vinegar, and salt. Cover the bowl, and let stand overnight at room temperature. The following morning, pack the mixture into an airtight, sterilized jar. Leave for at least 14 days at cool room temperature or in the refrigerator.

Variations
1 For a garlic mustard, replace the tarragon with 1 chopped garlic clove.
2 Replace the white wine with 3 tablespoons of cider vinegar and 3 tablespoons of honey.

The Woods and Fields

The woods and fields have long been a source of free
bounty for country dwellers. Prized game may
have been restricted to a privileged few, but rabbit,
hare, and pigeon, densely flavored wild
mushrooms, delicious nuts, and delicate wild plants
have always been free for all.

A hen pheasant in the snow.

Game

All wild animals hunted for sport or food are described as game. It is classified into two types: furred, like venison, rabbit, and hare; and feathered, like grouse, pheasant, and wild duck.

In the United States, there are regulations which prohibit selling animals and birds which have been shot in the wild, but interestingly, you can sometimes buy truly wild game which has been imported from other countries, such as Scotland. Therefore, unless you hunt, or have friends who hunt, nearly all of the game available in the States, either from the butcher, or by mail order (for sources, see page 250), has been farm-raised. Depending on how it was raised, what and/or how it was fed, and how much exercizing it did, it may be milder in flavor, and have a higher fat content, and thus be more tender than wild game.

Most game in Britain and the United States is protected by law and can only be shot or culled between certain dates, the rest of the year being a closed season. In my country, shooting starts on what is known as "The Glorious 12th" (August), when those privileged to own – or to have access to – a moor can shoot grouse or common snipe.

Often described as the finest of all game birds, the red or Scottish GROUSE lives on the moors of Scotland and the north of England. It feeds on heather and wild berries, which no doubt accounts for its subtle flavor. The ruffled, sage, and blue grouse are found in varying numbers in the wild in the U.S. But the only grouse usually available for sale in the States is imported Scottish grouse, generally sold by mail order.

Like all game birds, grouse should be aged, or hung; exactly how long is purely a question of taste. So, when buying, always ask how long it has been aged. However, not all game is handled in the same manner, and aging is a time-consuming and expensive process, which is rarely done in the States. Even imported game may not have been aged.

Britain is particularly rich in game birds; as well as pheasant and partridge, there are wild duck, snipe, and woodcock. Until quite recently in our cities, game was the preserve of the rich few. Nowadays, however, game has become increasingly popular in Britain, and to a lesser extent in the U.S.

With their relatively lowfat content, both furred and feathered game make healthy alternatives to other meats and poultry.

Pheasant

The pheasant is the most common of the game birds, both in Britain and in the United States. The ring-necked pheasant is the one found most often in the field, and most often farm-raised. Although the male bird is more attractive, with his showy colors and flowing tail feathers, it is the dumpy, dull-brown hen bird that makes better eating, with its tender, fine-textured, delicately flavored flesh.

This is also true of farm-raised pheasants; the females have plumper, leaner breasts. A pheasant will weigh between 2 and 3 lb, and will generally serve two, depending on how you divide breast and leg meat.

Ideally, pheasants should be allowed to age to tenderize the flesh and allow a good flavor to develop. How long they are aged depends on how "high" you like the meat, and the weather or aging temperature; anything from three to ten days is acceptable. But this "high" flavor is not as appreciated in the States as it is in Britain or France, so unless you age the bird yourself, or buy an imported pheasant, it will almost definitely not have been aged. Be sure to ask your supplier before buying the bird.

Pheasant, when farm-raised, has a mild-flavored meat, which is not unlike very full-flavored chicken. Pheasants found in the wild have darker-colored meat with a more pronounced gamy flavor.

For roasting, the smaller birds are the best choice. An average-sized pheasant needs about 45 minutes to 1 hour at 375°F. Remember that like all game birds, however, they have a tendency to dryness; so either roast them breast down, or cover the breast with some thin slices of salt pork or bacon. It is also a good idea to pop a knob of butter into the cavities, and to baste them regularly during roasting. Larger birds are older and tougher, so they need slower cooking and are best braised.

Pheasant with Celery

Cooking with a liquid in a heavy, covered Dutch oven is the ideal way to deal with frozen pheasants or older, tougher birds. If the liquid becomes quite greasy, let it stand a few minutes until the fat rises to the surface, then skim off the fat with a spoon. If you clarify this fat by reheating it gently and straining it through cheesecloth, you can use it instead of oil or butter for cooking.

To make pheasant stock, or indeed a game stock of any kind, simply follow the recipe for Chicken Stock (see pages 106–7), with the carcasses or bones of the game used in place of the chicken.

SERVES 6–8

2 tbsp butter
1 lb thick-sliced bacon, chopped
2 pheasants
salt and freshly ground pepper
2 heads of celery, trimmed and sliced
hot water
small pinch of celery seeds
2½ cups Game or Chicken Stock (see pages 106–7)
1¼ cups port wine

Preheat the oven to 325°F.

In a large Dutch oven which has a tight-fitting lid, melt the butter over medium heat. Add the chopped bacon and sauté until it is golden brown. Using a slotted spoon, remove the bacon from the pot and reserve.

Season the pheasants with salt and pepper to taste and brown them all over in the bacon drippings.

Meanwhile, put the celery in a bowl, cover with hot water, and let stand about 1 minute. Drain the celery and refresh it under cold running water.

PHEASANT WITH CELERY

Add the celery to the Dutch oven, along with the bacon and celery seeds. Pour in the stock and port wine. Cover the pot and cook in the preheated oven about 1 hour, or until the pheasants are tender.

Using a slotted spoon, transfer the pheasants to a suitable carving board. Carve into quarters and keep warm in a 150°F oven.

Strain the contents of the pot into a saucepan, adding any juices from the carved pheasant. Reserve the solids, and let the liquid stand about 5 minutes to allow the fat to separate and rise to the surface, then spoon it off and discard.

Process the bacon and celery in a food processor until smooth, adding a little of the cooking liquid if necessary. Return this purée to the saucepan and stir over low heat to reheat the sauce.

Pour the sauce over the pheasant and serve.

Partridge

With its pale meat, the gray or English partridge is highly prized, but quite rare. It is, however, available by mail order (see page 250).

The chukar is the most common type of partridge domesticated in the U.S., and it is related to the Scottish red-legged partridge. Wild partridges you will find in the States are the Hungarian and the chukar. The best time to eat the wild partridge is in autumn, specifically September, October, and November.

Allow one partridge per person and, like pheasant, the young birds are best roasted. An average-sized bird needs between 20–30 minutes roasting time at 400°F. Serve with roasted potatoes, a gravy made from cooking juices, and watercress.

If the partridges come with their livers, use them in a stuffing, or to enrich the gravy. Alternatively, lightly fry the livers, spread them on a piece of toast and serve the partridge atop the toast.

Salmis of Partridge

A classic salmis *is a rather complicated affair: Game, usually partridge, woodcock, pheasant, or wild duck, is two-thirds roasted and then cooking is finished in a saucepan with truffles. It is finally coated with a* demi-glace *sauce — a rich brown sauce that is simmered and skimmed for hours — made with the carcass.*

This recipe is simplified to bring it within the realms of possibility for every competent cook. As partridges are nowadays often sold without their livers, chicken livers are suggested as an alternative.

SERVES 2

2 young partridges, plus their livers or 3 oz chicken livers, trimmed and chopped
salt and freshly ground black pepper
3 tbsp unsalted butter
3 tbsp olive oil
2 carrots, trimmed and finely chopped
2 onions, finely chopped
2 shallots, finely chopped
1 sprig of fresh thyme
1 bay leaf
$1\frac{1}{2}$ tbsp all-purpose flour
$1\frac{1}{4}$ cups Game or Chicken Stock (see pages 106–7)
$1\frac{1}{4}$ cups dry white wine
2 tbsp brandy or Cognac

Preheat the oven to 400°F.

Wipe the partridges all over. Then pat them dry and season with salt and pepper. Melt 1 tablespoon of the butter and, using a pastry brush, paint the birds all over with it. Put them in a roasting pan and roast, basting occasionally with the butter and pan drippings, until tender, 20–25 minutes.

Meanwhile, melt the remaining butter with the oil in a skillet over medium to low heat. Add the chopped carrots, onions, shallots, thyme, and bay leaf and sauté about 5 minutes.

Cover, lower the heat, and sweat 10 minutes longer, or until the vegetables are soft. Stir in the flour and, stirring constantly, cook 1–2 minutes. Then pour in the stock, stirring to prevent lumps forming, turn up the heat and bring to a boil. Lower the heat and simmer about 5 minutes.

Remove the partridges from the oven and, using a slotted spoon, transfer them to a suitable carving board. Carve and keep warm. Crush the carcasses by pressing on them firmly with a rolling pin or the flat side of a large kitchen knife and set aside. Strain any juices back into the roasting pan.

Put the roasting pan over medium heat, pour in the wine, and stir and scrape the bottom with a wooden spoon to loosen any browned bits. Turn up the heat, and boil to reduce the liquid by about two-thirds.

Add the livers, and cook 3–4 minutes. Add the vegetables in their stock along with the crushed carcasses. Stirring constantly, bring to a boil.

Remove the pan from the heat. Pick out the carcasses and bay leaf and strain the sauce through a fine strainer, pressing down firmly to make sure that the livers are pushed through. Pour the sauce back into the roasting pan, turn the heat down to low, add the brandy or Cognac, and simmer 1–2 minutes.

Return the partridge meat to the roasting pan, season to taste, and simmer briefly to reheat, then serve.

Wood Pigeon

Wood pigeon is the British name for the wild squab. Although these birds are not found in the States, they are imported from Europe and sold by mail order (see page 250). In my country, they may be hunted year round, but the best time to shoot them is from May to October, when they are feeding from crops in the fields. The best way to cook wood pigeon is by stewing or braising. You can also bone out the breasts and roast these in a 425°F oven for 10 minutes, or panfry them in a little oil and butter for a few minutes. If you prefer to roast a whole bird, you should first tenderize it by marinating it overnight in a strong red wine mixed with olive oil, chopped vegetables, and a few minced cloves of garlic. Then roast it in a 400°F oven for 20–30 minutes. Allow one bird for every two people.

In the States, commercially raised squabs (which are in actuality rock doves) are quite easy to find, both at a good butcher shop, or by mail order, and make a good substitute for wood pigeon. As these rich-flavored and tender birds are small, weighing 12 to 16 oz, allow one per person. You may also be able to find them partially deboned, which is handy if you want to broil or grill the birds laid out flat, or if you are stuffing them.

Winter means sparse feeding for woodland birds and animals.

Squab in a Hole

Hannah Glasse, the eighteenth-century English cookery writer, devised this intriguing way of presenting squabs. It looks especially spectacular if the squabs are cooked in individual dishes — I find a small soufflé dish is an excellent fit — although on the other hand, one large dish is easier to cope with. This is not — I had better warn you — a dish for delicate eaters, as the best way of coping with the birds is to pick at them with your fingers.

SERVES 4

3 tbsp dark, seedless raisins
2 cups plus 2 tbsp dry red wine
4 tbsp butter
½ lb thick-sliced bacon, diced
1 carrot, trimmed and chopped
1 leek, trimmed and chopped
1 onion, sliced
2 garlic cloves, chopped
1 sprig of fresh thyme
4 small squabs, plus their livers or 2 oz chicken livers, trimmed
salt and freshly ground black pepper
grated zest of 1 lemon
1⅔ cups plus 2 tsp all-purpose flour
2 extra-large eggs, lightly beaten
2 cups milk
vegetable oil, for greasing

Put the raisins in a bowl with the 2 tablespoons of the red wine and let soak about 30 minutes.

Melt half of the butter in a skillet which has a tight-fitting lid over medium heat. Sauté the bacon, carrot, leek, onion, garlic, and thyme 10–15 minutes, until the vegetables are soft.

Meanwhile, prepare the squabs: Split them by first cutting them along the backbone with a sharp knife and then opening them up by gently pulling them apart. Turn them over, press them firmly on the breast to flatten them, and season them all over. Chop the livers finely, and set aside.

Place the birds on the vegetables in the skillet, add the lemon zest and remaining wine, cover, and simmer gently, or until the birds are tender, about 20 minutes.

Remove the squabs and keep warm. Strain the contents of the skillet through a strainer, and reserve both the bacon and vegetables and the liquid.

Preheat the oven to 425°F and lightly oil either 4 individual soufflé dishes each large enough for 1 squab, or one large, deep-sided ovenproof dish just large enough to hold the squabs in 1 layer.

Make the batter: Combine 1⅔ cups of the flour and a pinch of salt in a bowl. Add the eggs and slowly beat in the milk. Beat in ⅔ cup of the strained liquid from the skillet along with the raisins in their wine. Let rest about 15 minutes.

Toward the end of this time, heat the oiled dish(es) in the oven until they are sizzling hot, 3–5 minutes.

Remove the dish(es) from the oven and pour in the batter. Return to the oven and bake about 15 minutes or until the batter has risen.

Place the squabs on top of the batter and spoon a little of the strained cooking liquid over the squabs. Surround the birds with the reserved bacon and vegetables. Return the dish to the oven and bake 5 minutes longer, until the batter is golden brown.

Meanwhile, make the sauce: Melt the remaining butter in a clean skillet over medium heat and cook the chopped livers for 2–3 minutes.

Using a wooden spoon, stir in the remaining 2 teaspoons flour and scrape the bottom of the pan so the flour is well mixed in. Pour in the remaining strained cooking liquid, scraping the bottom. Turn up the heat, and simmer, stirring constantly, until the sauce is thick and smooth. Season to taste and serve with the squabs.

Rabbit

Every farmer will tell you that the countryside is overrun with rabbits, but it is unusual in my country to see a wild rabbit on sale, and game that has been shot in the wild in the States may not be sold. Wild rabbit has a much stronger taste and darker flesh than those which have been farm raised.

It is probably wise to avoid any wild rabbit, either that you hunted yourself, or one that was presented to you by a friend who hunts, which weighs more than about 3 lb, as it may well be quite old, tough, and powerfully flavored. You can, however, soak it overnight in milk flavored with herbs to soften the flavor somewhat.

Commercially bred rabbit, on the other hand, is much milder and has paler, milky soft flesh, not unlike

chicken. Many butchers, and some of the larger supermarkets, will sell cut-up rabbits, which may be roasted, braised, or brushed with oil and broiled, panfried, or barbecued.

Rabbit with Chili Pepper and Olives

SERVES 4–6

2 tsp sun-dried tomato paste, or 2 tsp finely chopped sun-dried tomatoes

1 tsp Oriental chili paste

1 garlic clove, chopped

2 tbsp finely chopped fresh thyme

1 tbsp finely chopped fresh oregano

$\frac{1}{4}$ cup olive oil, plus extra for brushing

coarse sea salt or kosher salt and freshly ground black pepper

1 rabbit, weighing about $2\frac{1}{2}$ lb, cut up, or 8–12 rabbit thighs

4 whole heads of garlic

4 sprigs of fresh thyme

1 onion, finely chopped

6 large green olives, pitted and sliced

$\frac{2}{3}$ cup dry white wine

$\frac{2}{3}$ cup Chicken Stock (see pages 106–7)

1 tbsp thick plain yogurt (see page 53)

small bunch of fresh flat-leaf parsley, finely chopped

Preheat the oven to 375°F.

In a bowl, mix together the sun-dried tomato paste, chili paste, garlic, 1 tablespoon of the chopped thyme, oregano, 2 tablespoons of the olive oil, and salt and pepper to taste. Using a stiff brush, paint the rabbit pieces with this paste. Let stand about 10 minutes.

Meanwhile, using a pastry brush, paint the heads of

garlic all over with olive oil. Place each head on a sheet of foil and sprinkle with the rest of the chopped thyme, the sprigs of thyme and the salt and pepper. Wrap loosely in foil, sealing the packages, and put them on a baking sheet.

Heat the rest of the olive oil in a Dutch oven over medium heat. Add the onion and sauté about 5 minutes, until soft. Arrange the rabbit pieces on top. Put the pot into the oven along with the prepared garlic packages and roast 30 minutes.

Remove the garlic and Dutch oven. Unwrap the garlic and let cool. When cool enough to handle, peel the cloves and set aside.

RABBIT WITH CHILI PEPPER AND OLIVES

Add the olives, white wine, and chicken stock to the pot. Bring to a boil, reduce the heat, and simmer about 30 minutes, or until the rabbit is tender. Using a slotted spoon, transfer the rabbit pieces to a warm serving platter and keep warm.

Process the roasted garlic cloves with about 1 tablespoon of the cooking liquid from the rabbit in a food processor until smooth. Stir this into the sauce in the Dutch oven, turn up the heat, and simmer the sauce to reduce it by about one-third. Remove the pot from the heat. Stir in the yogurt and parsley and season.

Pour the sauce over the rabbit and serve.

Hare

In Britain, hare has no closed season so it can be hunted year round, but it cannot be sold between the months of March and July to protect the numbers. The best time to eat it is between October and January, before the animals are too thin and worn out from the winter.

Wild hare is difficult to find in the United States, unless you hunt it yourself, and it is known as either jackrabbit or snowshoe rabbit. The blue or Scottish hare is sometimes imported from Europe and available by mail order (see page 250).

Hare has a far-earthier, fuller flavor than rabbit. Ideally, it should be aged for between three to seven days, depending on the size of the animal and the weather conditions. Traditionally, hare is aged with its head down and it is not drawn after being killed, so a bowl is placed underneath it to catch the blood, which may then be used in the classic dish, Jugged Hare.

Hares are either sold whole or cut into pieces. An average saddle will weigh 2–3 lb, and serves two to four people. The best way of cooking it is to roast it at 425°F for 20–35 minutes. For extra flavor, lay it on sliced onions flavored with sprigs of fresh thyme and rosemary.

Hare with Noodles

Based on a traditional old Tuscan recipe from The Gastronomy of Italy *by Anna del Conte, this is an economical way of dealing with a whole hare.*

Only the legs are used in this rich, full-bodied pasta sauce, which means that the saddle can be turned into a pâté (see Game Terrine, page 174) or roasted separately (see page 171).

SERVES 4

2 tbsp olive oil
2 thick slices of unsmoked bacon
1 small onion, finely chopped
1 celery stalk, trimmed and finely chopped
1 garlic clove, finely chopped
1 small sprig of fresh rosemary, finely chopped
the legs of 1 hare
2 tsp all-purpose flour
$\frac{2}{3}$ cup dry red wine
$\frac{2}{3}$ cup Game Stock (see page 106)
pinch of grated nutmeg
coarse sea salt and freshly ground black pepper
2 tbsp thick plain yogurt (see page 53)

Heat the oil in a heavy-bottomed large, deep skillet over medium heat. Add the bacon and sauté 2 minutes. Then add the onion, celery, garlic, and rosemary and cook until the vegetables are soft, stirring frequently.

Add the hare legs to the skillet and sauté them until lightly browned.

Sprinkle in the flour and cook about 1 minute, stirring constantly, until the flour is brown. Turn up the heat, stir in the wine, stirring to prevent lumping, and boil until it has reduced by about half.

Add about half of the stock, the nutmeg, and a pinch of salt and stir together. Turn down the heat to low, partially cover the pan, and simmer about 1 hour. Add

the remaining stock a little at a time to prevent the sauce from getting too thick.

Using a slotted spoon, lift the hare legs from the pan. Bone them, cut the meat into small pieces, and return these to the pan. Remove the pan from the heat and stir in the yogurt, season, and serve with large noodles.

A wild red deer stag.

Venison

Venison is the term for all deer meat, and sometimes, the meat from other large game, such as antelope, elk, caribou, reindeer, and moose. Deer is in season in the wild at different times of the year; and regulations for hunting depend on the area and the type of deer.

Wild venison needs to be aged for at least a few days. As with all game, the cuts from older, tougher animals are best braised or stewed.

Over the past few years, venison farming has become increasingly popular. Farmed venison, depending on how it was raised, is most often milder in flavor, and more tender than that found in the wild. Happily, some of the farm-raised venison may have been aged, which will increase its tenderness. New Zealand exports a great deal of farm-raised venison, which comes from the red deer, and 80 percent of the venison consumed in the States is from that country.

When roasting a tenderloin or saddle, either marinate it, or wrap it with bacon, and always remember to baste it as it cooks.

Venison Saint-Hubert

SERVES 4–6

2 onions
2 carrots, trimmed
1 celery stalk, trimmed and chopped
2 sprigs each of fresh marjoram, thyme, and flat-leaf parsley, tied
together in a bunch
3 juniper berries, crushed
3 whole black peppercorns, crushed
grated zest of 1 orange
2 cups red wine
3 tbsp red wine vinegar
1 boned and rolled haunch of venison, weighing about 2 lb
2 tbsp olive oil
6 oz salt pork, diced
3 tbsp all-purpose flour
1 tbsp tomato paste
1 cup Game or Chicken Stock (see pages 106–7)
3 tbsp brandy
$\frac{1}{4}$ cup red currant jelly
salt and freshly ground black pepper

Chop 1 of the onions and 1 of the carrots, and in a glass or stainless steel bowl suitable for marinating, mix with the celery, herbs, juniper berries, peppercorns, and orange zest. Add the vinegar and red wine and stir together to make a marinade.

Place the venison in the marinade, and let marinate in the refrigerator a minimum of 8 hours, turning the venison occasionally. (For a stronger flavor, you can let the venison marinate as long as 3 days.)

Preheat the oven to 400°F.

Remove the venison from the marinade, put it in a flameproof roasting pan, and roast about 50 minutes, basting it occasionally with the marinade.

Meanwhile, start making the sauce: Chop the remaining onion and carrot and heat the oil in a saucepan over medium heat. Add the salt pork and the chopped onion and carrot, and sauté until brown. Then stir in the flour and tomato paste, and cook 1 minute longer, stirring constantly. Strain the marinade and discard the solids. Stir the marinade liquid and stock into the saucepan, stirring to prevent lumping. Turn the heat down to low and simmer about 30 minutes.

When the venison is cooked, transfer it to a warmed serving dish. Let rest in a warm place about 20 minutes. Place the roasting pan over medium heat and, using a wooden spoon, stir and scrape the juices in the pan. Then pour in the brandy, heat it and flame it to burn off the alcohol. Add the sauce from the pan to the roasting pan, and stir in the red currant jelly. When it has melted, strain the sauce into a sauce or gravy boat. Season the sauce and serve with the venison.

GAME TERRINE

Game Terrine

A game terrine such as this should be made 2 or 3 days in advance, so the flavors have plenty of time to mellow and blend. It needs a mixture of game meat along with pork and pork fat for flavor, moisture, and texture. This recipe can be made with either hare, rabbit, or venison or even, as here, wild boar.

At one time WILD BOAR did run free, doing untold damage to the English countryside. However, unlike Italy, France, and Germany, where it is still hunted in the forests and hills, it has vanished in Britain. So what you buy there as "wild boar" is, in fact, a farmed wild boar/pig cross. It has a more gamy flavor than an ordinary pig, but is milder and fattier than a true wild boar.

In the U.S., it may be hunted in the Southwest. It is also available by mail order (page 250). You can, of course, always use regular pork instead. Buy the cheaper truffle peelings or pieces to use in this terrine, if you like.

SERVES 10–12

1 lb wild boar (peccary)
$\frac{1}{4}$ lb cooked ham, diced
$\frac{1}{4}$ lb pork fatback, diced

$\frac{1}{2}$ tsp ground allspice
pinch of ground cloves
pinch of grated nutmeg
$3\frac{1}{2}$ tbsp brandy
$3\frac{1}{2}$ tbsp dry Madeira wine
salt and freshly ground pepper
1 lb fresh side pork, cut into chunks
1 large egg
$\frac{1}{2}$ oz black truffle, finely chopped (optional)
$\frac{3}{4}$ lb sliced bacon

Cut half of the wild boar into finger-size strips. Mix the strips in a bowl with the ham, fatback, allspice, cloves, and nutmeg. Pour in the brandy and Madeira, season, and stir thoroughly. Cover the bowl and let marinate 1–2 hours, stirring the wild boar occasionally, to let the flavors blend.

Preheat the oven to 350°F.

Cut the remaining boar into chunks. Put the chunks of wild boar along with the pork side meat in a food processor and process until reduced to pieces about 1-inch thick. Strain the liquid from the marinade into this mixture. Break in the egg, add the truffle, if using, salt, and pepper, and process again until reduced to pieces about half the previous size. (Be careful not to over-process or chop too finely as this will result in a heavy and dense pâté.)

Line a 2- to 2$\frac{1}{2}$-pint terrine with the bacon, reserving 2 or 3 slices. Spread one-third of the chopped mixture on the bottom of the terrine and cover with half of the boar strip mixture. Repeat the process, and finish with a final layer of the chopped mixture. Cover the top with the remaining slices of bacon, and lay a sheet of parchment paper on top.

Place the terrine in a roasting pan and half fill it with boiling water. Bake for 1$\frac{1}{4}$–1$\frac{1}{2}$ hours, replenishing the hot water as necessary. To test whether the terrine is ready, insert a skewer into the pâté: If the juices that run out are clear, it is cooked.

Remove from the water bath and let cool slightly. Then place a plate or a piece of wood on top, and weight it down with about 2 lb of cans of food to press the terrine.

Wild boar is still hunted in some European countries.

Refrigerate at least 2 days before serving, to allow the flavors to mellow.

Nuts

Nuts are the fruit of certain trees. Some, such as almonds, cashews, coconuts, and pine nuts, are edible and contain a valuable source of fat and protein; others, like acorns and horse chestnuts, were eaten in former times, but have since been dropped from our culinary repertoire, as frankly they do not taste very good. Peanuts and water chestnuts, however, are not nuts; the former is the seed of a legume, the latter a bulb.

In Britain, at the beginning of the season, or if you are lucky enough to have a tree, you can often find "green" or immature ALMONDS and WALNUTS. These are young with a fleshy casing or "shuck," and a soft underdeveloped kernel. Although too bitter to eat raw, they are ideal for pickling; simply prick the skin all

Walnuts are a specialty of southwest France.

over, soak in a brine for a couple of days, then simmer in wine vinegar infused with spices and leave for several weeks. These are enjoyed in my country as a pickle, and are excellent served with cheddar cheese.

As the season progresses, I often buy "wet" or fresh nuts. Wet walnuts from France are particularly juicy, with a fresh oiliness, and a softer outer shell which can be cracked with your hands.

Although often confused, the horse chestnut and the sweet chestnut trees are not related. It is the SWEET CHESTNUT that we know, love, and eat, either roasted, in a sage-and-onion turkey stuffing, or as *marrons glacés*. In France, Italy, and Switzerland, this most floury and least oily of all nuts is ground into a flour which is then used to make cakes and puddings. Chestnuts may also be found in cans and jars, either whole in syrup or in water, or in a purée, again, sweetened or not.

Most of the nuts you buy in their shells are fully grown and sold dried so they will last for several weeks, provided you keep them in a loosely fastened plastic bag in a cool place. When choosing nuts, look for unbroken shells which have no traces of moisture. Try holding them in the palm of your hand: A good nut will weigh heavy for its size.

Shelled nuts are sold loose, or in packages, jars, or cans, and raw, toasted, or roasted, sometimes salted or flavored, and sometimes further processed by chopping, blanching, slicing, or grinding. If stored too long after being opened, nuts go rancid and bitter, and develop an unpleasant oily taste; so buy them in small quantities. Shelled nuts keep well in the freezer, and there is no need to thaw them before using in a recipe.

Chestnut Soup

Sweet chestnuts are in season from October through to the end of the year. Choose nuts with unbruised and undamaged skins, avoiding any which show traces of damp or mold. If you buy whole nuts, they must be peeled before use. This can be done relatively easily by slitting their skins and roasting them in a hot oven 5–10 minutes or by boiling them (see below).

Although freshly peeled chestnuts do have a stronger, fuller flavor, peeling them is time consuming. You may find it easier to buy them peeled and vacuum-packed in airtight jars or in water. You will need 12 oz. Make sure the jarred chestnuts are unsweetened, and reduce the cooking time in this recipe to about 30 minutes.

SERVES 4–6

1 lb fresh chestnuts in shell
1 tbsp olive oil
1 onion, finely chopped
1 celery stalk, trimmed and chopped
grated zest of 1 orange
5 cups Chicken Stock (see pages 106–7)
1 tbsp dry Madeira wine
salt and freshly ground black pepper
1 tbsp finely chopped fresh flat-leaf parsley

To peel the chestnuts, use a sharp knife to make a couple of slits in the skin of each nut. Put them in a saucepan, cover with boiling water, and bring to a simmer over medium heat. Simmer about 5 minutes and remove from the heat. Then take out the nuts a few at a time, drain, and refresh them under running cold water. Peel off their skins, which should be quite easy.

Heat the olive oil in a large saucepan over medium heat, add the onion and celery, and sauté gently 5 minutes, or until soft. Add the orange zest and peeled chestnuts and sauté 2–3 minutes longer.

Pour in the stock and bring to a boil. Turn down the heat to low, cover, and simmer about 45 minutes.

Working in batches, process the soup in a food processor until smooth. Return it to the pan, stir in the Madeira, season to taste, and bring back to a boil.

Serve the soup immediately sprinkled with the chopped fresh parsley.

Aïllade or Walnut and Garlic Sauce

Aïllade is at its most pungent when made with wet walnuts (see page 176). However, by all means use ready-shelled nuts — the result is still superb and excellent for serving with cold meats.

In the walnut-growing area of southwest France, aïllade is one of the treats of late August. I once visited a farm in the region that still presses its own walnut oil and the owner passed on an invaluable tip: Later on in the year, soaking the nuts overnight in hot milk gives the shells the glossy appearance of new walnuts and revitalizes the meat.

MAKES 1½ CUPS

3 garlic cloves
salt and freshly ground black pepper
1 cup walnut pieces
⅓ cup olive oil
½ cup crème fraîche (see page 52) or sour cream
3 tbsp finely chopped fresh parsley

Put the garlic cloves and a large pinch of salt in a food processor or blender and process until creamy. Add the walnuts and process again until they are finely chopped.

With the machine still running, gradually pour in the olive oil. When it is well blended, and the liquid is smooth and thick, pour in the cream and process a few more seconds. Fold in the parsley, season, and serve.

Fungi

Most of the mushrooms we eat are cultivated and grown in the dark. The most usual is the WHITE BUTTON MUSHROOM, sold in a variety of sizes from the small white button-size to the larger brown-beige open caps. When fresh, they are firm and unmarked with taut gills, and a mild flavor, tasting faintly of chicken. The white button mushroom was once the only mushroom readily available, but today, American mushroom growers are cultivating other mushrooms, once only found in the wild, under tightly controlled conditions. These mushrooms are often erroneously called wild, but since they are cultivated, the proper label is "exotic." Exotic mushrooms that you will find in gourmet stores, and at better supermarkets are: the delicate, softly textured OYSTER MUSHROOM; the more intensely – some would say almost overpoweringly – flavored brown SHIITAKE MUSHROOM, of which only the cap should be eaten, as the stem is too tough; and the CREMINI MUSHROOM, also known as the Italian Brown, which closely resembles the white mushroom, but has a more robust flavor.

In spite of constant efforts, no one has yet succeeded in taming the hundreds of other edible wild mushrooms to cultivate them. It is fair to say, that while the cultivated exotic mushrooms are quite good, there is nothing to compare with one found in the wild.

I remember a couple of years ago I spent my vacation in early September in Tuscany, high in the hills around Florence. My great treat was to go early in the morning to the Mercato Centrale, the covered food market. The streets were still empty, and the tourists had yet to appear, but the market was already doing a brisk trade. Built in the 19th century, it is a curious building a little like a Victorian railway terminal, with its cast-iron columns and glass sides; but it feeds all Florence and is known affectionately as "the belly of the city."

Luck was with me, I had arrived at prime mushroom time, and there were mounds of *porcini*, the most treasured of all Italian mushrooms, freshly gathered and being carefully inspected by the Florentine housewives – the Italians, like the French and Poles, take their wild mushrooms very seriously. The *porcini* (*cèpe* in French, called CEP or PENNY BUN in Britain), in season from early summer through to the autumn, has a densely meaty flavor and strange slippery – almost gelatinous – texture which are second to none. A fleshy mushroom with a thick white stem and a rounded bulbous soft brown cap, it is excellent eaten on its own, lightly brushed with oil and broiled, or panfried with garlic and chopped parsley, and finished with a little cream to be served with pasta. Dried *porcini* are sold throughout the year and add body and depth of flavor to stews, casseroles, and sauces.

Throughout Europe and the United States, there are hundreds of wild edible mushrooms. However, do let me give you a word of warning: Until you are sure of what you are picking, always check with an expert before you even think of eating your bounty. In France and several other European countries, every pharmacist must, by law, be trained to identify wild mushrooms. In Britain, and in the States, we are not so lucky. So to identify your wild mushrooms, seek advice.

As well as the large, open flat caps and mottled chestnut mushrooms, soft gray oyster and yellow chanterelle mushrooms are now cultivated.

One of the finest wild mushrooms, and one of the most famous, is the MOREL, usually the first wild mushroom of the season. The CHANTERELLE, which taste a little of the flesh of ripe apricots, mixed with an earthy mustiness, and a prick of pepperiness and subtle sweetness, is a prized mushroom.

In Britain, late summer and autumn, before the serious frosts, is the time to go mushroom picking. I look for soft shaggy INKY CAPS, often found near tree stumps, which may be used for making mushroom ketchup; giant PUFFBALLS, found in forests in the summer; delicate wild OYSTER MUSHROOMS; CHICKEN-OF-THE-WOODS, which may need to be first simmered in stock, before sautéeing; HONEY MUSHROOMS, which are good sautéed and braised, however, the stems may be tough; and BLEWITS, with stems brushed with purple, which grow abundantly.

If the thought of picking wild mushrooms terrifies you, a large selection may be found at top-quality gourmet stores. Although expensive, adding even a few to cook with cultivated mushrooms transforms the flavor. Also remember that some edible mushrooms may be toxic unless cooked.

Italy and France are also famous for their truffles, underground tubers which are dug up by specially trained dogs or pigs. The Italian WHITE TRUFFLE is superb grated raw, using a special truffle grater, over a risotto; and the BLACK TRUFFLE from France is used in pâtés, sauces, and stuffings, or even baked in batter like a miniature Yorkshire pudding and eaten whole.

Saffron milk caps are particularly appreciated in Europe.

Mushroom Caviar

Because this slow method of cooking mushrooms develops and intensifies their flavor, ordinary cultivated white button mushrooms will do. However, make sure that they are fresh, firm, and dry — once they develop a wet, slimy skin it is a sign that they are past their peak. Clean them gently by wiping them with a damp cloth rather than using running water.

SERVES 4

1 tbsp olive oil
1 onion, finely chopped
$\frac{3}{4}$ lb firm button mushrooms
salt and freshly ground black pepper
juice of $\frac{1}{2}$ lemon
3 tbsp sour cream
1 tbsp finely chopped fresh chives

Heat the oil in a skillet over medium to low heat, add the onion, and cook until they are soft, stirring, 3–5 minutes.

Process the mushrooms in a food processor until very finely chopped and almost reduced to a purée.

Add them to the skillet, season to taste and cook over low heat about 8 minutes, until the mushrooms are soft and creamy textured.

As the mushrooms exude a lot of juice while they cook, you will need to get rid of some of it. Simply turn up the heat to medium and stir the liquid and mushrooms together until the juices evaporate, then reduce the heat to low and carry on slow cooking. You will probably have to repeat the process 2 or 3 times.

Remove the pan from the heat and scrape the contents into a bowl. Stir in the lemon juice, sour cream, and chives, adjust the seasoning, and chill.

Serve with toasted slices of Walnut Brioche (see page 196).

Mushroom Ketchup

Late on Saturday afternoons, my local market often sells vegetables and fruits very cheaply, rather than having to keep them until Monday. If I get lots of mushrooms, I am tempted to make this ketchup as it is rich and spicy. No matter how much I make, it never seems to sit in my pantry for very long before it is all used up.

MAKES 2 CUPS

2 lb mushrooms, thinly sliced
$1\frac{1}{4}$ cups port wine
2–3 canned anchovy fillets, drained and chopped
2 garlic cloves, sliced
$\frac{1}{2}$ tsp ground allspice
$\frac{1}{4}$ tsp ground cloves
$\frac{1}{2}$ tsp ground mace
$\frac{1}{3}$ cup water
coarse sea salt or kosher salt and freshly ground black pepper

Put the mushrooms into a large saucepan along with the port wine, anchovy fillets, garlic, allspice, cloves, mace, water, salt, and plenty of pepper.

Bring to a boil over medium to low heat, reduce the heat, and simmer about 10 minutes.

Pour the hot ketchup into a warm, dry, sterilized jar and let cool. Seal and refrigerate about 10 days for the flavors to blend. Refrigerate for up to 4 weeks.

Risotto with Porcini

Use an arborio rice for this risotto as the grains absorb just the right amount of liquid while retaining their texture.

SERVES 4

¾ *lb fresh* porcini *(cèpes), sliced, or 11 oz fresh cultivated mushrooms, sliced, and 1 oz dried* porcini *(cèpes)*

6¼ *cups Chicken Stock (see pages 106–7)*

4 tbsp butter

3 tbsp olive oil

1 onion, finely chopped

1½ cups arborio or risotto rice

salt and freshly ground black pepper

½ cup freshly grated Parmesan cheese

If you are using dried *porcini*, soak them in a small bowl of hot water for 15 minutes, or until soft. Drain them, straining the soaking liquid through cheesecloth, and reserve the liquid. Chop the mushrooms. Bring the stock to boil, strain and add the mushroom soaking water. Reduce to a simmer.

Heat half the butter with the olive oil in a large skillet over medium heat, add the onion, and sauté until it begins to color. Add the sliced fresh mushrooms and cook 2–3 minutes, stirring occasionally. If using dried *porcini*, add to the pan and cook 1 minute longer. Stir in the rice and sauté 1–2 minutes, stirring constantly, until thoroughly coated with the butter and oil.

Add a ladleful of the hot stock to the rice. When the rice has absorbed the liquid, add another. Carry on stirring and adding stock until the rice is cooked *al dente*: This will take about 20 minutes and probably use up all the stock. The risotto should be creamy.

Season to taste, then stir in the remaining butter and the Parmesan cheese.

RISOTTO WITH PORCINI left, MUSHROOM CAVIAR (SEE PAGE 181), right.

Plants from the Woods

Food for Free, by Richard Maybe, struck a chord when it was first published in 1972 in Britain. It seemed that everyone had forgotten all about the wild edible foods growing in the countryside which were there for the picking.

Leaves from LAMB'S TONGUE, DANDELION, SORREL, and WATERCRESS (check first that the stream is fast-flowing) make excellent salads.

FIDDLEHEAD FERNS, which are the coiled fronds of several different types of edible ferns, make their colorful appearance in the spring. The ones with the best flavor being the brake fern or ostrich ferns. They may be steamed and served with melted butter, or stir-fried – the list is endless and the possibilities exciting.

Whatever you use, however, do make sure the plants have not been sprayed. Also, wash them thoroughly, and just to be on the safe side, when foraging, always consult a good reference book, or seek the advise of a local nature club.

Dandelion and Bacon Salad

Cultivated DANDELION *plants, grown specifically for salads, are blanched to make their leaves soft and sweet. However, as wild dandelions are so plentiful, it makes sense to put their leaves to good use, if you live near an area where they grow in abundance. Pick only the tiny inner leaves, as the larger outer ones can be quite hairy and extremely bitter.*

SERVES 4

5 oz tiny new potatoes, scrubbed
10 oz young dandelion leaves
2 oz sorrel leaves
coarse sea salt or kosher salt and freshly ground black pepper
$\frac{1}{3}$ cup extra-virgin olive oil
1 tbsp hazelnut oil
6-oz piece of thick-sliced bacon, trimmed and cut into 1-inch strips
2 shallots, very finely chopped
2 tbsp white wine vinegar

Cook the new potatoes in lightly salted boiling water in a saucepan over medium heat about 8 minutes, or until tender. Drain the potatoes and keep warm in a 200°F oven.

Mix the dandelion leaves with the sorrel in a salad bowl, tearing any of the larger leaves with your hands. Sprinkle with a little coarse sea salt or kosher salt to taste.

Mix all but 1 teaspoon of the olive oil with the hazelnut oil and season to taste with pepper. Add the potatoes to the bowl, pour the dressing over the salad, and toss it thoroughly with your hands.

Heat the remaining oil in a skillet over medium heat and fry the bacon strips until crisp. Add the shallots and fry 2–3 minutes longer, or until they just begin to turn golden. Using a slotted spoon, lift the bacon and shallots out of the pan and scatter them over the dressed salad leaves.

Turn up the heat to high, pour the vinegar into the skillet and, stirring and scraping any browned bits up from the bottom of the pan with a wooden spoon so the juices mix together, boil to reduce, about 1 minute. Pour this hot dressing over the salad, give it a final toss, and serve immediately.

DANDELION AND BACON SALAD

The Granary

Cereals were man's first staple food, their importance illustrated in their centuries-old role in harvest festivities and as a symbol of plenty. And they remain central to much country food — from breads and pies to pastries and pasta.

In the West, most of the flour we use is milled from wheat. There are, however, a number of different types of wheat flours, so the two most important points to bear in mind when buying flour are: the type of wheat from which it is milled, and its extraction rate – in layperson's terms, this means the percentage of whole wheat kernel left in after milling.

Very generally speaking, there are two different types of wheat: hard and soft. Hard wheat has a hard kernel with a high protein content. The more protein a flour contains, the more gluten (a part of protein) in the dough; therefore, BREAD FLOUR makes a dough which is more elastic and can trap the bubbles of carbon dioxide produced by the fermentation of the yeast, which causes the dough to rise. As bread flour produces a good crust and open texture, it should be used for bread-making, other yeast cookery, some batters and pasta. Hard wheat grows best in warm dry climates. In the States, it is grown in the high Plains regions, from Texas to North Dakota.

DURUM WHEAT, grown in North Dakota, is ground into semolina flour and used for pasta.

SOFT FLOUR is milled from soft wheat which grows in the temperate climates of the Pacific Northwest and in the eastern and southeastern United States. It has a soft grain, containing a higher level of starch than protein. It is lighter and far more fragile than flour made from hard wheat. Sold as CAKE or PASTRY FLOUR, it is a white flour ideally suited for pastry-, cake-, cookie-making and so on.

Flour also differs in the amount of kernel left in after milling. WHOLE-WHEAT FLOUR, what the British call WHOLEMEAL FLOUR, results from 100% extraction, meaning nothing has been taken away – or added – so the goodness of the grain is intact. It is heavier and denser than white flour The particular coarseness or fineness of the grind is not standardized; try several brands to find one you prefer. WHOLE-WHEAT PASTRY FLOUR is the milled whole grain of the soft wheat berry, suitable for some pastry and cookies, although it produces a heavier texture than white cake flour. ALL-PURPOSE FLOUR contains 75–76% of the wheat kernel, which means that most of the bran and wheat germ have been removed. It is sometimes bleached to make it a pure white color.

UNBLEACHED ALL-PURPOSE FLOUR, a cream-colored flour, is all-purpose flour which has received no bleaching.

By U.S. law, all flour not containing wheat germ must be enriched with thiamin, riboflavin, niacin, and iron in a effort to restore some of its goodness. Some flour may also be enriched with calcium, but it will say so on the label.

Some flours are also sold as STONE-GROUND FLOURS; this means that the wheat or other grain is ground by the old-fashioned method between two stones, rather than by the modern mass-production stainless-steel rollers. Stone-ground flour is usually more expensive; but, because the wheat is crushed at a cooler temperature, more of the grains' goodness is preserved, and it should have a higher nutritional value. However, it will not keep as long as commercially milled flour. Stone-ground flours are sold at health food stores, or by mail order (see page 250).

SELF-RISING FLOUR, used in some cakes, biscuits, and pastry, is a soft, generally white, flour to which a leavening agent, usually baking powder and salt, have been added.

All flour should be kept in an airtight storage jar in a cool, airy place. Unless you bake often, purchase flour in small quantities. As a general rule, all-purpose flour keeps four to six months; self-rising two to three months; and whole-wheat flour, because of its higher fat content, about two months. Flours tend to turn rancid if they are kept too long. I do remember one

Oats, wheat, and barley are used in many forms – cooked whole, ground to make flours, and even, in the case of barley, fermented to make alcoholic drinks.

Wheat is harvested in Gascony, southwest France.

bread-making enthusiast, however, telling me that he always kept his whole-wheat flour for months, most satisfactorily, in the freezer.

Flours are made from many other grains, cereals, nuts, or legumes, including barley, buckwheat, corn, rye, rice, and soybeans. OAT FLOUR, for example, is made by grinding oats after the husks have been removed. However, OAT BRAN is the ground outer casing of the oat. Chick-peas, or garbanzos, are ground into a rich creamy flour which is used to make dense crêpes called *socca*. RICE FLOUR, silky smooth and fine, does not contain any gluten, so it is useless in bread-making, but it still helps give cookies a light, crumbly texture. Shortbread made with rice flour substituted for a small amount of the all-purpose flour, for example, is most successful.

RYE FLOUR, an essential ingredient in Eastern European cooking, adds a distinctive flavor to anything made with it. The gluten content is low, so if you want to make rye bread, use some wheat flour as well.

The grain CORN, which the British call maize, is grown throughout the world and there are hundreds of different types, from the varieties used for popcorn, to those grown for their huge cobs. Their colors range from white and yellow to red, blue, and brown or even variegated. Yellow and white CORNMEAL are finely ground corn kernels, used to make such Southern favorites as corn bread and spoon bread. POLENTA is coarsely ground corn, but the Italians also use the term for a traditional dish made from boiling the meal in water with butter or olive oil, sometimes with a little added grated Parmesan cheese. HOMINY is hulled white or yellow dried corn, made by soaking and boiling the kernels in either slaked lime or lye until the outer skin of the kernel is soft enough to be rubbed off. When dried, it is then ground and made into hominy grits, a specialty of the South.

Thickening agents

Some flours also make effective thickening agents to be added to soups, stews, sauces, and so on. All-purpose flour and butter make a roux, the basis of many a white sauce. ARROWROOT, made from a tropical root of the same name, is effective in clear meat and fruit sauces, and is ideal because it thickens at a lower temperature, unlike cornstarch which needs to boil to reach its full thickening potential. It also gives sauces a glossy finish.

CORNSTARCH, interchangeable in many cases with arrowroot, is made by grinding and pulverizing the starch extracted from corn kernels, and it can be used to lighten cakes and pastries. POTATO FLOUR, made from dried and ground potatoes, needs to be cooked to thicken, and is particularly useful for anyone on a corn-free or gluten-free diet, and is completely tasteless.

Whole-wheat Bread

One of the simplest of all breads, whole-wheat bread is ideal for serving with farmhouse cheeses. For extra fiber, the bread can be further enriched by adding a teaspoon of fine wheat bran and then sprinkling it with a little more bran before baking. However, because of its higher bran and wheat germ content, bread made with whole-wheat flour tends to have a denser texture and rises less than bread made with white flour.

MAKES TWO SMALL LOAVES

2 tsp honey
1½ cups milk
1 oz fresh compressed yeast or 2 packages active dry yeast
6 cups whole-wheat flour
2 tsp salt, plus extra for glazing
1 tsp bran, plus extra for finishing
2 large eggs
6 tbsp unsalted butter, melted, plus extra for greasing

Put the honey with ⅓ cup of the milk in a saucepan and heat it over low heat until lukewarm. Remove from the heat, mix in the yeast thoroughly, cover and let stand in a warm place for 15 minutes, until it is frothy.

Put the flour and salt in a large bowl. Add the bran, eggs, and melted butter and pour in the yeast mixture with the remaining milk. Using a wooden spoon, mix until the dough comes together.

Knead on a flat, lightly floured surface for about 10 minutes, or until the dough is smooth. Cover with a cloth and let rise in a warm place until it has doubled in size.

Preheat the oven to 450°F and generously butter a baking sheet.

Punch down the dough by lifting it from the bowl and kneading it for a minute or so. Cut the dough in half and shape the pieces into 2 cigar-like loaves. Slash the tops with a knife.

Place the loaves on the prepared baking sheet, cover with a cloth and let rise. When they have doubled in volume they are ready to be baked.

Lightly brush the loaves with a salt glaze made by dissolving a pinch of salt in 2 tablespoons of hot water. Sprinkle the tops with more bran and bake for about 20–30 minutes, or until brown.

Remove from the sheet and let cool on a wire rack.

Hazelnut Bread

Traditional break-making in France opposite.

Slices of hazelnut bread are particularly good served lightly toasted with a little goat cheese melted on top. Instead of using bread loaf pans, I sometimes make fat, column-shaped loaves in 4-inch unused clay flower-pots. The pots should first be soaked for a short while in water; this creates the effect almost of steaming the bread, making it particularly moist.

This recipe can also be adapted for a walnut bread: Substitute the same quantity of walnuts for hazelnuts and use walnut instead of hazelnut oil.

MAKES TWO SMALL LOAVES

1 tsp honey

$\frac{2}{3}$ cup milk, plus 1 tbsp for glazing

$\frac{1}{2}$ oz fresh compressed yeast or 1 package active dry yeast

2 cups unbleached white bread flour

2 cups whole-wheat bread flour

1 cup coarsely chopped hazelnuts (filberts)

$1\frac{1}{2}$ tsp coarse sea salt or kosher salt

3 tbsp hazelnut oil, plus extra for greasing

$\frac{2}{3}$ cup water, plus 1 tbsp for glazing

$\frac{1}{4}$ cup rye flour

Combine the honey and the $\frac{2}{3}$ cup milk in a saucepan and heat it over low heat until lukewarm. Remove from the heat. Mix in the yeast and stir to dissolve. Let stand in a warm place until foamy, about 10 minutes.

Put the white flour into a large bowl, and stir in the whole-wheat flour, hazelnuts, and salt. Add the hazelnut oil and $\frac{2}{3}$ cup water to the yeast mixture and mix together well, then pour into the flour. Mix until the dough comes together.

Turn the dough onto a flat, lightly floured surface and knead for about 10 minutes, or until the dough is firm and elastic, adding a little white flour if necessary to prevent sticking. Cover with a cloth and let rise in a warm place for about 1 hour, or until the dough has

doubled in volume.

Lightly grease two 5- × 4- × 3-inch loaf pans (2-cup capacity) with a little hazelnut oil.

Punch down the dough by kneading it again for a few seconds, divide it in half, and shape each half into a loaf. Scatter the rye flour on a clean work surface and roll the loaves in it until they are well covered. Reserve any unused rye flour.

Put the dough into the prepared loaf pans, cover, and let rise in a warm place for 30 minutes, or until doubled in volume.

Meanwhile, preheat the oven to 425°F.

Using a pastry brush, paint the loaves lightly with a glaze made from 1 tablespoon of milk mixed with 1 tablespoon of water. Sprinkle the tops with the reserved rye flour, then bake for 35–40 minutes, or until the bread sounds hollow when tapped with your fingers.

Remove breads from the pans and let cool on wire racks.

Grissini or Breadsticks

Until recently, I thought all breadsticks came in packages from huge industrialized bakeries. It was only when I visited Turin—the home of grissini—that I realized how wrong I was. There I found endless flavors and variations of these charming, irregularly-shaped sticks on sale in small local bakeries.

They are often made with semolina flour which, as it is such a hard flour, can be difficult to work unless mixed with bread flour. SEMOLINA consists of the largest particles of the endosperm found when the outer skin, or bran, is stripped from the Durum wheat berry. It is sold either as grains or ground into flour. Malt extract syrup is a yeast food used to promote bread rising and a golden crust. It can be found in some supermarkets and in health-food stores.

MAKES ABOUT 20

1¼ *cups warm water* (105°–115°F)

1 *tbsp malt extract syrup*

pinch of granulated sugar

½ *oz fresh compressed yeast or 1 package active dry yeast*

2 *tbsp olive oil, plus extra for greasing and brushing*

3 *cups unbleached white bread flour*

⅔ *cup* + ½ *cup semolina flour, plus extra for cutting and rolling*

large pinch of coarse sea salt or kosher salt

Pour 1¼ cups of warm water into a large mixing bowl and stir in the malt extract syrup, and sugar. Add the yeast and stir to dissolve. Let stand in a warm place about 10 minutes, until foamy.

Stir in the olive oil. Add the white flour, the ⅔ cup of the semolina flour, and the salt, and mix until the dough comes together. Turn it onto a flat, lightly floured surface and knead for about 8–10 minutes, or until the dough is smooth, shiny, and elastic, adding a little white flour if necessary to prevent sticking.

Lightly oil a baking sheet. Shape the dough into a rectangle to fit the baking sheet and place it on the sheet. Using a pastry brush, lightly paint the top with oil. Cover with plastic wrap and let rise in a warm place for about 1 hour, or until it has doubled in volume.

Preheat the oven to 450°F.

Sprinkle the dough with semolina flour before cutting and rolling. Using a sharp knife, cut the dough into 20 equal pieces and, using your hands, roll each one on the work surface into sticks about 12 inches long and ¾ inch wide. It does not matter if they are irregularly shaped. Sprinkle the remaining semolina flour on the surface and roll the sticks in it to coat.

Put the breadsticks back on the baking sheet so they are not touching, and then bake in the preheated oven for 20 minutes. Transfer to wire racks and let cool.

Variations

Replace the semolina flour in which the breadsticks are rolled with ½ cup sesame seeds or poppy seeds.

Olive Oil Bread

The taste of olive oil bread depends upon the quality of olive oil used to make it: The best is an extra-virgin olive oil, with its defined flavor and low acidity.

The amount and quality of the salt is equally important. All bread needs salt for flavor, and if you leave the salt out or do not mix it in thoroughly, the dough lacks springiness and rises in a misshapen fashion. I always use Maldon sea salt as it has a robust flavor and is also very easy to mix in. Unlike other sea salts, it is soft and crumbles into tiny particles when rubbed between the fingers. Kosher salt is a good substitute.

MAKES 1 LARGE OR 2 SMALLER LOAVES

pinch of granulated sugar
1 cup warm water (105°–115°F)
$\frac{1}{2}$ oz fresh compressed yeast or 1 package active dry yeast
3 cups unbleached white bread flour, or a mixture of $1\frac{1}{2}$ cups whole-wheat bread flour and $1\frac{1}{2}$ cups unbleached white bread flour
$1\frac{1}{2}$ tsp coarse sea salt or kosher salt, plus extra for finishing
3 tbsp extra-virgin olive oil, plus extra for greasing and glazing

Dissolve the sugar in 1 cup of warm water. Add the yeast and stir to dissolve. Let stand in a warm place until foamy, about 10 minutes.

Put the flour with the salt into a large bowl. Add the olive oil to the yeast mixture, mix together, and pour into the flour. Mix until the dough comes together.

Turn the dough onto a flat, lightly floured surface and knead for about 10 minutes, or until the dough is smooth and elastic, adding a little flour if necessary to prevent it from sticking. Place the dough in a clean, lightly oiled bowl and turn it over to coat with oil. Cover with plastic wrap and let rise in a warm place for about 30–40 minutes, until it has doubled in volume.

OLIVE OIL AND ROSEMARY BREAD top, OLIVE OIL AND GREEN OLIVE OIL BREAD bottom.

Traditionally, olive oil bread is very thin, so turn the dough onto a flat, lightly floured board and, using a rolling pin, roll it out into 1 large or 2 small ovals, each about $\frac{1}{2}$ inch thick.

With a sharp knife, make several diagonal cuts on the tops of the dough ovals and then gently pull the cut edges apart slightly to open them up, giving the loaves a latticed appearance.

Preheat the oven to 450°F. Lightly oil a baking sheet. Place the loaves on the prepared baking sheet. Brush the tops with olive oil and sprinkle with sea salt. Cover, and let rise in a warm place for about 20 minutes, or until doubled in volume.

Bake the loaves for 20–30 minutes, or until they are golden brown and sound hollow when tapped with your fingers.

Remove the bread from the baking sheet and cool on a wire rack.

Variations

1 Olive Oil and Green Olive Bread: After the dough has been rolled out into an oval, immediately put it on a baking sheet. Use your fingertips to make 24 holes in the surface of the dough, place a pitted green olive in each indentation, and brush with olive oil. Proceed as above, omitting sprinkling with the salt.

2 Olive Oil and Red Onion Bread: Toss 1 thinly sliced red onion in a couple of tablespoons of olive oil and season with salt and freshly ground black pepper to taste. When the dough has been shaped into ovals and placed on a baking sheet, spread the onions over the top and press them lightly into the dough. Brush with olive oil, sprinkle with salt, and proceed as above.

3 Olive Oil and Rosemary Bread: Add 1 tablespoon of finely chopped fresh rosemary to the bowl with the flour and proceed as above.

4 Olive Oil and Sun-Dried Tomato Bread: Add about $\frac{1}{2}$ cup drained, chopped, oil-packed sun-dried tomatoes to the bowl with the flour and proceed as above.

Brioche

Brioche is made from a yeast dough enriched with eggs and butter.

A good unsalted butter is essential for brioche, and those made in Gisors and Gournay, great French butter-producing centers, were particularly famous.

It may have have been in one of these towns that they dreamed up the brioche mousseline, *a diet-defying concoction in which an extra 4 tablespoons of butter is added to every pound of dough, which is then baked in a tall mold further heightened by tying a band of buttered parchment paper or foil around the top.*

In the United States, good-quality butters are increasingly available from small dairies, especially in the Northeast.

MAKES TWO SMALL LOAVES

3½ tbsp granulated sugar

2 tbsp warm water (105°–115°F)

½ oz fresh compressed yeast or 1 package active dry yeast

3¼ cups + ¼ cup unbleached white bread flour

pinch of coarse sea salt or kosher salt

5 extra-large eggs

1 stick softened unsalted butter, cut into small pieces, plus extra for greasing

Combine ½ tablespoon of the sugar with the 2 tablespoons of warm water in a mixing bowl. Add the yeast and stir to dissolve. Let stand in a warm place until foamy, about 10 minutes.

Mix together 3¼ cups of the flour, the salt, and remaining sugar in another large bowl. Beat 4 of the eggs into the yeast mixture, mix together, and pour into the flour. Mix until the dough comes together.

Turn the dough onto a flat, lightly floured surface and knead for about 15 minutes, until smooth and elastic. As the dough is very sticky, flour your hands every so often during the kneading process.

When the dough begins to come away from your fingers easily, place the butter, a few pieces at a time, on top of the dough and push them in. Squeeze the dough through your fingers to mix the butter in and then knead the dough with the palms of your hands. Carry on squeezing and kneading until all the softened butter has been incorporated.

Sprinkle some flour around the sides of the bowl and put the dough in. Cover, and let rise in a warm place for 2–3 hours, or until it has doubled in size.

Punch down the dough by kneading it for a few seconds. Generously grease 2 brioche molds with butter. Divide the dough in half and then cut one-third off each piece. Roll all the pieces of dough into balls. Put the larger balls into the molds, and, using your thumbs, make a circular indentation in the top center of each. Put a smaller ball in each indentation and press it down firmly. Cover and let rise again for about 1 hour or until doubled in volume.

Meanwhile, preheat the oven to 400°F.

Beat together the remaining egg and 1 tablespoon of water and, using a pastry brush, brush the brioches all over with the glaze. Bake in the preheated oven for 30 minutes, brushing them again with the glaze after 15 minutes baking.

Remove the brioches from the molds and set on wire racks to cool.

Variation

Walnut Brioche: Add 1 cup of chopped walnuts to the flour before mixing in the yeast mixture, and proceed as above.

BRIOCHE AND CORN MUFFINS (see overleaf)

Corn Muffins

Well-known in cornbread, cheery yellow cornmeal is also used in such all-American favorites as hoecakes, hush puppies, and muffins, as below. Serve these for breakfast or brunch, or, of course, as part of the Thanksgiving feast.

MAKES ABOUT 14

1 stick butter, melted and cooled slightly, plus extra for greasing

2¼ cups yellow cornmeal

1 cup self-rising flour

⅓ cup granulated sugar

1 tbsp baking powder

1 tsp salt

2 large eggs

1¼ cups milk, warmed

Preheat the oven to 400°F. Generously butter about 14 muffin-pan cups and fit them with paper liners also greased with butter.

Mix the cornmeal, flour, sugar, baking powder, and salt in a large bowl and make a well in the center. In a separate bowl, lightly beat the eggs and stir in the melted butter and warm milk. Mix together and pour this into the center of the dry ingredients. Using a wooden spoon, mix together until the batter is just smooth and blended.

Pour the batter into the prepared paper liners, and bake in the oven for about 20 minutes, or until well risen and golden brown.

Transfer the muffins to a wire rack and let cool slightly. Serve while still warm.

Variation

Fry ¼ pound of sliced bacon until really crisp, drain thoroughly on paper towels, crumble into small pieces, and add to the flour. Proceed as above, cutting the quantity of salt by half.

Plum Bread

This is actually more like a fruitcake than a bread. It will keep for several days, wrapped in foil, and stored in an airtight tin. Make this cake a few days before serving since the flavor improves over time.

MAKES TWO SMALL LOAVES

2 sticks cold unsalted butter, cut up, plus extra for greasing

2½ cups all-purpose flour

2 tsp baking powder

1 tsp freshly grated nutmeg

1 tsp ground cinnamon

1 tsp ground ginger

pinch of salt

½ cup chopped blanched almonds

1½ cups dried currants

1½ cups golden raisins

⅓ cup chopped mixed candied citrus peel

⅔ cup chopped candied cherries

1 cup packed light brown sugar

4 large eggs

a little milk, as necessary

Preheat the oven to 350°F and generously butter two 5- × 4- × 3-inch loaf pans (2-cup capacity).

Mix together the flour, baking powder, nutmeg, cinnamon, ginger, and salt in a large bowl. Cut the butter into the flour mixture, using a pastry blender or 2 knives, until the mixture is the texture of fine crumbs.

Stir in the almonds, currants, raisins, mixed peel, cherries, and sugar until thoroughly mixed.

In a separate bowl, beat the eggs lightly. Stir them into the mixture, adding a little milk if necessary, until it is smooth and just drops from the spoon.

Spoon the batter into the prepared pans, dividing evenly and bake for 45 minutes to 1 hour. If a metal skewer inserted into the center comes out clean, the loaves are ready. Turn onto a wire rack and let cool.

Basic Pie Pastry

This recipe results in a light, short pastry ideal as a base for savory tarts and quiches. If you prefer using a whole-wheat flour, or a mix of whole-wheat and white flours, the pastry will be heavier. You can also use it as a sweet pastry if you add the sugar.

MAKES ¾ LB, ENOUGH FOR TWO 8-INCH SHELLS

1⅔ *cups all-purpose flour*
pinch of salt
1 *tsp superfine or granulated sugar (for sweet pastry)*
1 *stick cold unsalted butter, cut into small pieces*
3–4 *tbsp cold water*

If making the pastry by hand, mix the flour, sugar, if using, and salt into a large bowl. Cut the butter into the flour mixture, using a pastry blender or 2 knives, until the texture of fine crumbs. Slowly add 3–4 tablespoons of cold water, tossing with a fork, until the dough comes together.

Alternatively, put all the dry ingredients and butter into a food processor and process for a few seconds until the mixture has reduced to the texture of fine crumbs. With the machine still running, slowly pour in the 3–4 tablespoons water and process until the dough comes together to form a ball.

To shape the dough, use your hands to form into a ball, and flatten slightly.

Wrap the dough in plastic wrap and let it rest in the refrigerator for 15–30 minutes before using.

Rich Pie Pastry

This recipe creates a delicious crust for fruit tarts, particularly when enhanced with various flavoring ingredients as discussed on page 243.

MAKES 1 LB, ENOUGH FOR TWO 9-INCH SHELLS

1¾ *cups all-purpose flour*
1½ *tsp superfine or granulated sugar*
pinch of salt
1 *extra-large egg*
1 *stick cold unsalted butter, cut into small pieces*
2–3 *tbsp cold water*

Mix together the flour, sugar, and salt in a large bowl. Make a well in the center and break in the egg. Add the butter and slowly work the pieces in with a pastry blender or 2 knives, drawing in the flour as you go.

When the dough is crumbly, pour in 2–3 tablespoons of cold water, tossing with a fork, until the dough comes together to form a ball.

Alternatively, put all the dry ingredients and butter in a food processor and process until crumbly. With the machine still running, pour in the water, a little at a time, and process until the dough forms a ball.

Knead the dough on a flat, lightly floured surface 2 or 3 times with the palm of your hand until it is completely smooth. Wrap it in plastic wrap or a plastic bag and chill for several hours to let it rest before using.

If wrapped, it should keep for several days in the refrigerator.

Certosino or Italian Christmas Cake

The taste of this cake is far more aromatic than the traditional British Christmas cake. Instead of apples I have also made it with puréed quinces (see page 224), puréed pears, or a mixture of the two, and each time the spiced, moist fruit flavor was superb. The cake matures and mellows with keeping, so do make it at least a week before you want to eat it.

CERTOSINO

SERVES 8–10
MAKES A 9-INCH CAKE

4 tbsp unsalted butter, plus extra for greasing
½ cup golden raisins
1½ tbsp rum
9–10 oz tart apples, peeled, cored and sliced
1 tsp fresh lemon juice
1½ tbsp superfine or granulated sugar

6 tbsp + 2 tsp water

1 cup honey

1 tsp ground cinnamon

1 tbsp anise seed

2½ cups all-purpose flour

1½ cups coarsely chopped blanched almonds

2½ oz bittersweet chocolate, coarsely chopped

1 cup chopped candied orange and lemon peel

½ cup pine nuts

1½ tsp baking soda

3 tbsp apricot jam

walnut or pecan halves and candied fruit, to decorate

Preheat the oven to 325°F and generously butter a 9-inch springform pan or savarin mold.

To prepare the fruit, put the golden raisins in a small bowl with the rum and let soak for 30 minutes. Meanwhile, combine the apples, lemon juice, sugar, 1 tablespoon of the butter, and 2 tablespoons of the water in a saucepan. Simmer gently for 10–15 minutes or until reduced to a soft purée. Pass the purée through a strainer, measure ¾ cup, and let cool.

Put the honey in the top of a double boiler, or in a bowl set over a saucepan half-filled with warm water, and warm over medium heat. Add the remaining 3 tablespoons butter and 3 tablespoons of water, and stir until the butter has all melted. Then stir in the cinnamon and anise seed and remove from the heat.

Put the flour into a large bowl. Slowly pour in the honey mixture, stirring vigorously with a wooden spoon, until it is well blended. Stir in the apple purée, the almonds, chocolate, candied peel, and the raisins with the rum. Carefully fold in the pine nuts so as not to crush them. Dissolve the baking soda in 2 teaspoons of water and stir this into the batter also.

Spoon the batter into the prepared pan and bake in the preheated oven for 1¼–1½ hours. To test whether the cake is done, insert a metal skewer into the center: If it comes out clean, the cake is ready. Unmold it onto a wire rack and let cool.

To decorate the cake, melt the apricot jam with 1 tablespoon of water in a saucepan over low heat. Brush the top of the cake with the jam, then stud the walnut or pecan halves and candied fruit over the top. Finally brush the cake all over with the jam to set the nuts and fruit in place.

As well as being used in many Italian and French cakes, candied fruits are a traditional gift at Christmas and New Year.

Chestnut and Orange Cake

Chestnut flour is made from dried and ground sweet chestnuts (see page 176) and is used frequently for baking in Italy, France, and Switzerland. Unfortunately, it is rather difficult to buy in the States, so I have adapted this recipe to use fresh chestnuts. This gives a less smooth, but more interesting texture. So even if you can buy the right flour, I still think the cake should be made with a mixture of chestnut flour and chestnuts. You can then be sure of deriving some of the benefit from the whole nuts.

SERVES 8–10

MAKES AN 8-INCH CAKE

$1\frac{1}{2}$ *sticks unsalted butter at room temperature, plus extra for greasing*

$\frac{3}{4}$ *cup chestnut flour plus $\frac{3}{4}$ cup unshelled chestnuts,*

or 9–10 oz ($2\frac{1}{4}$–$2\frac{1}{2}$ cups) unshelled chestnuts

$\frac{1}{2}$ *cup + 2 tbsp superfine or granulated sugar*

2 extra-large eggs

grated zest and juice of 2 large oranges

$\frac{1}{2}$ *cup + 2 tbsp self-rising flour*

$\frac{1}{2}$ *tsp salt*

2 cups soft white bread crumbs

1 cup confectioners' sugar

Preheat the oven to 375°F and generously butter two 8-inch layer cake pans. Line them with disks of buttered parchment paper.

To prepare the chestnuts, use a sharp knife to make a couple of slits in the skin of each. Put them in a saucepan, pour on enough boiling water to cover, and simmer for about 5 minutes. Take out a few chestnuts at a time, drain, and refresh them under cold running water. Then peel off their skins, which should come off

Modern machinery makes harvesting much less strenuous than in previous centuries, left. Sweet chestnuts, right.

quite easily. Return them to the pan with 2 tablespoons of water and simmer for 10–15 minutes, until soft. Drain, measure $\frac{1}{2}$ cup (or $1\frac{1}{2}$ cups if not using chestnut flour), and chop them finely.

In a large bowl, beat 1 stick of the butter with the superfine or granulated sugar until light and fluffy. In another bowl, lightly beat the eggs, then beat them into the butter mixture, a little at a time, taking care not to curdle the mixture. Stir in the orange zest, reserving about 1 teaspoon. Sift together the chestnut flour, if using, the self-rising flour, and the salt and fold them into the butter-egg mixture along with the bread crumbs and chopped chestnuts.

Pour the batter into the prepared pans, dividing evenly, and smooth the tops. Bake in the preheated oven for about 45 minutes. To test whether the cakes are done, insert a metal skewer into the center: If it comes out clean, the cakes are ready.

Let them cool for a few minutes in their pans, then unmold them onto a wire rack, peel off the parchment paper, and let cool completely.

To prepare the frosting: In a clean bowl, beat the remaining $\frac{1}{2}$ stick butter until soft and smooth. Sift in the confectioners' sugar and fold it in with the remaining orange zest. Beat in the orange juice, a little at a time, until the frosting is soft and easy to spread.

Spread the bottom of each cooled cake with a thick layer of frosting and put the frosted sides together.

Chill for about 15 minutes before serving.

The Best-Ever Chocolate Cake

This is not self-promotion, but a claim that I make on behalf of Josceline Dimbleby, whose recipe this is. Not only is this cake unrefusable, but it is also incredibly easy. The secret, according to Jossie, is to make it with really fresh bread crumbs, either from a white or whole-wheat loaf.

One of my best friends is also a demon baker, and she makes this cake at the drop of a hat, aided and abetted by her three sons: three-year old twins and their older brother, aged five. Last year they made it as my birthday cake, and we all wolfed it down almost before the candles were blown out. You cannot get a better recommendation than that.

SERVES 8–10

MAKES AN 8-INCH CAKE

2 sticks unsalted butter at room temperature, plus extra for greasing
8 oz semisweet chocolate, cut into pieces
1 cup + 2 tbsp superfine or granulated sugar
6 large eggs
2⅔ cups ground hazelnuts (filberts) (see page 64)
4 cups soft bread crumbs, whole-wheat or white
grated zest of 1 orange
2 tbsp orange marmalade

for the glaze:
4 oz semisweet chocolate, cut into pieces
4 tbsp unsalted butter, cut into pieces
2 tsp honey
1 oz white chocolate (optional), to decorate

Preheat the oven to 375°F and generously butter two 8-inch layer cake pans. Line these with disks of buttered parchment paper.

Melt the semisweet chocolate in the top of a double boiler, or in a bowl set in a saucepan half-filled with warm water, over medium to low heat, stirring until smooth. Remove from the heat and let cool slightly.

In a large bowl, beat the butter until smooth. Then beat in the sugar, a little at a time, until the mixture is light and fluffy. Beat in the eggs, 1 at a time, beating well after each addition. If the mixture looks a little curdled, do not worry. Beat the melted chocolate into the mixture, and stir in the hazelnuts, bread crumbs, and orange zest.

Spoon the batter into the prepared pans, dividing evenly, and smooth the tops. Bake in the preheated oven for 20–25 minutes, or until the center is firm to a light touch.

As these cakes are quite fragile, let them cool in their pans. Meanwhile, melt the marmalade in a small saucepan over medium heat, stirring. Loosen the cake edges with a knife, then unmold one of the cakes onto a serving plate, and remove the paper disk. Using a knife, lightly spread the cake with the marmalade. Carefully unmold the other cake onto a board, peel off the paper disk and place it on top of the marmalade-spread cake.

To make the glaze: Put the chocolate, butter, and honey in the top of a double boiler, or in a bowl set in a saucepan half-filled with warm water, over medium to low heat and stir until smooth. Remove from the heat and continue beating until the glaze thickens. Pour over the cake and spread evenly with a spatula. Let set before serving.

If you want to decorate the cake: Before the glaze has set hard, hold the piece of white chocolate over the cake and use a vegetable peeler to shave off thin slivers, allowing them to fall onto the cake.

Thin Crackers

These crackers bear absolutely no relation to commercially manufactured crackers, as they are far crisper and have a much more interesting taste.

Traditionally, these were rolled out using a "biscuit break," a cunning invention consisting of a heavy adjustable roller attached to the pastry table. It could be rolled back and forth over the dough, thus relieving the cook of the hard work of flattening it. As this piece of equipment no longer seems to exist, you will just have to press extra hard on your rolling pin!

These crackers have a short shelf-life and should really be eaten on the day they are made. If you do want to keep them, put them in a container while still warm along with a sheet of wax paper to prevent them from going soggy. You can always revive them by warming them briefly in the oven.

MAKES 15–20

4 tbsp cold butter, cut into small pieces, plus extra for greasing
2 cups unbleached white bread flour
$\frac{1}{8}$ tsp salt
1 tsp baking powder
6 tbsp light cream
1 tbsp water, if necessary
coarse sea salt or kosher salt, for sprinkling

Preheat the oven to 350°F and generously butter a baking sheet.

Mix together the flour, salt, and baking powder in a large bowl. Cut the butter into the the flour mixture with a pastry blender or 2 knives until it is the texture of fine crumbs. Stir in the cream, then gather the mixture together with your hands to make a firm dough, adding 1 tablespoon of water if necessary.

On a lightly floured, flat surface, roll out the dough very thinly, about $\frac{1}{16}$ inch, pressing down hard on the rolling pin. Using a 3-inch round cookie cutter, cut the dough into circles. Arrange the circles on the prepared baking sheet, prick them all over with a fork, and sprinkle with a little sea salt. Bake for 10–15 minutes, or until golden. Transfer to wire racks and let cool.

Pistachio Tuiles

French in origin, tuiles are light cookies with a slightly sticky texture derived from their high egg white and sugar content. Classically they are made with ground almonds instead of flour, and then scattered with sliced almonds. Whatever the content, they must be bent over a rolling pin to give them their characteristic shape of curved roof tiles or tuiles.

MAKES ABOUT 30

1 stick unsalted butter, melted, plus extra for greasing
4 large egg whites
1 cup + 2 tbsp superfine or granulated sugar
$\frac{3}{4}$ cup all-purpose flour
$\frac{1}{2}$ cup peeled and coarsely chopped pistachio nuts

Preheat the oven to 375°F and generously butter a baking sheet.

In a large clean bowl, beat the egg whites until frothy. Beat in the sugar until blended, then add the melted butter. Sift in the flour, and mix together gently.

Put a teaspoon of the batter on the prepared baking sheet and, using the back of the spoon, spread it out into a thin round. Sprinkle some chopped pistachios on top. Repeat the process allowing space for them to spread. Bake only 10 at a time so there is enough time to remove and shape the cookies before they harden.

Bake in the preheated oven for about 6 minutes, or until they are a pale golden brown. Immediately lift off the cookies with a metal spatula.

While they are still soft and pliable, quickly mold each one over a rolling pin so it is set in a curved shape. Let cool on a wire rack; store in airtight containers.

Brandy Snap Baskets

Although the conventional way of serving brandy snaps is to curl them around the handle of a wooden spoon and let them cool, and then pipe them full of brandy-flavored whipped cream, I like to mold them into individual small baskets and then fill them with fresh berries or an ice cream or sorbet. Larger pieces of the mixture molded over small bowls also make delightful serving dishes.

MAKES 20–30

1 stick unsalted butter, plus extra for greasing
$\frac{1}{3}$ cup light corn syrup
1 cup + 2 tbsp granulated sugar
$\frac{3}{4}$ cup all-purpose flour
pinch of salt
2 tsp ground ginger
1 tsp fresh lemon juice

Preheat the oven to 325°F. Generously butter a baking sheet and several small cups or round molds for shaping the brandy snaps.

Combine the butter, corn syrup, and sugar in the top of a double boiler, or in a bowl set in a saucepan half-filled with warm water, over medium to low heat and stir until melted.

Remove from the heat. Mix in the flour, salt, ginger, and lemon juice. Beat until the batter is smooth.

Put teaspoonfuls of the batter on the prepared baking sheet, spacing them about 6 inches apart to allow room for them to spread. Bake in the preheated oven for 8–10 minutes, or until golden brown. Let cool for a few moments (they should hold together but still be very pliable).

Using a slotted spatula, lift each slightly cooled brandy snap off the baking sheet and press it over a mold. If you let cool too long, they will snap when you try to press them into shape; return them to the baking sheet and reheat them in the oven for a couple of minutes and try again.

Once shaped, let them cool. Serve filled with a sorbet or ice cream (see page 247) or store them in an airtight container until ready to use.

Almond Cookies

Cornstarch added to flour lightens the texture when baked, so these cookies are particularly rich and crumbly.

MAKES ABOUT 20

2 sticks unsalted butter, plus extra for greasing
$1\frac{1}{4}$ cups all-purpose flour
$\frac{1}{2}$ cup cornstarch
$\frac{1}{4}$ cup confectioners' sugar
$\frac{1}{4}$ cup whole blanched almonds, finely ground
grated zest of 1 orange
$\frac{1}{4} - \frac{1}{2}$ tsp orange extract
about 20 almonds

Preheat the oven to 350°F and butter a baking sheet.

In a saucepan, melt the butter over low heat. Remove from the heat. Sift the flour, confectioners' sugar, and cornstarch into the butter. Add the ground almonds, orange zest, and orange extract to taste and beat to a smooth paste with a wooden spoon.

Break off small amounts of the paste and roll them lightly into balls between your palms. Put the balls on the prepared baking sheet and flatten them slightly with your thumb. Arrange an almond in the center of each, pressing it down gently.

Bake in the preheated oven for about 20 minutes, or until a golden brown. Transfer the cookies to a wire rack and let cool.

Store, separated with wax paper, in an airtight container until ready to use.

Bread and Butter Pudding

It takes a famous Swiss chef like Anton Mosimann, formerly of London's Dorchester Hotel, to transform a traditionally heavy pudding into something light and wonderful. His recipe relies on a creamy, flourless, vanilla-scented custard and slices of fresh, soft bread rolls.

SERVES 4–6

3 tbsp unsalted butter, plus extra for greasing

1¼ cups milk

1¼ cups heavy cream

1 vanilla bean, split, lengthwise

3 large eggs

½ cup + 2 tbsp granulated sugar

3 small soft bread rolls, cut into thin slices

¼ cup golden raisins or sultanas, soaked in warm water and drained

2 tbsp apricot jam, heated

2 tbsp confectioners' sugar

Preheat the oven to 325°F and generously butter a deep, 2½-quart, oval casserole dish.

In a heavy-bottomed saucepan, combine the milk, cream, and vanilla bean and slowly bring to a boil over low heat. Just as it is about to reach boiling point, remove from the heat.

In a large bowl, beat together the eggs and granulated sugar until the mixture is pale yellow. Then slowly pour in the milk and cream mixture, stirring continuously.

Butter the slices of roll with one-quarter of the butter and arrange them on the bottom of the dish. Sprinkle with the raisins, then pour the milk and egg mixture through a strainer over the bread. Do not worry if the bread floats to the top. Dot with the remaining butter and cover with parchment paper.

Place the dish in a deep roasting pan and add enough hot water to come halfway up the side of the casserole dish. Bake for 35–45 minutes, or until firmly set around the sides but still wobbly in the center.

Remove from the oven and let cool for a short while. Then, using a pastry brush, lightly brush the top with a thin coating of heated apricot jam. Sift the confectioners' sugar over the top and serve warm.

BREAD AND BUTTER PUDDING opposite

Buckwheat Crêpes

BUCKWHEAT GROATS or KASHA, the hulled, crushed buckwheat kernels, come in fine, medium, and coarse grinds and can be used for making dumplings or for stuffing geese or carp, or to serve with Beef Stroganoff instead of rice.

BUCKWHEAT FLOUR, gray in color speckled with black, is ground from the seed. It is used primarily in Eastern Europe and northern France, either plain or mixed with wheat flour for crêpes, galettes or blinis, — crêpes leavened with yeast which are usually served with caviar.

MAKES ABOUT 12

$\frac{3}{4}$ *cup unbleached white bread flour*

$\frac{1}{2}$ *cup + 1 tbsp buckwheat flour*

$\frac{1}{2}$ *tsp salt*

3 large eggs, lightly beaten

3 tbsp unsalted butter, melted

1 cup milk

1 cup water

corn oil, for frying

Make the batter by mixing together the white flour, buckwheat flour, and salt in a bowl. Make a well in the center and beat in the eggs, then slowly beat in the melted butter, milk, and water. Beat until smooth.

Alternatively, combine the milk, water, and eggs in a food processor and process together. Then, with the machine still running, slowly add the buckwheat flour, followed by the white flour, salt, and melted butter and process again until smooth.

Either way, let the batter stand in a cool place to rest for about 1 hour before use.

To cook the crêpes: Heat a heavy-bottomed omelet or crêpe pan over medium heat until very hot. Using a pastry brush, brush the inside all over with a little oil, then return it to the heat. Pour in about 1 tablespoon of the batter and swirl it around the pan until it is spread in an even, thin layer over the bottom.

Cook it for 2–3 minutes, loosening the edges with a metal spatula. Then, with a flick of the wrist, toss the crêpe in the air and catch it as it lands, uncooked side down. Cook it for 2 minutes longer. (If the idea of tossing a crêpe terrifies you, just use the spatula to flick it over.) Turn the cooked crêpe onto a warmed dish and keep warm in a 200°F oven.

Continue cooking the rest of the batter in the same way. Fill each crêpe with Fruit Compote (see below) and serve with crème fraîche (see page 52).

Fruit Compote

MAKES 3 LB

$\frac{1}{2}$ *lb dried apricots*

$\frac{1}{4}$ *lb pitted prunes*

$\frac{1}{4}$ *lb dried figs*

$\frac{1}{4}$ *lb dried pears*

$\frac{3}{4}$ *cup raisins*

1 tea bag

$\frac{3}{4}$ *cup packed light brown sugar*

grated zest and juice of 2 oranges

$\frac{1}{2}$ *cup rum*

1 cinnamon stick

$\frac{1}{8}$ *tsp freshly grated nutmeg*

pinch of ground cloves

pinch of ground ginger

Put the apricots, prunes, figs, pears, and raisins in a large bowl along with the tea bag. Pour on enough warm water to cover and let soak overnight.

Remove the tea bag and put the fruit into a saucepan which has a tight-fitting lid. Add the sugar, orange zest

After the harvest in Tuscany.

and juice, rum, cinnamon, nutmeg, cloves, and ginger. Stir together and bring to a boil over medium to low heat. Just before it reaches boiling point, turn the heat down to low, cover, and simmer for about 45 minutes, or until the fruit is soft.

Remove the cinnamon stick. Serve with the Buckwheat Crêpes, or use as a filling for Winter Pudding (see page 239), or serve with yogurt for breakfast.

Savarin

The savarin is named after Brillat-Savarin, the celebrated French lawyer and gastronome. He supposedly devised the syrup used to soak the cake, which is traditionally made in a large ring mold, now commonly known as a savarin mold.

SERVES 4–6

4 tbsp unsalted butter, melted, plus extra for greasing

1 cup unbleached white bread flour

pinch of salt

$1\frac{1}{2}$ tbsp superfine or granulated sugar

2 large eggs

$\frac{1}{4}$ oz fresh compressed yeast or $1\frac{1}{2}$ tsp active dry yeast

1 tbsp warm water $(105°–115°F)$

for the syrup:

$1\frac{1}{4}$ cups superfine or granulated sugar

2 cups water

2 tsp rose water

for the filling:

$\frac{1}{2}$ lb mixed berries, including strawberries, red currants, blackberries, etc.

Generously butter an 8- to 9-inch savarin mold.

Mix together the flour, salt, and sugar in a large bowl. Add 1 of the eggs and stir together with a wooden spoon. Dissolve the yeast in the 1 tablespoon of warm water and add to the flour with the remaining egg. Mix together thoroughly. Knead in the bowl until smooth and elastic, 5–10 minutes Then beat in the melted butter.

Press the dough evenly into the prepared mold, cover, and let rest in a warm place for about 30 minutes.

Preheat the oven to 400°F. Bake the savarin for 20–25 minutes. Unmold onto a wire rack and let cool.

Make the syrup: In a saucepan over a low heat, combine the sugar and 2 cups water and slowly heat until the sugar is dissolved. Turn up the heat and boil for about 5 minutes until it starts to thicken. Remove from the heat and stir in the rose water.

Set the savarin on the rack over a bowl and baste it with the syrup, leaving it to soak through to the center.

Place the savarin on a serving plate, fill the center with the berries, and spoon over any remaining syrup.

SAVARIN

The Orchard and Soft Fruit Garden

*Spring blossoms herald a rich harvest throughout
summer and autumn. Few other foods provide such a
spectacular range of intense tastes and colors as the
fruits of the orchard trees, soft-fruit canes and bushes,
and the tangled branches of the hedgerows.*

Due to the vastness of the United States, and the varied climates, soils, and growing conditions, a huge variety of fruits are grown. While you may not see all varieties in your supermarkets, and certainly not at all times of the year, availability is improving and, due to increasing consumer interest, the less commercial varieties are seen more often as well. And, of course, there are always gourmet shops, greengrocers, farm markets and stands selling sparklingly fresh in-season fruits, sometimes organically grown.

Britain, on the other hand, is a much smaller country, with a shorter growing season, and while some excellent fruit is produced locally, much of what we see in our markets has been imported. While I don't have anything against imported fruit, I wish that the range of varieties that we *do* grow was better represented.

We can't grow citrus fruits in the British climate, but they grow abundantly in Florida and California, and to a lesser extent, in Texas, Arizona, Louisiana, and Georgia. The citrus family is a large one and members include the highly useful LEMON, and the closely related, less tart, but more fragrant, LIME; the astringent yellow-fleshed GRAPEFRUIT, and its sweeter ruby-red cousins; and, of course, the ORANGE, of which there are supposedly 2,000 varieties world-wide, although, in fact, only 200 of these are grown on a commercial scale.

The majority of oranges grown and sold in the States are sweet oranges from either Florida or California, providing fresh fruit 12 months of the year. As a rule, Florida oranges are better for juice, while California oranges are better for eating. The most popular varieties sold are Valencias and navels.

Another important member of the citrus family is the smaller, easier-to-peel and sometimes seedless MANDARIN ORANGE, and its close relatives, including the CLEMENTINE, TANGERINE, MURCOTT, TEMPLE ORANGE, TANGELO, and the dome-shaped MINNEOLA. As citrus fruits can be crossed so easily,

many hybrids have been developed and new crosses are constantly being produced, so it is quite difficult to keep up with all the latest developments.

When buying citrus fruits, choose fruit which feel heavy for their size, as this is a sure sign of juiciness. The skin must be firm and it must look and feel as if it contains plenty of moisture, as once it starts to crinkle or shrivel, the fruit is getting tired and old. Do not be put off by discolored skin or a skin with green spots, as these do not affect the flavor.

Oranges, lemons, and limes are vital for cooking and baking. Not only do you need their juice for flavoring, but their zest can also be added to great effect, as it gives a bitter-sweet, fruity taste that adds subtlety to many a dish, ranging from soups to cakes.

Unfortunately, the skins of citrus fruits, and oranges in particular, are often dyed to produce a brighter color, and then coated with wax to prolong their life during transportation. If you are going to use citrus zest, make sure to either buy uncoated fruit or organically grown fruit, or first scrub the skin with a stiff brush, hot water, and a tiny drop of dishwashing liquid, then rinse it thoroughly and pat dry.

Particularly keen gardeners claim to be able to grow grapes, figs, apricots, peaches, nectarines, and melons in our rather doleful British climate. All these fruits need remorseless sun, like that in California, to ripen and sweeten them, and to allow them to develop their heady, succulent flavor.

It goes without saying that the best GRAPES come from the areas that boast a Mediterranean-type climate, such as the Mediterranean region itself, California, and parts of South Africa and the Americas. Although generally thought of simply as either black, red, or green, grapes can be any color from a deep, rich purple, through a ruby red, to a pale creamy yellow. Table grapes, those for eating rather than making wine, come in endless varieties and choice must depend on preference and their taste and color. Fortunately, as

Morello cherry blossom

grapes are so small, it is often possible to sample them before buying. My favorite variety of grape is the large, richly scented muscat: sweet and heavy with a full flavor, these grapes are one of the treats of autumn. If cooking with grapes, buying a seedless variety saves a lot of time and trouble. However, remember it is always possible to strain a sauce to remove the seeds and skins.

Depending on the variety, the skin of the FIG can range from a pale yellow, through a bright green to a deep purple; and their fleshy insides can be anything

from a pale pink to a deep scarlet. In fact, it is the ripeness of the fruit rather than the color which is an indication of flavor: For really ripe fruit look for soft figs which are just beginning to split at the bottom. Avoid any figs with spotted skins, as this means that the fruit has turned sour. Fresh figs should always be eaten within a couple of days of purchase.

PEACHES, with their soft downy skin, the smoother, more vividly colored NECTARINES, and smaller, juicy APRICOTS all require a similar warm, sunny climate to achieve perfection. Although far less easy to buy, it is worth trying the white-fleshed peach found at farm stands and farmers' markets, as its flesh is softer and much more aromatic than the yellow-fleshed varieties.

The perfect MELON relies on the spring rains to swell its fruit and the summer sun to give it a ripe lusciousness and complex spiciness.

There are many types of melons, but those most commonly sold in the States are cantaloupe, crenshaw, and honeydew. Cantaloupes have golden-orange flesh, and are at their best from June through November. Look for a firm, unbruised melon with light, yellow colored skin, which has a ripe fragrance, and gives slightly to gentle pressure. Let them ripen further at room temperature and chill when ripe or after cutting. The best melons come from the Western states; although some are grown east of the Mississippi, their flavor is nowhere near as sweet and the flesh may be watery. Crenshaws are available from August to December. The skin of this large melon should have a golden color and the aroma should be sweet. Let it ripen further at room temperature. Honeydew melons, unlike cantaloupes and crenshaws, will not ripen once off the vine. Look for a light yellow skin that feels soft, and yields to gentle pressure, and a fragrant, perfumed scent.

Summer's bounty of luscious nectarines, cherries, peaches, and plums.

Fruit from the Trees

During the summer and early autumn, the orchards are heavy with fruit. First come the CHERRIES; then the PLUMS start to appear, the best of the U.S. varieties being the red-skinned Santa Rosa, an excellent plum, with unfortunately, a very short growing season, the darker El Dorado, and the deep amber-skinned Friar. In Britain, the pale, sugary GREENGAGE plum is a real treat, and a comparable plum grown in the U.S. — although it's not a true greengage — is the Kelsey. The other members of the plum family include the Italian-type prune-plums, such as the FELLENBURG, and the DAMSON (which are only found at farmers' markets, and are much too tart to be eaten raw).

Some APPLES are ripe for eating by mid-August, as are some PEARS; but you will have to wait until October to enjoy QUINCES. Most of the quinces in the States are from California and of a variety called the pineapple quince. They were once quite popular, especially for making quince jelly and marmalade, but they can be difficult to obtain.

Apples

For once, the British climate works to our advantage in producing ideal conditions for growing a fruit. Apples need plenty of rain to swell the fruit, comparatively low temperatures for slow ripening, weak sun to color the fruit, and cool nights to intensify the flavor; this pretty much sums up the British summer. As I sit shivering in the cool of August, I console myself with the thought that at least the apples are thriving and developing those well-rounded complex flavors.

The northern half of the U.S., especially New York, Michigan, and Washington State, produces fine apples, due to the cool nights and moderate temperatures, providing the proper ratio of acids to sugars.

The British National Fruit Collection lists over 3,000 named varieties of apple — heaven knows how many there are in the world! No two apple varieties are ever alike, and no other fruit has such a wide range of tastes, aromas, textures, colors, and shapes. In the States alone, there are about 2,500 types of apple grown; however, only about 15 of those make up 90 percent of the apples commercially produced.

There are two basic uses for apples: cooking and eating, but most apples can be used for either. While some varieties of apples in Britain are grown solely for cider production, most cider and apple juice in the States is produced from the types of apples grown normally, utilizing the smaller, not-perfect specimens.

Cooking apples have a higher acid content and the best varieties include: Newtown Pippin, Rhode Island Greening, and Gravenstein. They are perfect for cooking to a purée for applesauce, for an old-fashioned double-crust pie, or a crisp. The Rome apple is considered a good baking apple, and it is often baked whole, and sometimes cored and stuffed, but I find it lacks flavor and tends to have a mealy texture.

The simplest way to make applesauce is to peel and core a couple of apples and simmer them over a low heat with a little water or white wine, a knob of butter, a stick of cinnamon, a couple of cloves, and sugar to taste. Often the best pies and crisps are made from two or more types of apples, chosen for their different qualities. A perfect combination could be: Greenings for a good tart bite; Jonathans, because they hold their shape; and Golden Delicious or Cortlands for sweetness.

Often, when I make an apple tart or Tarte Tatin (see page 222) I prefer to cook with apples more commonly used for eating, such as Granny Smith or Golden Delicious, as they will hold their shape better.

The apples I have most enjoyed in the States include: McIntosh, which when fresh is crisp, tart, and dripping with juice; Granny Smith, which was originally imported from New Zealand and is now grown on the East and West coasts, and available year round. It has a sweet-tart flavor and crisp texture, good for cooking and baking, as well as eating raw; Jonathan, which is a small apple with a fine texture and a rich, semitart flavor, the best being grown in Michigan; Empire, a cross between a Red Delicious and a McIntosh, which at its peak is a truly superior, firm, crunchy, and juicy apple; Ida Red, grown in the Northeast, is a tart, firm apple, particularly good for baking; Cortland, grown in the Northeast down through the Mid-Atlantic States, is an apple which resists browning, making it a good choice for fruit salads.

When buying apples avoid any with bruises, although a blemished, broken or wrinkled skin does not necessarily mean that it will not taste good. The size can be a controversial issue; some varieties produce smaller fruit, for example, the Jonathan, and the supermarket chains often insist on larger apples. So growers are then forced to comply with their specifications by stringent pruning and breeding.

Unfortunately, in Britain and the States, we are in danger of losing some of the old-fashioned and less well-known apples that are grown on too small a scale to satisfy the quantities which the supermarkets demand. Admittedly, some may grow irregularly, do not travel well, bruise easily, make small fruit or have a short shelf life, so they can be difficult for any ordinary wholesaler or retailer to handle. You can still, however, find these unusual varieties at farmers' markets, from road-side farm stands, from the orchards themselves (it's a great treat to go and pick them yourself), or by mail order (see page 250), and it is worth seeking them out: Not only do some taste superb, but it is vital that we all make every effort to preserve what is, in effect, part of our culinary heritage. A few of my favorites are: Baldwin, a wonderful all-purpose apple which can now be found only in the apple country of New York State; Northern Spy, grown in the Northeast and northern Midwest, is a crisp, spicy, all-purpose apple; Winesap, which happily seems to be more available now, has a tangy, wine-like flavor, and also is pressed into a superb cider; Wealthy, found in the Northeast, is the highest quality apple to use for applesauce.

Old-fashioned apple varieties often have more interesting, complex flavors.

Tarte Tatin

This classic French tart needs a firm variety of apple, which holds together well, and preferably also one with a sweet, dense flavor. I suggest using an apple such as Jonathan, Golden Delicious, Cortland, or Granny Smith.

It is up to you whether you peel the apples. Frankly, I don't bother, as I like the contrast of the soft flesh and the skin. However, as you start cooking the apples on top of the stove, you must use a heavy-bottomed flameproof dish or pan that will not buckle over direct heat. I find a cast-iron skillet is ideal.

SERVES 4–6

6 tbsp butter, plus extra for greasing

$\frac{1}{4}$ cup superfine or granulated sugar

$1\frac{1}{2}$ lb apples (see above), cored and halved

$\frac{1}{2}$ tsp ground cinnamon

$\frac{1}{2}$ lb Rich Pie Pastry (see page 199), chilled and rested

Preheat the oven to 400°F and generously butter a 10-inch flameproof dish, a heavy-bottomed cake pan, or a cast-iron skillet. Sprinkle the bottom evenly with about half of the sugar.

Depending on the size of the apples, cut each half lengthwise into slices about $\frac{1}{2}$ inch thick. Arrange the slices of apple, overlapping, in the dish, sprinkle with a little of the cinnamon and sugar, and dot with some of the butter. Repeat the process until all the apple, butter, cinnamon, and sugar are used up.

Put the pan over medium to high heat and cook for 10–15 minutes, until the sugar has caramelized, taking care not to let it burn. If a lot of liquid is produced, as sometimes happens if you are using very juicy apples, simply pour some of it off into a small saucepan (hold a lid against the apples to keep them in place while draining). Boil the liquid in a small saucepan over a high heat to reduce it until it is thick and syrupy, and then pour it back over the apples.

Roll out the pastry dough into a round about $\frac{1}{4}$ inch thick and slightly larger than the top of the pan. Fold in the edge of the dough to make a border, press it flat, and crimp the edges. Pierce the pastry all over with a fork to make tiny holes through which the steam can escape.

Lay the pastry over the apples, folded side down, and bake in the preheated oven for about 25 minutes, tenting the pastry with foil if it begins to get too brown. Remove the tart from the oven and unmold it upside-down by placing a serving plate over the pan and carefully inverting them.

Serve hot or warm with a huge bowl of whipped cream or crème fraîche (see page 52).

Apple and Quince Soufflé

The QUINCE *is a subtly fragrant fruit with a heady, honeyed perfume. The type most familiar in Britain is similar to a rounded pear in shape and it can be easily distinguished by its golden-yellow skin covered with a dusty down.*

Quince cannot be eaten raw as it is too hard and acidic. When cooked with sugar, however, the flesh turns a soft pink and makes wonderful jam, jelly, or paste. Interestingly, the Spanish name for the fruit is marmelo, *and it is thought marmalade was originally made with quinces, the use of Seville oranges being a later adaptation.*

Available from August, sometimes through the winter, quinces may be hard to find where you live. So if you are tempted by this recipe and cannot find the right fruit, try it with pears instead, adding a little lemon juice to the poaching water.

SERVES 4–6

2 tbsp butter, cut into pieces, plus extra for greasing
3 tbsp superfine or granulated sugar
½ lb quinces, peeled and cored
⅓ cup water
½ lb Empire, Ida Red, or Golden Delicious eating apples, peeled and cored
2 whole cloves
1 tbsp Calvados, or apple brandy
3 extra-large eggs, separated
1 tsp confectioners' sugar

Wicker baskets hang ready for apple-picking.

Preheat the oven to 400°F and butter an 8-inch, 2-quart soufflé dish. Put I tablespoon of the superfine or granulated sugar into the dish and turn it around to coat it evenly with the sugar.

Chop the quinces into small dice and place in a heavy bottomed saucepan with the water. Chop the apples into slightly larger pieces and scatter them on top along with the cloves.

Cover the pan with a lid and simmer over medium to low heat for 10–15 minutes, or until the juices run and the fruits soften. Remove the lid, turn up the heat, and simmer rapidly, stirring occasionally for 5–10 minutes, or until the mixture has reduced to a soft, but still dry, consistency.

Purée the fruit in a food processor or by passing it through a strainer. Stir in the butter until melted, the Calvados, and superfine or granulated sugar to taste (make the purée on the sweet side, as the sweetness will be diluted by the beaten egg whites), and beat in the egg yolks while the mixture is still warm.

In a separate bowl, beat the egg whites until they form stiff peaks. Using a metal spoon, carefully fold them into the fruit purée. Pour the mixture evenly into the prepared soufflé dish and put the dish on a baking sheet. Place in the oven and bake for 20 minutes.

Open the oven door, carefully pull out the baking sheet just far enough to be able to reach the soufflé, and sprinkle the top with confectioners' sugar. Close the door gently and bake for another 5 minutes. Serve.

Spiced Crab Apples

Once the countryside was full of wild crab apple trees bearing tiny sour fruit. Because of their high acidity, these apples were never eaten raw but were used to great effect in cider or in pickles and jellies. It is their very astringency which makes them ideal for pickling, as their sharpness counteracts the vinegar and spices and their flavor is never overpowered.

This pickle is delicious with roast goose (see page 117) or Homemade Sausages (see page 150).

Contrary to popular belief, our native wild crab apple trees are a different species from our eating apples. The latter come from an Eastern strain which were crossbred to produce the cultivated variety. The term crab apple has also come to cover the ornamental nonedible varieties introduced from China and Japan, which grow in many gardens.

Since crab apples are often grown as propagators in orchards and, as I hate to see anything going to waste, this is the ideal solution for coping with the sour fruit.

MAKES 4½ LB

2¼ lb crab apples
1¼ cups white wine vinegar
1 cup packed light brown sugar
1 heaping tbsp peeled and coarsely chopped fresh ginger
6 whole allspice berries
3 whole cloves
½ cinnamon stick, crushed
½ tsp freshly grated nutmeg

Put the apples in a large kettle or pot along with enough water to cover, bring to a boil over medium heat, lower the heat, and simmer for about 5 minutes, or until the apples just begin to soften.

Using a slotted spoon, transfer the apples to warm, dry, sterilized I-pint jars and reserve the liquid.

In a clean saucepan over medium heat, combine the vinegar, ginger, allspice, cloves, cinnamon, and nutmeg. Bring to a boil, lower the heat, and simmer for 10 minutes. Add 1¼ cups of the liquid in which the apples have cooked, turn down the heat, and simmer for another 5 minutes.

Pour the hot syrup over the apples and let cool before sealing the jars.

Refrigerate for about 7 days to allow the flavors to mellow before eating. Store in the refrigerator.

Pears

The perfect dessert pear is juicy with a buttery texture and a mellow, sweet flavor. They should be eaten on their own or accompanied by shavings of a mature hard cheese, such as Parmesan. During the late summer in France and Italy, you can buy tiny, bright-yellow pears which look as if they might be straight out of a still life, with skins lightly russeted and brushed with a watercolor pink. When I see them — and I must confess I cannot name the variety — I buy them immediately.

In Britain, and in the States, we are not often as lucky. For shipping and handling purposes, most of our commercially grown pears are picked when still quite unripe. However, pears do not ripen on the tree successfully; a tree-ripened pear may be soft and mushy. You can sometimes buy ripe fruit at the store, but it may not have been ripened under ideal conditions. A better idea is to plan ahead and buy a less mature fruit and ripen it at home at a cool room temperature. To hasten the ripening process, put the pears in a brown paper bag.

Like apples, there are several varieties of pears and each one has a distinctive flavor and a natural season, which, also like apples, has been extended by controlled storage. The best I've tasted in the States are: BARTLETT, known in my country as the Williams pear. Buy them when they are green in color; when ripe, they will turn pale yellow and have a soft, particularly yielding flesh. Red Bartlett pears, while they look beautiful, are not nearly as flavorful. Many people consider COMICE the most flavorful of all pears with a rich, juicy sweetness. The BOSC has heavily russeted green skin, and, unlike other pears, is best eaten when firm and crunchy. Interestingly, this pear ripens both at room temperature and in the refrigerator. SECKEL pears are truly an American pear, and very small in size. While they are good eaten raw, they are most often poached or home-canned in a syrup aromatic with cinnamon and cloves.

The trouble with buying pears is that the quality can vary widely. Their texture can be mealy or dryly fluffy and they may have started rotting on the inside. If you can, try to get your greengrocer to cut one up to allow you to sample it to see what condition it is in.

Pears Poached in White Wine with Cassis

In Victorian times in Britain, a distinction was made between stewing and eating pears. The former had a firm, almost hard, texture, lacked flavor, were long keeping, and were ideal for cooking as they kept their shape; the latter were softer, buttery, acid but sweet, and had to be eaten as soon as they were ripe.

Nowadays, however, this distinction has disappeared, but only certain pears really cook well. Anjou, Bosc, Seckel, and Comice are ideal for poaching. If you can't find any of these, however, choose any

pear with an even shape that has yet to soften.

Once cut, all pears discolor readily, so it is a good idea to immerse them in water acidulated with lemon juice.

SERVES 6

¾ cup superfine or granulated sugar
2½ cups water
1¼ cups dry white wine
grated zest of 1 large orange
1 cinnamon stick, broken into pieces
6 firm pears, peeled and cored
2 tbsp crème de cassis (black currant liqueur)

Make a simple sugar syrup in a saucepan just large enough to hold the 6 pears upright: Combine the sugar and water in the pan and stir over low heat until dissolved. Turn up the heat and bring to a boil, then boil to reduce by about one-third. Stir in the wine, orange zest, and cinnamon.

Put the pears in the pan, standing upright, turn the heat down to low, and poach, covered, for about 15 minutes, or until the pears are just beginning to soften.

Using a slotted spoon, lift out the pears. Then turn up the heat, stir in the crème de cassis, and boil to reduce the liquid by about two-thirds, or until it is quite thick and syrupy.

Turn down the heat to low and remove the cinnamon pieces. Return the pears, standing upright, to the pan and simmer for 3–5 minutes, spooning the liquid over the pears so they become streaked with the rose-colored syrup.

Transfer the pears to a serving dish, pour the syrup over the pears, and let cool before serving. The pears can also be served chilled.

PEARS POACHED IN WHITE WINE WITH CASSIS

Pears in a Brioche

I once tried this recipe with Perry pears, the descendants of the wild pear introduced to England by the Normans and which are still grown especially for their juice. The result was a bittersweet dessert with an unexpected pungent, woody flavor.

SERVES 4

2 tbsp unsalted butter, plus extra melted butter for brushing
1 lb firm pears, peeled, cored, and sliced
1 tbsp granulated sugar
1 tbsp eau-de-vie de Poire William (pear liqueur)
$\frac{2}{3}$ cup heavy cream
1 Brioche (see page 196)
3 tbsp sliced unblanched almonds

Preheat the oven to 350°F.

Melt the butter in a skillet over low heat. Put in the pears, sprinkle with the sugar, and cook gently, turning them occasionally, for about 5 minutes, or until tender.

Stir in the Poire William and cream, turn up the heat, and boil briskly to reduce the liquid to a reasonably thick, coating consistency. Remove from the heat and keep warm.

Cut out a wide circle in the top of the brioche and remove enough of the brioche to make a hollow deep enough for the pear slices. Brush the brioche all over with melted butter.

Place the brioche on a baking sheet with the almonds scattered around it, and toast in the oven for about 10 minutes, or until the almonds turn golden.

Remove the brioche from the oven. Spoon the pears into the hollow dribbling some of the sauce down the sides, and scatter the toasted almonds over the top.

Serve immediately, cutting like a cake.

Plums

Many a child has, at least once during a long summer, hidden under a plum tree away from the watchful eyes of grown-ups and crammed themselves fit to bursting with the brightly colored, juicy treasures from the tree.

You can always tell a plum is fresh by its firm skin, tautly stretched over the succulent flesh, and its gentle bloom giving it a look as if it has been lightly smeared with chalk. The trouble with ripe plums, however, is that they spoil and bruise so easily; so usually those on sale in shops just do not match the juicy fleshiness of those picked from the garden.

Pears range in color from bright green to deep scarlet opposite. The Victoria plum is one of the best-known varieties below.

Plum and Pear Jam

Ripe plums are full of natural sugar and pectin, so they can be used in one of the few jam recipes that needs absolutely no extra sugar. You must, of course, use very soft, ripe plums and pears in this recipe to achieve the right sweetness and set. It is, therefore, an ideal way of coping with a windfall, provided you cut out any bruises.

This recipe is more like a purée than a true jam in texture, but it will keep for months in the refrigerator.

MAKES 3–4 LB

2 lb ripe eating plums, pitted and halved
grated zest and juice of 1 orange
1 cinnamon stick, crushed
2 whole cloves
1 cup water
2 lb ripe pears, peeled, cored, and roughly chopped
grated zest and juice of 1 lemon
2 tbsp sweet dessert wine, such as Beaumes-de-Venise

Combine the plums, orange zest and juice, cinnamon, cloves, and water in a heavy bottomed kettle or pot. Over a low heat and stirring frequently, simmer for about 20 minutes, or until the fruit is quite soft.

Add the pears, lemon zest and juice, and sweet wine, if using. Simmer, stirring occasionally, for 1 hour, or until the fruit has reduced to a thick pulp. Add more water, if necessary, at any time to prevent the fruit from sticking to the bottom of the pan.

If you like jam very smooth and more like a purée or paste, pass it through a strainer or process in a food processor; otherwise, spoon it as it is into warm, dry, sterilized ½-pint jars. Let it cool before sealing the jars and store in the refrigerator.

BLACKBERRY AND SCENTED GERANIUM LEAF JAM (SEE PAGE 244), PLUM AND PEAR JAM left. The cherry-picking period in orchards is a short one, generally no more than a week above right.

Cherries

MONTMORENCY or SOUR CHERRIES are one of the few fruits that can successfully be grown on a north-facing wall. Their use is admittedly rather restricted as they are far too sour to eat without sweetening; but they can be pricked all over with a needle and left to soak for months in vodka to make a fiery, fruity drink, or baked in a pie, or turned into a sharp sauce to accompany roast duck or goose.

SWEET CHERRIES need plenty of sun to ripen and they are best grown in warm, sunny climates. They should be juicy with a good ratio of fruit to pit. The way to judge their freshness is to look at the stems: If they are intact and still green, it means they have been recently picked, but after a few days the stems start to dry up and turn brown or fall off.

The cherry season is short; in the States, from late May to July. The largest crop comes from Washington State, and the best, and most popular variety is the Bing cherry. The two types of white or light-colored cherries grown in the U.S. are Royal or Queen Anne and Rainier; these bruise very easily and are available in only limited supplies.

Clafoutis

For a clafoutis, or cherry cake, choose the plumpest, firmest cherries you can find. If they are slightly tart, simply add a little extra sugar.

Some recipes suggest that you cook the cherries whole without pitting them, as this gives the clafoutis a stronger flavor. However, I find the pits irritating.

SERVES 4

3 large eggs
1½ cups all-purpose flour
½ cup superfine or granulated sugar
pinch of salt
1 cup warm milk
1 tbsp light rum
3 tbsp unsalted butter at room temperature
1 lb (1 pint) fresh cherries, pitted
1 tsp confectioners' sugar

Separate 1 of the eggs, put the egg yolk with the 2 whole remaining eggs in a large bowl, and beat them lightly. Sift together the flour, superfine or granulated sugar, and salt into the eggs, then stir together. Pour in 2 tablespoons of the milk and beat until the mixture is smooth. Then, gradually stir in the remaining milk and the rum. Beat the batter until it is smooth and shiny. Let it rest for 1 hour in the refrigerator.

Preheat the oven to 425°F and use about half of the butter to grease a 9-inch round gratin dish or a one-piece quiche dish.

Beat the remaining egg white until it forms stiff peaks and fold it into the batter. Pour the batter into the prepared dish, drop the cherries in (don't worry if they sink because they will rise to the top during cooking), and dot the top with the remaining butter.

Bake for 35–40 minutes, or until the batter is puffed up and golden brown.

Remove from the oven, sift the confectioners' sugar over the top, and serve immediately.

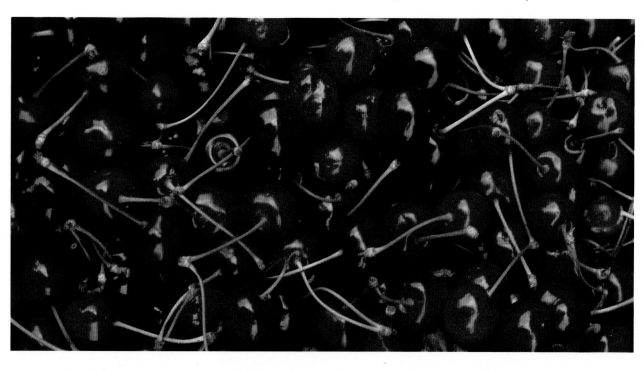

Fruit from the Bushes

In Britain, summer is the season for soft fruit. We have a profusion of BLACK, RED, and WHITE CURRANTS; tiny irridescent cooking GOOSEBERRIES; STRAW-BERRIES in all their juicy glory; the softer subtler RASPBERRY; and the larger, darker LOGANBERRY, with its sharper taste. Finally, comes the BLACK-BERRY, which may be picked from the hedgerows right up to mid-October, although according to old country lore blackberries should never be touched after the old Michaelmas Day; the day the Devil is said to spit on the fruit to spite his rival, the Archangel Michael.

In the States, it is easy to find strawberries,

Sweet cherries left

raspberries, and, depending on where you live, usually blackberries and loganberries. Loganberries, grown on the West Coast, are available from June to July. Blackberries are generally in season from May to August. Red currants and gooseberries are sometimes found at farmers' markets; while white currants are quite rare, and black currants are at times imported from New Zealand.

BLUEBERRIES are well known, but have you ever heard of, let alone tasted, ELDERBERRIES, purple-black in color, used for wine, or mixed with apples in a pie; HUCKLEBERRIES, ranging in color from red to black, are native Northwest berries that are never cultivated; CLOUDBERRIES from New England resemble amber-colored raspberries, and make a lovely jam; or the OLALLIEBERRY, a native to the West Coast, resembling blackberries.

Soft fruits damage easily, and are best left unwashed, although you can gently wipe firmer fruit with a damp cloth. If you must wash the berries, do so only just before using.

Most soft fruits make excellent fruit vinegars. Put a handful of lightly mashed fruit in a jar and cover with wine vinegar or cider vinegar and infuse for a week. Then, strain through cheesecloth; add the same volume of sugar as liquid (or less for a sharper vinegar), boil 10 minutes and store in clean, corked bottles until needed.

You can also purée soft fruit to make a coulis, or fruit sauce. Choose very ripe fruit, such as raspberries or strawberries, and purée in a food processor and strain or press through a fine strainer. Add sugar to taste.

Strawberries

Strawberries herald all the joys of summer. Served with lashings of rich, fresh cream, they take pride-of-place at parties and picnics — and, of course, at events like Wimbledon.

The juicy, ripe, bright red strawberry, with its perfect balance of sweetness and acidity, is a fruit to be treasured. The tiny wild, or alpine, strawberry has a heady, intense flavor, but I still prefer the larger, more luscious fruit of the cultivated varieties. They come in all shapes: from round or pendulous to globular, and even irregular. California is the largest producer of strawberries in the United States. With over 21,000 acres planted, the most widely planted varieties are: Chandler, which grows in southern California, and is the first to ripen, available from March to June; Pajaro, grown in the north of the state, which first appears in late May and is available, depending on the weather, until September; and Selva, a late-season variety of berry, which is available from June and on through September.

If they grow in your area, the best way to buy strawberries is to go to pick-your-own farms; you can then be certain that the fruit is in peak condition. They should be slightly soft, yielding to the gentlest of squeezes, and highly and evenly colored. If their color fades away to white (although many California varieties have white shoulders which do not affect taste), or if the strawberry is a pale green, they are not ripe. When choosing, look out for signs of bruising, and check that the calyx and stem are still a fresh bright green.

Ideally, strawberries should never be washed and certainly not under a running faucet as this literally drowns their flavor. However, they may be sandy, and you can never be certain whether or not they have been sprayed (unless, of course, you buy certified organic fruit). Either wipe them gently with a damp cloth, or put them into a bowl of cold water, lifting them gently out with your hands, then drain on paper towels. Any sand will sink to the bottom of the bowl. Strawberries are best eaten raw and the laziest way to serve them is to pile them into a dish without even hulling them. Just leave your friends to pick them up and dip them into a bowl of crème fraîche or lightly whipped cream.

Marinated Strawberries

Strawberries at their peak cannot be improved upon and need nothing more than cream. Unfortunately, it is all too rare to be able to buy them at their best, so a sweet steep will improve their flavor.

SERVES 4

2 lb (3 pints) fresh strawberries
½ cup superfine or granulated sugar
grated zest of 1 and juice of 2 large oranges
⅓ cup Grand Marnier, or other orange-flavored liqueur
1 tbsp chopped fresh mint leaves (optional)

Hull the strawberries and put them in a large bowl, allowing plenty of room so they are not overcrowded or they will bruise. If they are quite large, cut them in half with a sharp knife. Sprinkle with the sugar and orange zest, add the juice and Grand Marnier, and stir together carefully so as not to crush or bruise the berries.

Cover the bowl and let marinate in the refrigerator for about 2 hours, stirring carefully from time to time. Serve chilled, accompanied by lightly whipped cream flavored with a few chopped mint leaves, if desired.

Strawberry Tart Brûlée

When choosing the strawberries for this tart, it is better to buy very firm, slightly under-ripe fruit. If they are too juicy and squashy, they will not retain their shape or texture when cooked.

SERVES 4–6

15–20 large, firm strawberries
1 tbsp brandy
$\frac{1}{3}$ cup superfine or granulated sugar
$\frac{1}{2}$ lb Rich Pie Pastry (see page 199)
2 cups heavy cream
4 large egg yolks
butter, for greasing

Preheat the oven to 375°F and lightly grease a 10-inch tart or quiche pan with butter.

Using a sharp knife, cut the strawberries in half and put them in a large bowl. Pour the brandy over the berries and sprinkle with half of the sugar. Stir gently so as not to crush or bruise the strawberries and let marinate for 1 hour.

Roll out the pastry dough on a flat, lightly floured surface to a thickness of about $\frac{1}{4}$ inch, and line the tart pan with it. Trim the edges of the pastry and prick the bottom with a fork. Cover the pan with a sheet of parchment paper weighted down with some baking beans or rice and bake "blind" for 15 minutes.

Meanwhile, pour the cream into a saucepan. Warm it over medium heat for 1 minute. Put the egg yolks into a heatproof bowl and beat in the warmed cream.

Set the bowl over a pan of boiling water and, stirring constantly, cook the mixture for 5 minutes, until slightly thickened. Do not let it boil or the eggs will curdle. Then strain it into a clean bowl and let cool.

Drain the strawberries, reserving the juices, and arrange them flat-side down in a single, close-fitting layer on the pastry. Stir their drained juices into the cream mixture, pour the cream mixture over the fruit, and chill for 2 hours.

Preheat the broiler. Sprinkle the top of the tart with the remaining sugar, set 4–6 inches from the broiler, and broil until the sugar caramelizes into a golden brown, turning the pan from time to time so that it browns evenly. Be careful not to burn the sugar.

Serve warm or chilled.

Strawberries and roses are synonymous with summer.

Raspberries

With their velvet texture and a bloom like a soft kid glove, raspberries are very definitely a fruit for eating raw. Always choose them when slightly soft but without a blemish or bruise.

Although keen fruit-growing gardeners recommend the yellow raspberry and insist that it is even more delightful than its soft wine-red cousin, this is not much use to those of us who can't find them, as they are rarely to be seen in the stores. However, if you do find them, snap them up.

Recently re-reading Elizabeth David's *Summer Cooking*, I came across what has now become my definitive recipe for raspberry jam – the only exception I ever make to not cooking the fruit. It preserves almost intact the fresh flavor of the berry, and, if you can resist eating it, it will last for up to a year. Put equal quantities of raspberries and sugar in a large glass baking dish in an oven preheated to 350°F, and bake for 20–30 minutes, until soft. Then crush the fruit to a purée with a wooden spoon and pack into warm, dry, sterilized $\frac{1}{2}$-pint jars. Seal with a circle of waxed paper dipped in brandy, and, when cool, cap with the jar lid.

Raspberry and Hazelnut Shortbread

SERVES 4

3 sticks unsalted butter, chilled and cut into small pieces,
plus extra for greasing
$1\frac{1}{3}$ cups hazelnuts (filberts)
$1\frac{2}{3}$ cups all-purpose flour
$\frac{1}{3}$ cup semolina flour
$\frac{1}{2}$ cup + 2 tbsp superfine or granulated sugar
pinch of salt
1 cup heavy cream, whipped
1 lb ($1\frac{1}{2}$ pints) fresh raspberries
1 tsp confectioners' sugar

Preheat the oven to 375°F and lightly butter 2 baking sheets. Scatter the hazelnuts on an ungreased baking sheet and toast in the oven for 10–15 minutes, or until golden brown. While they are still warm, rub them in a dry cloth to remove the skins.

Put the nuts in a food processor and process until they are the texture of coarse crumbs. Add the flour, semolina, sugar, and salt into the processor. Add the butter and process until the mixture comes together to form a ball. Wrap this pastry dough in a plastic bag and refrigerate for about 30 minutes, until chilled.

Divide the pastry into thirds. Roll out each piece on a flat, lightly floured surface into a circle about $\frac{1}{4}$ inch thick and, using an 8-inch round cake pan as a guide, cut each into identical circles. Put the dough circles on the buttered baking sheets and bake for 15–20 minutes, until edges are lightly browned.

Let them cool slightly on the sheets before transferring them to a wire rack. When they are cool, assemble them into a layer cake: Spread some of the

Scotland is known for its fine-flavored raspberries.

cream on one of the shortbread circles and then arrange half of the raspberries on it. Spread these with a little more cream and place a second shortbread circle on top. Repeat the process, using the remaining cream and raspberries, and finish with the remaining shortbread.

Sift the confectioners' sugar on top and serve chilled.

Variation

You can, if you prefer, divide the shortbread dough into 12 pieces to make 4 individual shortbread.

Summer Pudding

This is truly one of the great treats of summer, and can be made with
most soft fruits in any combination — the mixture is up to you.

If black and white currants are unavailable, use all red currants,
or substitute equal amounts of mixed berries such as raspberries and
blackberries.

SUMMER PUDDING

SERVES 8–10

1 lb (1½ pints) raspberries
1 cup + 2 tbsp superfine or granulated sugar
½ lb (1 pint) black currants (see above)
½ lb (1 pint) red currants (see above)
½ lb (1 pint) white currants (see above)
1 tablespoon crème de mure (blackberry liqueur)
2 tablespoons dry white wine
1 loaf of day-old white bread, unsliced
heavy cream, lightly whipped, to serve

Put the raspberries in a bowl and sprinkle with the 2
tablespoons of sugar. In a separate bowl, put the black
currants, red currants, white currants, and the rest of
the sugar and gently stir to combine. Set the fruits aside
for 3–4 hours, or until the juices start to run.

Transfer the mixed currants to a saucepan and add
the crème de mure and white wine. Bring almost to a
boil over medium heat. Simmer for 2–3 minutes to
cook the fruit lightly, then remove from the heat and,
when cool, mix in the raspberries.

Trim the crusts from the bread and cut it into slices
about ¼ inch thick. Cut a circle out of 1 of the slices to
fit the bottom of a 1-quart round pudding mold or
bowl, and then cut wedges of bread to fit snugly around

the sides – there should be no gaps. Spoon in the fruit and juice and cover the top with 2 slices of bread, trimming the edges to make a neat finish.

Cover the mold with a plate small enough to fit just inside the rim, place something heavy on top to press it down, and let it stand, refrigerated, overnight.

To serve the pudding, warm the blade of a sharp knife under running hot water, then ease the blade around between the pudding and the mold. Place a serving dish upside-down on top and turn the whole thing over quickly, giving it a short, sharp shake.

Serve the pudding cut into slices, with lightly whipped cream.

Variation

You can also make a Winter Pudding using the Fruit Compote (see page 210) and very-thinly-cut slices of whole-wheat bread.

In a saucepan over low heat, dissolve the sugar in the water. Then turn up the heat, bring to a boil, and simmer for 5 minutes.

Remove the pan from the heat, add the leaves, cover the pan, and let stand to infuse for 4–5 hours (or overnight if you wish, for a stronger scent and a deeper-green sorbet).

Pour the liquid through a strainer, pressing down quite hard on the leaves to extract their flavor and all the syrup. Stir in the lemon zest and juice.

Freeze in an ice-cream machine, according to the manufacturer's directions. Alternatively, put the mixture into a shallow freezerproof pan and freeze until the sides are firm but the center is quite runny (the actual time will depend on the efficiency of your freezer). Remove it from the freezer, pour it into a chilled bowl, and beat it thoroughly until smooth. Return it to the freezer until almost solid.

Black Currant Leaf Sorbet

Black currants

Light, delicate, and refreshing, this sorbet is made with the leaves of the edible black currant plant (the ornamental species does not have the same flavor). Black currant leaves are curiously aromatic, and when soaked in a sugar syrup, they infuse the liquid with a heady perfume which is not dissimilar to the muzzy taste of elderflowers. Be sure to pick young, tender leaves free from frost and insect damage, and wash and refresh them in ice cold water before use.

SERVES 4

$\frac{2}{3}$ *cup granulated sugar*
$2\frac{1}{2}$ *cups water*
3–4 handfuls of young black currant leaves, or other aromatic, edible leaves, such as elderflower
grated zest of 2 lemons and juice of 3 lemons

Fruit Tarts

Most fruit can be used in a fruit tart. Rhubarb needs special treatment (see overleaf); some, however, such as plums, apricots, gooseberries, blueberries, red or black currants, peaches, cherries, and figs, can either be poached first in a sugar syrup (see Pears Poached in White Wine with Cassis page 226) or baked directly in the tart shell in the oven. Or, if they are very ripe, they may simply be pitted, sliced, and arranged in the cooked pastry shell. Other fruits, especially strawberries and raspberries, should never be cooked.

The best pastry dough to use is a Rich Pie Pastry (see page 199), and you can subtly alter its flavor by including ground nuts or other flavorings.

Once the pastry shell has been baked "blind" and cooled, the bottom should be spread with a Confectioner's Custard (see page 243) or a jam of your choice and then baked with the fruit; if the tart is not going to be baked again, you can also use whipped cream or a fruit coulis or purée (see page 233).

Finally, the fruit should be glazed: Either sprinkle the fruit with granulated sugar and pop it under a preheated broiler until it starts to caramelize; or melt a jam or jelly and reduce it slightly, then paint this over the fruit.

The important thing to remember is to choose ingredients and flavors that complement each other.

OPEN FRUIT TARTS: from left to right, STRAWBERRY, RASPBERRY, GOOSEBERRY, RED CURRANT, CHERRY.

Rhubarb and Marmalade Tart

Rhubarb tends to collapse into a "mush" when cooked and the excess moisture can spoil the pastry in a tart. To prevent this, cook the rhubarb first with some sugar, just until its juices start to run but still firm enough so the pieces stand upright in the tart.

SERVES 4–6

1 tbsp unsalted butter, plus extra for greasing
½ lb Rich Pie Pastry (see page 199), chilled and rested
1 lb rhubarb
2 tbsp superfine or granulated sugar
¼ cup coarse-textured orange marmalade
1 tbsp Scotch whisky

RHUBARB AND MARMALADE TART

Preheat the oven to 375°F and generously butter an 8-inch tart pan with a removable base or 4 individual tartlet molds with removable bases.

Roll out the pastry dough on a flat, lightly floured surface into a circle about ¼ inch thick and slightly larger than the pan. Line the pan (or molds), trim the edges, prick the bottom(s) with a fork, and cover with parchment paper weighted down with some baking beans or rice. Bake "blind" in the preheated oven for 15 minutes. Remove from the oven, remove the beans and paper, and let cool slightly. Turn up the oven to 450°F.

Cut the rhubarb into 2-inch pieces. Combine the rhubarb with the sugar in a saucepan and cook gently over low heat for 5–7 minutes, shaking the pan occasionally, until the rhubarb releases some of its juices but is still firm enough to handle and hold its shape. Drain, reserving the juices, and let cool.

Gently heat 2 tablespoons of the marmalade in a small saucepan, until melted. When the pastry is slightly cooled, paint the bottom and sides with the melted marmalade. Stand the pieces of rhubarb upright in the pastry shell(s), packing them in tightly. Dot the top with the butter, cover with parchment paper, and bake in the preheated oven for about 15 minutes, until the pastry is lightly golden. Remove from the oven and let cool slightly.

To make the glaze: In a saucepan, boil the rhubarb juices over high heat to reduce to about 1 teaspoon. Stir in the remaining marmalade and the whisky and, stirring constantly, continue boiling to reduce by about half; be careful not to burn the glaze. Using a pastry brush, paint the glaze over the top of the fruit and let cool before serving.

Open Tart Variations

1 Replace 6 tablespoons of the flour in the Rich Pie Pastry with ground almonds, use Confectioner's Custard (see right) for the base, fill with $1\frac{1}{2}$ lb halved and pitted plums, then bake in a preheated 400°F oven for 20 minutes, and brush with melted apricot jam.
2 Add 1 teaspoon of grated orange zest to the Rich Pie Pastry, use Confectioner's Custard (see right) for the base, fill with $1\frac{1}{2}$ lb halved and pitted greengage plums or Shiro or Kelsey plums poached in a sugar syrup (see page 240) for 5 minutes, and sprinkle with granulated sugar, then glaze under the broiler.
3 Add 1 teaspoon of ground cinnamon to the Rich Pie Pastry, use whipped cream for the base, fill with $1\frac{1}{2}$ lb pitted and sliced apricots poached in a sugar syrup for 3 minutes, then brush with melted apricot jam.
4 Replace 6 tablespoons of the flour in the Rich Pie Pastry with ground hazelnuts, use Confectioner's

Custard (see right) for the base, fill with 1 lb mixed black currants, red currants, and white currants poached in a sugar syrup (see page 240) for 5–7 minutes, sprinkle with sugar, and then glaze under the broiler. Alternatively, red currants can be used.

Confectioner's Custard

2 large egg yolks
2 tbsp superfine or granulated sugar
1 cup milk
1 vanilla bean

In a bowl, thoroughly whisk the egg yolks with 1 tablespoon of sugar, until they become pale and form a light ribbon on the surface.

Slowly bring the milk to a boil in a saucepan with the vanilla bean and the remaining sugar. Remove from the heat and slowly pour the milk into the egg yolks, whisking constantly. Remove the vanilla bean and return the mixture to the saucepan over a low heat. Using a wooden spoon, stir until the mixture thickens and begins to coat the back of the spoon. Do not let it boil. Strain the custard into a cold bowl, then cover with greaseproof paper to prevent a skin forming. Refrigerate until needed.

Blackberry and Scented Geranium Leaf Jam

The basis of a good jam is ripe fruit with a high sugar and pectin content. So choose, or pick, the ripest and sweetest blackberries possible and discard any broken or crushed ones.

Scented geranium leaves, with their content of volatile oil, add an extra dimension of flavor to the jam. The best variety to use here is lemon verbena.

MAKES 3LB

2 lb (2 pints) ripe blackberries
3 scented geranium leaves
$\frac{3}{4}$ cup water
superfine or granulated sugar (see below)

Put the blackberries in a heavy-bottomed kettle or pot with the geranium leaves and the $\frac{3}{4}$ cup of water, or just enough to prevent them from sticking to the pan.

Stew the fruit over a low heat, stirring frequently, until they are very soft. Strain them to get rid of their seeds, pressing down very hard on the strainer to extract all the juice and pulp.

Measure the pulp and return it to the kettle or pot. For every $2\frac{1}{2}$ cups of pulp, add $2\frac{1}{4}$ cups of sugar. Stir over a low heat until the sugar is dissolved. Turn up the heat and bring to a boil and cook rapidly, stirring continuously, until the jell point is reached. This stage can take anywhere from 10 to 30 minutes, depending on how fiercely the jam is boiling and how ripe the fruit was, but you must stir continuously otherwise it can stick and burn in the pot.

To test whether the jell point has been reached, put a small amount on a saucer and cool it in the refrigerator; after 5 minutes it should have the right consistency, or set, of a jam. Ladle into warm, dry, sterilized $\frac{1}{2}$-pint jars, leaving $\frac{1}{4}$-inch headspace; refrigerate up to 6 months.

Honey

Honey comes from nectar collected by bees from flowers on plants, shrubs, and trees. No two nectars are the same, as they vary in the quantity and type of sugar and other trace elements. For this reason the taste, aroma and color of honey change according to the nectar from which it is made.

Beekeepers often move their hives around the countryside: In the spring, they may hire out their bees to pollinate the orchards or crops in the fields; then, depending on the time of the year, they will move the hives to the moors, woods, fields, or meadows so the bees can concentrate on a particular herb or blossom. Even then such plans can be thwarted, as bees are known to travel up to two miles for food.

Most of the honey we buy is "blended" or made from mixtures of different types and flavors from a variety of flowers; the base of blended honey is usually clover or alfalfa honey. The advantage of such blending is that it produces a consistent, if bland, taste; it is like buying a generic wine which cannot possibly offend anyone, as all its characteristics and idiosyncrasies have been ironed out. Blended honeys are the least expensive, and fine for using in baking or cooking. Like most honeys, they are sold in a clear, liquid form, and may have been heat-treated, or pasteurized, to remain liquid.

Bee hives are often moved from site to site, so the bees can collect nectar from specific flowers or herbs.

"Polyfloral," or mixed flower, honey is produced from a mixture of flowers or blossoms from a particular part of the country, from which the bees have collected nectar, or it is a blend of honeys from multiple floral sources. It may be labeled WILD FLOWER HONEY, but if it is blended, the label must say so.

"Monofloral," or single flower, honey is made of nectar from the flowers or blossom of a single species. At their best, these honeys can be superb, with a unique flavor and aroma that can range from delicate to strong, depending on the flower source. In my country, I have access to THYME HONEY from Greece, LIME and LAVENDER HONEY from France, CHESTNUT HONEY from Italy, and RASPBERRY HONEY from Scotland. In the States, some of the single-flower honeys you may find are: BUCKWHEAT, ORANGE BLOSSOM, DANDELION, LINDEN, HEATHER, SPEARMINT, ACACIA, EUCALYPTUS, and TUPELO. These honeys are like estate-bottled wine; they each have a distinctive character and taste, which varies from year to year according to the climate. They also cost more than other honeys.

Should your honey crystallize in storage, it is worth remembering that it can always be made liquid for cooking by simply standing the jar in a bowl of warm water for a few minutes.

If the honey is crystallized rather than clear and liquid, stand the jar in a bowl of hot water. Whip the cream until it forms soft peaks, then fold in the honey and lavender flowers.

Freeze in an ice-cream machine according to manufacturer's directions. Alternatively, put the mixture into a shallow freezerproof pan and freeze until the sides are firm but the center is quite runny (the actual time will depend on the efficiency of your freezer). Then remove it from the freezer, scrape it into a chilled bowl, and beat it thoroughly until smooth. Return it to the pan and freeze until solid.

You could just let this ice cream freeze without even beating it; it will not be quite as smooth but, because it has quite high sugar and fat contents, it should not form any of the large ice crystals, which can ruin the texture of ice cream.

Variations

1 Use lime blossom honey with 2 teaspoons of grated lime zest.

2 Use an orange blossom or acacia honey with 2 tablespoons of grated orange zest.

3 Use a thyme or herb honey with 1 teaspoon each of grated lemon zest and finely chopped fresh lemon thyme or plain thyme.

Honey and Lavender Ice Cream

For the most exciting honey ice cream, I use a single-flower honey with a distinctive, well-rounded flavor.

SERVES 6

$\frac{1}{2}$ *cup lavender honey*
2 cups heavy cream
2 tsp unsprayed lavender flowers, lightly crushed

HONEY AND LAVENDER ICE CREAM IN A BRANDY SNAP BASKET (SEE PAGE 207) left. Lavender fields in Provence below.

Seasonal Menus

Spring

SIMPLE LUNCH
Roulade with Asparagus (page 129)
Poached Cod with Capers (page 81)

LUNCH FOR FRIENDS
Liver Mousse with a Basil and Tomato Sauce (page 108)
Roast Sea Trout with Stewed Cucumbers
(page 72 and page 30)
Gooseberry Tart (page 240)

SIMPLE SUPPER
Fish Cakes with Hollandaise Sauce (page 82 and page 128)
Pears in a Brioche (page 229)

VEGETARIAN SUPPER
Pasta with Spring Vegetable Sauce (page 34)
Tarte Tatin (page 222)

DINNER
Terrine of Lemon Sole with Shrimp (page 89)
Navarin of Lamb (page 145)
Rhubarb and Marmalade Open Tart (page 242)

Summer

BRUNCH
Mirror Eggs (page 127)
Grissini or Breadsticks (page 192)
Black Currant Leaf Sorbet in Brandy Snap Baskets
(page 239 and page 207)

PICNIC
Chicken in a Loaf (page 113)
Spinach, Ricotta, and Raisin Tart (page 61)
Marinated Strawberries (page 234)

SEAFOOD SUPPER
Fish Soup (page 86)
Mixed Poached Seafood with Salicornia (page 95)
Savarin (page 212)

DINNER
Lettuce and Chervil Soup (page 41)
Turbot in Rock Salt (page 88)
Paper Bag Potatoes (page 21)
Honey and Lavender Ice Cream with Pistachio Tuiles
(page 247 and page 206)

Fall

SAVORY LUNCH
Game Terrine with Onion Marmalade
(page 174 and page 23)
Toasted Brioche (page 196)
Pears Poached in White Wine with Cassis (page 226)

SIMPLE LUNCH
Jambon Persillé with Whole-wheat Bread
(page 155 and page 191)
Warm Red Cabbage Salad (page 27)

SUPPER
Hare with Noodles (page 172)
Buckwheat Crêpes with Fruit Compote (page 210)

DINNER FOR FRIENDS
Chestnut Soup (page 176)
Pheasant with Celery (page 165)
Apple and Quince Soufflé (page 224)

HARVEST SUPPER
Zucchini and Corn Chowder (page 30)
Braised Pork with Wild Mushrooms and
Juniper Berries (page 147)
Plum Tart (page 243)

Winter

BRUNCH
Homemade Sausages with Onion Marmalade and Coarse-grain
Mustard (page 150, page 23 and page 159)
Kedgeree (page 101)
Scrambled Eggs (page 131)
Corn Muffins (page 198)

LUNCH
Oxtail with Grapes (page 138)
Bread and Butter Pudding (page 209)

DINNER
Curried Parsnip Soup (page 16)
Roast Loin of Pork Studded with Ham (page 148)
Roast Vegetables with Thyme (page 38)
Buckwheat Crêpes with Fruit Compote (page 210)

CHRISTMAS DINNER
Tartare of Salmon with Cucumber Salad (page 70)
Roast Goose with Spiced Crab Apples (page 117 and page 224)
Henrietta's Roast Potatoes (page 21)
Certosino or Italian Christmas Cake (page 200)

Mail Order Sources

BACON, HAM, AND SAUSAGE

Aidells Sausage Company: 1575 Minnesota Street, San Francisco, CA 94107. (415) 285-6660

Basse's Choice Plantation Ltd: P.O. Box 1, Smithfield, VA 23430. (800) 678-0770

Nodines Smokehouse: P.O. Box 1787, Torrington, CT 06790. (800) 222-2050

Smithfield Collection: P.O. Box 487, Smithfield, VA 23430. (800) 628-2242

CHEESE

Craigston Cheese Company: 45 Dodges Row, Box 267, Wenham, MA 01984. (800) 365-6299

Goat Folks Farm: 8528 Tunison Road, Interlaken, NY 14847. (607) 532-4343

Grafton Village Cheese Company, Inc: P.O. Box 87, Grafton, VT 05146. (802) 843-2221

Hollow Road Farms: Box 93, Hollow Road, Stuyvesant, NY 12173. (518) 758-7214

Ideal Cheese Shop Ltd: 1205 2nd Avenue, New York, NY 10021. (800) 382-0109

Laura Chenel's Chèvre: 1550 Ridley Avenue, Santa Rosa, CA 95401. (707) 575-8888

Little Rainbow Chèvre: Box 379, Rodman Road, Hillsdale, NY 12529. (518) 325-3351

Maytag Dairy Farms: P.O. Box 806, Newton, IA 50208. (800) 247-2458

Shelburne Farms: Junction of Bay and Harbor Roads, Shelburne, VT 05482. (802) 985-8686

Vella Cheese of California, Inc: 315 2nd Street E., Sonoma, CA 95476. (800) 848-0505

FLOUR AND GRAINS

Gray's Grist Mill: P.O. Box 422, Adamsville, RI 02801. (508) 636-6075

King Arthur Flour Bakers Catalogue: RR2 Box 56, Norwich, VT 05055. (800) 827-6836

FRUITS AND VEGETABLES

Fresh & Wild, Inc: P.O. Box 2981, Vancouver, WA 98668. (206) 737-3652

Grafton Apple Company, Inc: Route 121, RR3, Box 236D, Grafton, VT 05146. (800) 843-4822

Mission Orchards: 3501 Kaylor Drive, Ukiah, CA 95482. (800) 333-1448

Sunshower: 48548 60th Avenue, Lawrence, MI 49064. (616) 674-3103

Tom Towers Apple Farm: P.O. Box 400, Youngstown, NY 14174. (716) 745-9538

Wood Prairie Farm: RFD 1, Box 164, Bridgewater, ME 04735. (207) 429-9765

GAME

D'Artagnan: 399–419 St. Paul Avenue, Jersey City, NJ 07306. (800) 327-8246

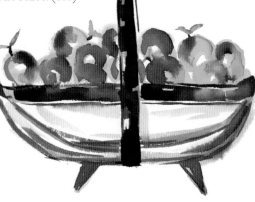

Native Game Company, Inc: P.O. Box 1046, Spearfish, SD 57783. (800) 952-6321

Oakwood Game Farm: P.O. Box 274, Princeton, MN 55371. (800) 328-6647

Polarica Game U.S.A. The Game Exchange: 105 Quint Street, San Francisco, CA 94124. (800) GAME-USA

Wild Game, Inc: 2315 West Huron Street, Chicago, IL 60612. (312) 278-1661

ORGANIC CATALOGUES

Deer Valley Farm: RD 1, Guilford, NY 13780. (607) 764-8556

Rising Sun Organic Food: I–80 Rte. 150, P.O. Box 627, Milesburg, PA 16853. (814) 355-9850

Walnut Acres: Penns Creek, PA 17862. (800) 433-3998

ORGANIC MEAT AND POULTRY

Benson and Stapelman Meats: Rte. 2, Box 61A, Belden, NE 68717. (203) 866-6282

Sugar Hill Farm, Inc: Smith Hill Road, Box 50, Colebrook, CT 06021. (800) 526-2748

SMOKED FISH

Dean & DeLuca, Inc: Mail Order Department, 560 Broadway, New York, NY 10012. (800) 221-7714

Ducktrap River Fish Farm, Inc: 57, Little River Drive, Belfast, ME 04915. (207) 763-3960

ideal enrichment for soups and sauces. Spoon over fresh fruit or other desserts in place of whipped cream.

Flageolet Beans: Small, tender French kidney beans, ranging in color from light green to creamy white. They can be purchased dried in better supermarkets, gourmet food stores, and health food stores.

Garam Masala: A blend of dry-roasted, ground spices from India, which can include black pepper, cinnamon, cloves, coriander, cumin, dried chilies, and other spices. Garam masala can be purchased in Indian markets or in the gourmet section of some supermarkets.

Harissa Paste: A fiery-hot Tunisian flavoring made from hot chili peppers, garlic and other spices. It is used to accent soups, stews, sauces, and other dishes. You can find it in jars and cans in stores specializing in Middle Eastern ingredients.

Juniper Berries: Grow on the juniper bush. Fresh, they are so bitter as to be inedible and must be dried before using. Most often, they are sold already dried and ready-to-use to flavor meats, stews, sauces, stuffings, and a whole host of other preparations. The berries are responsible for the characteristic flavoring of gin.

Lemon Grass: An important ingredient in Thai cooking, lemon grass has a sour-lemon flavor and fragrance. Lemon grass, fresh or dried, can be found in Oriental markets. Thin strips of lemon peel can be substituted.

Rock Salt: Rock salt comes in chunky crystals and is often used as a bed for serving oysters and clams and for mixing with ice to make ice cream in a crank-style ice cream maker. Ask your fish purveyor where to obtain rock salt for you.

Sorrel: A sour-flavored perennial herb, sorrel is available in limited supply year-round with the best in the spring. Cooked sorrel in jars and cans can be purchased in some gourmet food stores.

Glossary

Crème Fraîche: A rich, thickened cream with a tangy flavor, crème fraîche is available in the refrigerated section of some supermarkets and gourmet food stores. Since crème fraîche can be boiled without curdling, it's an

Index

Page numbers in *italic* refer to illustrations

Acknowledgments

There are so many people whom I would like to thank for their help with *A Glorious Harvest*: Gwen White for the hours spent on her word processor and, with her chef/husband Colin, for their generous contribution to the recipes; Denise Bates, my editor, for her tireless coaxing and patience; Lewis Esson for his eagle eyes and strivings for exactitude; Andrew Hewson, my agent; Rebecca Delegano and Rebecca Morley for their patience in the kitchen while testing; Paul Welti for his splendid designs; Jess Koppel and Lyn Rutherford for, respectively, photographing and recreating my recipes; the endless farmers, growers, producers, and retailers who have generously given of their time and expertise; and finally, all my friends who have manfully stayed the course and eaten up the food.

Recipe acknowledgments

Claiming a recipe as my own can be a moot point, as so often it may be a classic which I have absorbed into my repertoire. Some may come from more recent acknowledged sources, but in cooking them several times I may have changed the balance of flavors with a twist here, a tweak there and made them my own. Others I have reproduced in their entirety and would therefore like to thank: Raymond Blanc for *Tartare of Salmon with Cucumber Salad*; Anna del Conte for *Chicken Breasts with Orange* and *Hare with Noodles*; Elizabeth David for *Oxtail with Grapes* and *Broiled Calves' Liver Kabobs with Lettuce Sauce*; Josceline Dimbleby for *The Best-Ever Chocolate Cake*; Peter Graham for *Whiting with Cottage Cheese*; the late Jane Grigson for *Curried Parsnip Soup* and *Eels in Green Sauce*; Ian McAndrew for *Liver Mousse with a Basil and Tomato Sauce* and *Breast of Guinea Fowl with Lentils*; Patricia Lousada for *Corn Muffins*; Deborah Madison for *Zucchini-Corn Chowder* and *Green Tomato, Raisin, and Mint Chutney*; Anton Mosimann for *Bread and Butter Pudding*; Rick Stein for *Terrine of Sole with Shrimp*; and Mary Taylor Simetti for *Chicken in a Loaf*. Other writers to whom I owe a particular debt are Marcella Hazan, Joy Larkcom, Marie-Pierre Moine, Roger Phillips, and Claudia Roden. Thank you one and all.

The publishers would like to thank the following photographers and organizations for their permission to reproduce photographs in this book:

10–11 J. Ducange/Agence Top; 12 J.-P. Couderc/Agence Top; 13 Mike England; 14 Michael Boys/Boys Syndication; 23 P. Hussenot/Agence Top; 26 Michael Boys/Boys Syndication; 29 Michelle Garrett; 33 Michelle Garrett; 36 Lucy Mason; 40 Jess Koppel; 46–7 Debbie Patterson; 49 Michael St. Maur Sheil/Susan Griggs Agency; 53 Robert Harding Picture Library; 58 S & O Mathews; 62 F. Jalain/Explorer; 64 Jacqui Hurst; 66–7 Michelle Garrett; 70 Anthony Blake Photo Library; 72 Zefa Picture Library; 75 Gary Rogers; 76 Anthony Blake Photo Library; 87 S & O Mathews; 90 S & O Mathews; 92 Glyn Satterley; 98 Glyn Satterley; 99 Jacqui Hurst; 101 Glyn Satterley; 102–3 Michael Busselle; 104 Nicholas/Pix; 106 S & O Mathews; 114 Zefa Picture Library; 116 Anthony Blake Photo Library; 119 Anthony Blake Photo Library; 125 J.M. La Roque/Explorer; 132–3 Michael Busselle; 135 Glyn Satterley; 140 S & O Mathews; 142 Mike England; 148 Edward Parker/Hutchinson Library; 152 P. Hussenot/Agence Top; 158 R. Tixador/Agence Top; 160–1 Zefa Picture Library; 162 Zefa Picture Library; 167 Landscape Only; 172 Glyn Satterley; 175 Zefa Picture Library; 176 Laurence Delderfield; 180 Anthony Blake Photo Library; 186–7 John Miller; 190 Laurence Delderfield; 193 Jerrican; 201 Timothy Winter/Robert Harding Picture Library; 202 Michael Busselle; 203 Linda Burgess/Insight Picture Library; 211 Enrico Rainero/Robert Harding Picture Library; 214–15 F. Jalain/Explorer; 217 Jacqui Hurst/Boys Syndication; 221 George Wright; 224 Linda Burgess/Insight Picture Library; 228 Hank Delespinasse/Image Bank; 229 John Lewis Stage/Image Bank; 231 Anthony Blake Photo Library; 232 Jacqui Hurst; 235 Jacqui Hurst/Boys Syndication; 237 Lucy Mason; 239 Lucy Mason; 244–5 Bansse/Pix; 245 J.N. Reichel/Agence Top; 247 Catherine Bibollet/Agence Top.

Special photography by Jess Koppel: 2, 19, 20, 24–5, 31, 35, 39, 43–4, 50–1, 56, 60, 63, 65, 68, 71, 74, 77, 79, 81–3, 88, 91, 94, 96–7, 108, 111, 117, 118, 121, 122, 126–30, 137, 143–4, 149, 151, 153–4, 164, 169, 171, 174, 179, 182–5, 189, 194, 197, 200, 205, 208, 213, 218, 223, 227, 230, 238, 240–2, 246.

Sedgewood® Press would like to extend its thanks to the following for their generous assistance:

Alaska Seafood Marketing Institute, Elizabeth Alston, American Egg Board, American Lamb Council, Bob Anderson, California Artichoke Advisory Board, California Strawberry Advisory Board, Edward Edelman, Steven Hauff, Michelle Fleming, Jefferson Market Butchers, Richard Lord, Fulton Fish Market Information, Mushroom Council, National Broiler Council, National Goose Council, National Honey Board, National Millers' Federation, National Pork Producer's Council, National Potato Board, National Turkey Federation, Nichols Turkey Breeding Farm, Marlin Schiltz, Jean Taylor, Tom Tower, United Dairy Industry Association, Wisconsin Milk Marketing Board, Kaye Zubow.